SELECTED THEATRE CRITICISM

Volume 2: 1920-1930

Edited by
Anthony Slide

The Scarecrow Press, Inc.
Metuchen, N.J., & London 1985

JA '88

In the Same Series

Selected Theatre Criticism, Volume 1: 1900–1919
Selected Theatre Criticism, Volume 3: 1931–1950

Also Edited by Anthony Slide

Selected Film Criticism: 1896–1911
Selected Film Criticism: 1912–1920
Selected Film Criticism: 1921–1930
Selected Film Criticism: 1931–1940
Selected Film Criticism: 1941–1950
Selected Film Criticism: 1951–1960
Selected Film Criticism: Foreign Films 1930–1950

Library of Congress Cataloging-in-Publication Data
(Revised for vol. 2)
Main entry under title:

Selected theatre criticism.

    Includes indexes.
    Contents: v. 1. 1900–1919 -- v. 2. 1920–1930.
    1. Theater--New York (N.Y.)--Reviews. I. Slide,
Anthony.
PN2277.N5S44 1985   792.9'5'097471   85-2266
ISBN 0-8108-1811-6 (v. 1)
ISBN 0-8108-1844-2 (v. 2)

CONTENTS

Preface

vi

PREFACE

Selected Theatre Criticism: 1920-1930 collects contemporary reviews, reprinted in their entirety on almost 200 New York stage productions. The productions represented here include dramas, comedies, musicals, and revues, and have been selected on the basis of their contemporary and historical importance, both in terms of critical and popular regard. Reviews relate to original productions only; revivals have only been included if they were particularly notable.

Reviews included in this volume were chosen from American Mercury, American Review, The Bookman, The Drama, The Commonweal, Life, The New York Dramatic Mirror, New York Journal, The New Yorker and Shadowland. Among the critics/reviewers to be found in this anthology are Robert Benchley, Louis Bromfield, Alan Dale, Kenneth Macgowan, George Jean Nathan, and Richard Dana.

Productions are listed alphabetically by title. Following the name of each production is given the name(s) of the author, the theatre and the opening date. Additional credit information may be found in the Best Plays series.

For help in the preparation of this volume I would like to thank the staffs of the Library of Congress, the Los Angeles Central Library and the Doheny Memorial Library of the University of Southern California.

The reviews from The Commonweal are reprinted by permission of Commonweal Foundation, and the magazine's publisher, Edward S. Skillin.

Reviews on pages 18, 29, 132, 181, 191, and 193 by Charles Brackett and "G.W.G." reprinted by permission; © 1926, 1928, 1929, and 1930. The New Yorker Magazine, Inc.

Anthony Slide

ABIE'S IRISH ROSE (Anne Nichols; Fulton Theatre, May 23, 1922)

On the night following the presentation of The Rotters, residents of Broadway, New York City, were startled by the sound of horses' hoofs clattering up the famous thoroughfare. Rushing to their windows they saw a man, in Colonial costume, riding a bay mare from whose eyes flashed fire. The man was shouting as he rode, and his message was: "The Rotters is no longer the worst play in town! Abie's Irish Rose has just opened!"

Abie's Irish Rose is the kind of play in which a Jewish boy, wanting to marry an Irish girl named Rosemary Murphy, tells his orthodox father that her name is Rosie Murphesky, and the wedding proceeds.

Any further information, if such possibly be necessary, will be furnished at the old offices of Puck, the comic weekly which flourished in the '90's. Although that paper is no longer in existence, there must be some old retainer still about the premises who could tell you everything that is in Abie's Irish Rose.
                                        --Robert C. Benchley in Life (June
                                        8, 1922), page 18.

                              *   *   *

*We are probably the last person in the world qualified to argue with Miss Anne Nichols over the reason for the horrible success of Abie's Irish Rose, but when she says, as she did on the occasion of the play's two-thousandth performance, that people like it because it preaches tolerance and brotherly love, we brave the jeers and taunts of the populace and protest that Miss Nichols doesn't know her own strength. It is our opinion (now quoted in the open market at .04 cents on the dollar) that just exactly the opposite is true.

Up until the final act, Abie's Irish Rose is teeming with racial hatred and intolerance, and if there is one thing that an American audience laughs at more than another it is a good, acrimonious,

---

*Each year, following his initial negative review of the long-running Abie's Irish Rose, Robert Benchley published a new review; this is one of the more interesting.

snarling fight on the stage. If there is one character in a play who
hates everybody else, who is constantly muttering maledictions on
them, who flies into a rage the minute an object of his hate enters,
that character is a sure-fire comedy hit. Abie's Irish Rose has not
only one such character--it has two. Mr. Cohen and Mr. Murphy
can not abide each other's presence. When Mr. Cohen is on stage
and Mr. Murphy enters, the audience screams with anticipatory delight before even a word is spoken. All classes of theatregoers, including this reviewer, love a good, disagreeable character who is a
facile spleen-venter. And there is more spleen vented in the first
two acts of Abie's Irish Rose than in all of Shaw put together.

Just run over in your mind the comedy characters at which
you have laughed hardest, and unless our office statistician is a
liar, you will find that seven out of ten have been either venomous
misanthropes (like the mother in The Show-Off), or timid souls whose
life has been made miserable by the verbal assaults of some bitter
hectorer (like the series of William Collier persecutions). Brotherly
love, me eye!

It is quite possible that the tolerance motif in the last act of
Abie's Irish Rose serves to flatter the audience into an emotional
confidence that their hearts are in the right place and sends them
home in a glow of righteousness, but the show is a hit long before
the last act and it is the old spirit of the Roman gladiatorial combats
which has made it so.

Some day we should like to get together with Miss Nichols and
give her a few pointers on how to please the public.
                                        --Robert C. Benchley in Life
                                        (February 3, 1927), page 19.

AMERICAN BORN (George M. Cohan; Hudson Theatre, October 5,
     1925)

Mr. Cohan, in a curtain-speech at the riotous opening of
American Born, modestly denied being necessary to the "important
theatre." If he but knew it (and of course he does), he is tremendously necessary to the "important theatre," as he is the only
producer in America with a genuine sense of burlesque, the only one
who can go mad. American Born, however, is not necessary to anything. And Mr. Cohan knows that, too.

It is simply one of those Yanks-are-coming pieces, in which
two young Americans make all Britishers look very silly (and, incidentally, the two young Americans pick on one tiny Englishman in
actual physical encounter, from which the cad emerges quite credit-
ably, whether he was meant to or not), and spend their time wishing

they were back in God's country. Any play with Mr. Cohan himself
in it is worth seeing, however.

> --Robert C. Benchley in Life (Octo-
> ber 29, 1925), page 18.

ANIMAL CRACKERS (Book by George S. Kaufman and Morrie Ryskind,
  lyrics and music by Bert Kalmar and Harry Ruby; 44th Street
  Theatre, October 23, 1928)

If we were one, or all four, of the Marx Brothers we should
be a little confused by the judgments passed on us by the two visiting British journalists now on the staff of the N.Y. World. Mr. St.
John Ervine, exercising his unquestioned prerogatives as the guest
of a free country, was not pleased with the new Marx show, Animal
Crackers. On the other hand, his countryman and colleague, Mr.
William Bolitho, was so impressed by it that he wrote an appreciation
in the same journal which must have thrown Die Gebrüder Marx into
a panic of apprehension. We are afraid that from neither critic did
they derive much practical help in their work.

Mr. Ervine had probably heard too much about how funny the
Marx Brothers were, a fatal preparation for any critical viewing.
Someone might have told him, however, that Zeppo Marx is not supposed to be funny and thus have saved him from being so upset by
the discovery when he made it. It must be difficult, in dealing with
so strange a tongue as American, to tell right off-hand whether an
actor is supposed to be funny or not. We may also perhaps attribute
a little of Mr. Ervine's coolness in the face of Groucho Marx's barrage
of wise-cracks to a certain unfamiliarity with the words used. For,
from Mr. Ervine's own genial attempts to be colloquial in the vulgate,
we are quite sure that he couldn't have understood more than a third
of Groucho's highly modern references. Chico Marx, in spite of
having the answers in one of the most devastatingly mad scenes in
modern drama, left Mr. Ervine neither one way nor another, and it
was only Harpo, who speaks the universal language of pantomime
(and lechery), who registered with the visiting commentator. All
in all, pretty nearly a wasted evening for Mr. Ervine.

But even Mr. Ervine's disapproval must have been more compre-
hensible to the Marx family than Mr. Bolitho's enthusiasm, for the
latter understood them better than they probably understand themselves. As so often happens these days among earnest critics, deep
and significant symbolisms were read into this harlequinade which,
if generally accepted, would lower clowning to the level of a Channing
Pollock morality drama. Harpo is, to Mr. Bolitho, "the simplest member to understand," and yet he is a "suppressed wish-complex." We
wonder, or rather Mr. Bolitho wonders, "at the inviolable mutism he
keeps proper to his extrahumanity, at his phantom tricks which be-

long to a largely incommunicable dream world." Harpo should know
about this.

   "Groucho," says Mr. Bolitho (and he may be right), "is at the
same time less elemental and more complicated." We learn that he is
the sublimation of the Jews' attitude toward life, "the exteriorization
of this faithful power of laughing at themselves." The group, as a
family, may possibly "immortalize themselves and become stock characters as enduring as the angel and the devil of the Talmudic legend."
Of the two British opinions, we think we would rather have Mr. Ervine's condemnation. At least, he can plead ignorance of what it
was all about.

   The Marx Brothers ought to be very easy to enjoy. We find it
absurdly simple. In the first place, we know the language, which is
a great help, and, in the second place, we don't stop to think whether we are laughing at Harpo's inviolable mutism or because he is just
comical. When Groucho says to Chico: "You look like Emanuel Ravelli," and Chico says: "I am Emanuel Ravelli," and Groucho retorts: "No wonder you like like him. But I still insist there is a
resemblance," we detect no symbolism of an oppressed Jewry, but
rather a magnificently disordered mind which has come into its own.
And in Chico's suggestion that, in order to see if the stolen painting
is perhaps hidden in the house next door they first build the house
next door, we can find nothing which would qualify the brothers for
participation in a Talmudic legend, but rather something which makes
them a frantically transitory comet formation which we can proudly
tell our grandchildren of having seen one night in 1928. For we
doubt that the Marx Brothers have any successors.

                                        --Robert C. Benchley in Life (No-
                                           vember 16, 1928), page 14.

ANNA CHRISTIE (Eugene O'Neill; Vanderbilt Theatre, November 2,
     1921)

   If someone were to say to you, "Would you like to hear Mischa
Elman play 'Alexander's Ragtime Band'?" you would at once answer
yes. Because after all is said there are but eight notes and a great
artist can make any combination of those eight notes worth hearing.
Of course, there are combinations that are better than others, and
that is what I thought as I saw Eugene O'Neill's Anna Christie.
He takes a simple theme and a simple melodramatic combination and
plays it as an artist. With whether you would have preferred him to
take a greater theme or a greater combination I am less concerned,
because it is for us to consider not what he has not taken but what
he has. And then what he has done with it.

   And what he has taken is the simplest of stories. That of the

daughter of an old sailor who returns to him after some fifteen years.
She left him as a child. She has returned a woman of the brothels.
She goes to live with him on his barge. A crew of another vessel
is shipwrecked. They are picked up. One of the crew, an Irishman,
falls in love with the girl and the girl with him. The father opposes
the marriage. The girl blurts out the truth of her life. The sailor
rushes away but returns to marry the girl.

But it's honest. It doesn't stoop to theatrical effect in line
or in situation or in story for that matter. Basically it may be of
the theatre, but O'Neill writes it so that it becomes genuine, real,
and true.

The acting? Pauline Lord, a great actress. She deserved the
cheers. And George Marion as the old Swede. And Frank Shannon
as the Irish sailor.

> --S. Jay Kaufman in The New York
> Dramatic Mirror, November 20,
> 1921, page 701.

* * *

Every once in a while Pauline Lord comes along and shows us
what real acting is like. Her work in Anna Christie is so distinguished
that the ordinary phrases in a reviewer's vocabulary (and most of
them are ordinary) sound worse than saying nothing about it at all.
So deep is her etching of the part of Anna Christopherson that it
becomes a permanent delineation on the beholder's mind and remains
a part of his own experience.

Eugene O'Neill's play is not so momentous as Miss Lord's contribution to it, but, for its first act alone, Anna Christie should be
classed high among the season's important plays. In the second act
we are asked to accept not only love at first sight but love at practically no sight at all, as the almost simultaneous meeting, courtship
and proposal are carried on in a dense fog at night on the deck of a
coal barge. And in the last act there is that phenomenon which we
always thought would just precede the collapse of Pike's Peak--an
O'Neill happy ending. The author would have done well to put that
fourth act in an open boat with food and water for three days and
turn it out into the sea off Provincetown before sending the play into New York.

But with its first and third acts, and especially with Pauline
Lord and the support given her by George Marion, Frank Shannon
and Eugenie Blair, Anna Christie becomes one of the plays to be
seen if you are old enough to vote.

> --Robert C. Benchley in Life (No-
> vember 24, 1921), page 18.

THE AWFUL TRUTH (Arthur Richman; Henry Miller Theatre, September 18, 1922)

    Passing on now into the sunshine, we come to The Awful Truth, which is excellent entertainment. Mr. Arthur Richman has written a smart comedy which marches, and in the hands of an almost perfect cast, including Ina Claire, Bruce McRae, Paul Harvey and George Barraud, it seems much better than it probably is. The story of a divorcee who discovers that her first husband is more desirable than her prospective second is not particularly new, and a rather ponderous device toward the end upsets the balance a bit, but it is restful to sit back and feel that whatever happens, Miss Claire and Mr. McRae, with their able associates, are there to take care of it.
                              --Robert C. Benchley in Life (October 5, 1922), page 18.

BEGGAR ON HORSEBACK (George S. Kaufman and Marc Connelly; Broadhurst Theatre, February 12, 1924)

    Just to be mean, this department has always tried to find the faults in the opera of the Messrs. Kaufman and Connelly and dwell on them at perhaps a disproportionate length. In Dulcy, To the Ladies! Merton of the Movies and The Deep Tangled Wildwood we dragged out little flaws for inspection, chiefly because we feared that if we said how much we really liked them we should be investigated by the Senate and found guilty of once having had lunch with the team of playwrights in question.

    But in the face of Beggar on Horseback we must break down and admit that the boys are good. In fact, when it comes to satiric manipulation of the smug elements in our complacent civilization, such as business efficiency, literary standardization, artistic streetwalking, and other evidences that the Man in the Street is King, there seems to be no one in the field of playwriting to-day who is within shouting distance of this pair.

    Of course, there have been dream-plays before. And there have been impressionistic attacks on some of the things attacked in Beggar on Horseback, notably in The Adding Machine and Roger Bloomer. So the authors of the present opus can scarcely be called pioneers, although it is, as a matter of fact, a development of the claim which they did stake out as pioneers in Dulcy and which they have dug at in every play they have done since: the kidding of the great Business Bunk and Allied Bunks in other fields.

    What makes Beggar on Horseback remarkable is that, wholly aside from its message, it is very funny. It is a good show. Roland

Young, as the young musician who has one of the longest Freudian experiences in the history of dreams (8:30 until 11 p.m.), is an actor of such gentle skill that he has illuminated many inferior roles in the past and now finds himself in something worthy of his efforts, if you can call his smooth and quiet technique an effort. The rest of the cast, especially George Barbier in the delectable trial scene, couldn't be much better than they are, and, although we are one of the peasant type of playgoer who starts squirming along about the third minute of a pantomime, we must admit that, if a pantomime must be had, the one devised by Deems Taylor and executed by George Mitchell and a six-million-dollar blonde by the name of (let's see) Ruzt-Nissen is the best possible way out of the difficulty.

As an added feature, a mock newspaper is distributed between the acts which alone contains enough gorgeous clowning to make the paltry price of admission a privilege to pay.

--Robert C. Benchley in *Life*
(March 6, 1924), page 20.

* * *

"The whole enterprise," says the reviewer for the New York *Herald*, writing of the Messrs. Kaufman's and Connelly's *Beggar on Horseback*--"beginning with the purchase of a German original by Winthrop Ames, who read it and then threw it into the scrapbasket-- is a fine achievement." What we have here, however, is a much more commendable and thrilling display of 100 per cent Anglo-Algonquinism than an acquaintance with the facts, for Mr. Ames threw much less of Paul Apel's *Hans Sonnenstösser's Trip to Hell* into the scrapbasket than the *Herald's* comradely booster and patriot believes. It is true that the American adaptors have put several original and diverting scenes into the play, but that play, for all their embroideries, remains in theme, structure, intimate plan, characters, climaxes and numerous details considerably like the play that was produced in Berlin twelve years ago. The adaptors have Americanized the characters in the matter of externals, have brought up to date and localized satirically portions of the dream-body of the manuscript, have made their young composer hero play a composition by Deems Taylor instead of Chopin's Prelude in C minor, as in the Berlin production, have converted Apel's gramophone into a hurdy-gurdy and caused it to play a jazz tune instead of Paul Lincke's appallingly popular "Give Me a Little Bit of Love" from the then current musical comedy success, *Berliner Luft*, and have contrived a number of other such patent alterations, but, though they have done their job dexterously, they have brought little sound humor and fancy to the text that were not in it originally. Their deletion of the parrot, a highly comical device of the original; their conversion of the ear-torturing orchestra of the original into a singing jury; their mere suggestion of the nerve-racking phonograph that drives the young composer to distraction--these are as unfortunate as their literal adherence to the amusing murder scene at the end of the first

act, to the manner of the epilogue and prologue, and to the device
of the irksome heiress and the dancing waiter is the opposite.

The best elements in the local version of the play consist in
the adroitly humorous touches with which the adaptors have tricked
out the ends of several scenes in the original which, had they been
left as they were, would doubtless have trailed off somewhat ineffectively for an American audience, as well as in a thoroughly charming pantomine incorporated into the play by Deems Taylor--the most
delicately lovely thing of its kind I have seen since Madame Donnet's
little ballet, "La Pomme d'Or," and a vastly hilarious Kaufman-
Connelly burlesque of an American newspaper which is peddled among
the audience during the entr'acte. Roland Young has the rôle of
the young composer whose nightmare of what life would make of him,
were he to marry money at the expense of artistic happiness, brings
him back into the arms of a waiting Cinderella. His performance is
generally well managed, although one might wish that, inasmuch as
he cannot play the piano, he would at least learn the relative posi-
tions of the keys so that his digital manoeuvers might less drolly
fail to follow and synchronize with the off-stage playing.

> --George Jean Nathan in The Amer-
> ican Mercury (Vol. 1, No. 4),
> April 1924, pages 499-500.

BERKELEY SQUARE (John L. Balderston; Lyceum Theatre, November
    4, 1929)

After having seen a good deal of Ibsen done by Ye Little
Vanitie Case Players and a good deal of Shipman done by the coarse,
commercial managers along Broadway, I have gone before a notary
and signed a paper to the effect that I prefer seeing a bad play
well done to seeing a good play botched. That is just by way of
making a general rule of conduct for myself. It keeps me in Broadway. It is true that one may see an appalling number of bad plays
botched in Broadway, but one will never, never find a good play
well done in the Village. Good plays do get themselves done well
occasionally in Broadway and the event is worth waiting for. It is
happening at the moment at the Lyceum Theatre.

Berkeley Square is a good play beautifully done. It has to
do with a young American come to take possession of his Queen Anne
house in Berkeley Square and loving the past which it evokes. He
loves that past so passionately that he manages, by calling up the
jinnee who lives in his forebrain, to turn up as his own ancestor
in the London of 1784 and move through a few days of the life of
the time. Next to falling heir to an Invisible Cloak, it is the thing
that most of us would rather have happen to us than anything else
in the fairy tales.

The affair is eerily, romantically, superlatively fetchingly played by Leslie Howard, by Margalo Gillmore, and by the rest of the cast. Mr. Howard's last minute and a half on the stage contain as fine a bit of acting as one could hope to see.

It is a great comfort to see the art of acting at last catching up with the scenery; to stumble on a set of actors who live up to the doors through which they enter and exeunt. When real, wooden doors, swung on proper hinges and set in fixed jambs, first began to replace canvas doors on the stage, the effect, at least on me, was to shatter completely the illusion. The doors were so much more solid and satisfactory than the plays in those dark days, and the actors so much more wooden than the doors, that everything suffered horribly by contrast. I could believe that the ham hero was dashing off to carry the dispatches through the Confederate lines, against staggering odds, if he dashed off through a make-believe door and left the side wall of Fortress Monroe quivering and bellying in the breeze behind him. But when the early Belascos had union carpenters in to build genuine doors into the scenery, the far from genuine actors became about as convincing as a toupee.

These matters are particularly happily balanced in Berkeley Square. The production is Gilbert Miller's and Leslie Howard's, and, since there is no one better at scenery than Mr. Miller, and no one better at acting than Mr. Howard, the production is soul-satisfyingly right from beginning to end. If there is a tiresome spot here and there in the play itself, there is always something to look at and think about until it is over. There is, for example, a portrait of Mr. Howard's ancestor, supposedly painted by Sir Joshua Reynolds, which not only looks like Mr. Howard, but actually looks from the front as though it might have been painted by Reynolds. This is, as far as I know, the first use in any theatre of a portrait which did not look as though it had been painted by one of the stage hands. The picture turns up in the second act in its unfinished state; and there it is, sitting on Sir Joshua's own easel, sketched in sepia, just as Sir Joshua would have done it. I think these trifles are of tremendous importance.

>   --Ralph Barton in Life (November
>   22, 1929), page 24.

BEYOND THE HORIZON (Eugene O'Neill; Morosco Theatre, February
    3, 1920)

It is a grim study of misdirected lives which Eugene G. O'Neill offers in Beyond the Horizon, his first long play, and which introduces Richard Bennett's repertory season under the direction of John D. Williams. O'Neill has inherited a fine sense of the theater. He has demonstrated it in a number of stirring one-act plays of sea folk, presented in obscure parts of New York. In <u>Beyond the Horizon</u> he branches out most promisingly, taking up the mood which has inspired Ervine, Synge, Tchekov and other European dramatists--a mood which aims at reflecting all phases of life, the sombre and tragic, the gay and whimsical.

It is a play written with imagination and dramatic feeling. There is a pitilessly ironic undertone to its symbolism. The characters are drawn with accuracy and intelligence, and the dialogue in the main is forceful and true to the life it represents. For two acts it moves grippingly toward its relentless climax, but the last act shows a too conscious effort to attain this relentlessness, too little variety in the telling.

When the curtain rises you see a young dreamer, physically frail, sitting by the roadside gazing beyond the horizon at the sun setting upon the distant sea. He is about to take up a seafaring life with his uncle which will gratify, he believes, all his vague longings for a life of adventure and romance. His brother, a burly, unimaginative but generous fellow, is to remain on the farm.

There enters the girl from the neighboring farm--gay, wholesome but lacking sensitiveness. She pours out her heart and induces him to abandon his idea of a sea life. He agrees, marries her and remains on the farm while the brother takes his place on the ship.

Destiny plays its grotesque prank. The dreamer is a ghastly failure as a farmer and the property fast goes to ruin under his direction. Eventually he learns from his wife's own lips that she does not love him, that she knows she is more suited to the burly brother. But he finds solace in his child and his books.

More disaster overtakes him and he develops tuberculosis and while the brother has struck it rich in Buenos Aires, he lives ploddingly, hopelessly on the little farm--alone with his wife, now sodden in her despair, and her crippled nagging mother, who clings to life with usual tenacity. His mind is still on the open road that leads over the hills and beyond the horizon and the curtain falls upon him feverishly seeking it. He knows he is finally to go "to the far places." He has finally realized his dream.

Richard Bennett gave an excellent performance of the dreamer-- a difficult part to play with its shadows and subtleties. He must revel in it, for he hasn't had such an acting opportunity in years. Helen MacKellar brought a rugged simplicity and naturalness to the wife. Edward Arnold was convincing in the role of the brother. Louise Closser Hale gave a realistic portrayal of the crippled mother, a garrulous pessimist but ever so agile in maneuvering her wheelchair. Erville Anderson was capital as the proud old father. Max

Mitzel and George Riddell were effective as a profane sea captain and
a physician respectively.

--Louis R. Reid in The New York
Dramatic Mirror (February 14,
1920), page 258.

A BILL OF DIVORCEMENT (Clemence Dane; George M. Cohan Theatre;
November 10, 1921)

 A Bill of Divorcement throws an even more poignant gloom into
the soul of the beholder, probably because it is a better play.* In
the year 1932 a man who has been insane since the war returns
home, suddenly rational, to find his wife divorced from him and about
to marry another man. It is his daughter, a member of the much-
warned and maligned younger generation, who saves the situation, if
you can call a situation saved which sends you away beating your
temples and moaning softly to yourself.

 Allan Pollock, who has himself just returned to the stage from
the war hospital, is tremendously pitiful as the husband, and Katharine Cornell takes the remarkably written part of the girl and fills
it with abundant life and understanding. The play itself is subtly
depressing, perhaps because its bitter events take place on Christmas Day, but it is the kind of depression which brings with it exal-
tation.

--Robert C. Benchley in Life (November 3, 1921), page 18.

* * *

 A Bill of Divorcement by Clemence Dane is a carefully, cunningly wrought play. It treats of a phase of the divorce question which
is English, not American. The audience is even asked to suppose
that an amendment to the English divorce law which is pending has
been passed. We may suppose that the play was written as propaganda in support of this English law. It is frankly a thesis play,
and the thesis is one which has little to do with life in this country.
Yet the impossible happens. So vivid is the story into which the author transmutes her thesis that the thesis, happily, is entirely forgotten; or rather it is absorbed into the story and serves if anything
to stiffen it and root it even more deeply in reality.

 It is rooted deeply in the realities of human experience. That
is why it quickly transcends the special, local conditions which provide its background. That is why it is as poignantly moving in this

---

*Than The Claw.

country as it was in England. After all the special pleading is secondary. After all the play really grows out of the very human frailties of the three members of the Fairfield family, and each of them is really struggling for the right to live.

Margaret Fairfield, as we come to know her in the beginning, is not a particularly strong woman; she is now, and always has been, swayed by her daughter and the others about her. She is deeply in love with a man who is deeply in love with her, but is not quite sure that her duty does not lie with her insane husband. It is true that she married him in the fervid war days, when values were distorted; for sixteen years he has been in the insane asylum as a result of shell shock; but still she is not quite comfortable in taking up a new life without him. She is afraid her happiness is too good to last, and her indefinable trepidation communicates itself to us.

Her daughter, Sydney, is a different type. She is sharp and buoyant and modern; but in her there is a suggestion of the highly strung, over-sensitive temperament of the father who, even before his appearance, casts a sinister shadow over the household. Sydney, too, is engaged to be married; and in her case also we have that curious sense that her happiness is too good to last.

Then Fairfield comes. He has been cured of his insanity and has escaped from the asylum and returned to his home. A grey shell of a man he is, sane, but still a quivering convalescent, seemingly trembling on the verge of madness.

In his eyes Margaret is still his wife. With his old nervous fervor he beseeches her to return to him--he pleads for his right to live. Her love for him is gone. She has given her love to another man--and she has the right to live. Vacillating still she is ready to forego her happiness; but in the end it is Sydney who makes the sacrifice after she learns that her father's madness was in reality inherited, and that she herself may have the taint in her blood.

When a play with a mission turns out to be such a superb play one always wonders whether the play was written to serve the mission or whether the mission was appropriated to serve the play. And we invariably suspect the latter.

> --Kenneth Andrews in The Book-
> man, Vol. 54, No. 4 (December
> 1921), pages 376-377.

BITTER SWEET (Noel Coward; Ziegfeld Theatre, November 5, 1929)

Noel Coward is unquestionably the cleverest young man alive. At the age of twenty-nine, he can write plays, revues and operettas,

stage them, and act any of the rôles in them. He can compose songs
and lyrics, and sing them, accompanying himself on the piano, the
clavichord, the Irish harp, the hurdy-gurdy, or (by singing through
his nose, American fashion) on the trombone. He is the tennis and
badminton champion of Ebury Street; he tangoes and roller-skates
divinely, sketches ravishingly in aquarelle, and can recite the Gla-
golitic alphabet. I have heard it said that he once won an argument
from Florenz Ziegfeld over the selection of a chorus girl, but this
rumor may perhaps be put down to exaggeration born of his admir-
ers' enthusiasm. No man is as clever as that.

As for Mr. Ziegfeld: it would not only be flagrant lèse-
majesté, but pure dunderheadedness, to suggest that anyone on the
planet can touch him at the great-big, expensive production business.
He invented it, he made it what it is today, and what it will be for
a good many tomorrows. Whenever any other producer hires two
show girls, he is, if he is serious about his work, already beginning
to imitate Mr. Ziegfeld. This matter is no secret from the public.
If one of Mr. Ziegfeld's first-night audiences should be wiped out by
a wave of poison gas, the Social Register and Bradstreet's would be
forced to suspend publication until the next generation grows up.

As for Evelyn Laye: England has never produced a fairer
damsel--and I don't mean this the way it sounds. I mean that Miss
Laye is really devastatingly beautiful and alluring. She is beautiful
and alluring here in America, where all the women are masterpieces
of the Almighty's.

And yet (and this is the part of this review that I have been
dreading all week and trying to put off for a column):

I thought Bitter Sweet was pretty dull.

I suppose I should go and stand in the corner for having said
that--but that is the way I felt. The beat of the operetta never quite
caught up with the rivet-metronomed pit-a-pat of my New York heart.
They were playing "Hearts and Flowers" while I was whistling "Yankee
Doodle" and the effect was a not very amusing cacophony. I am sure
that if one stepped out of the Haymarket into His Majesty's Theatre,
where Bitter Sweet is playing in London, its graceful sentimental
rhythm wouldn't clash so violently with the outside world to which
one has become accustomed. But when one battles across Sixth
Avenue, after a series of hair-raising races with the traffic lights,
with one's eyes fixed on the façade of the Ziegfeld Theatre (so, by
the way, like a book-end magnified 1,000 times) as a goal, one's
appetite is whetted for a catchy tune and a funny comedian, not to
mention a platoon of Tiller Girls.

Bitter Sweet haughtily disowns catchy tunes, comedians and
Tiller Girls. It is as like the dear, dead 1880's and 1890's, in which
its story is laid, as a horsehair sofa--that is to say, it is quaint and

fetching and makes you fidget. The best things in it lose force by
being connotative. For example, the quartet of "greenery, yallery,
Grosvenor Gallery, foot-in-the-grave" young men would make up for
the absence of comedians to one soaked in the lore of Patience, of
The Yellow Book, of Hichens and Holbrook Jackson--if you could
find such a one along Sixth Avenue. So with the costumes, the
settings in Belgrave Square and Vienna, the story, the music and
the rest of the entertainment. It is an exact, delicate and intelligent reproduction of the mood of 1880-1890, miraculously well done
and fitting very awkwardly into tough, low-down 1929.

Of course, if you don't like 1929 (I am completely gone on it,
myself) Bitter Sweet would be just the thing to help you get away
from it all for a couple of hours, and for a very pleasant couple of
hours, too.

                              --Ralph Barton in Life (November
                                29, 1929), page 20.

BLACK BIRDS OF 1928 (Lyrics by Dorothy Fields, Music by Jimmy
    McHugh; Liberty Theatre, May 9, 1928)

Going to the theater these fine spring evenings is a little depressing, especially as there are no theaters to go to. A season
which died several months ago has just officially been pronounced
dead, the final blow having been given it when our opera hat was
smashed against the roof of a taxicab going over a bump. A couple
of plays tried to open after that, but the old carnival spirit was
gone.

There was one, however, which had plenty of life and enough
rhythm to make the entire theater hitch from left to right on its
foundations. Black Birds of 1928 may be just another one of those
colored revues, but it seemed to us to be exceptionally full of good
stuff.

Negro revues, as a general thing, seem to rely on a genial
spirit of willingness rather than on any particular merit to put themselves across. This one has several performers who are as good in
their lines as any performers could possibly be--and, once or twice,
even better. Mr. Bill Robinson, when he taps his way up and down
his own personal stairs, and Mr. Milton Crawley, when he tortures
his clarinet into some of the meanest sounds heard in these parts
since public whipping was abolished, both are artists that need no
bush. Then there is a "Porgy" number at the opening of the second
act which utilizes lavender shadows to excellent effect, and some
lyrics by Dorothy Fields which are not only sung distinctly but are
worth singing distinctly, especially "I Must Have That Man," as rendered by Adelaide Hall.

If this sounds like an enthusiastic notice of <u>Black Birds of</u>
<u>1928</u>, it is because we meant it to. Very few of our colleagues
seemed to see the difference between it and the average colored
show, but very few of our colleagues feel as we feel about hot clarinet work and tap-dancing.

> --Robert C. Benchley in <u>Life</u> (May
> 31, 1928), page 20.

BLOSSOM TIME (Book and Lyrics by Dorothy Donnelly, Music by
Franz Schubert and H. Berete; Ambassador Theatre, September
29, 1921)

It will be known as the Shubert-Schubert triumph. <u>Blossom</u>
<u>Time</u> with but a slight blemish of so-called "comedy" in the second
act (out by now no doubt) is so far above the <u>May Times</u> and <u>Blue</u>
<u>Paradises</u> with which it is being compared that when they are for-
gotten this will still be touring. Or being revived. The music over-
whelms, but even music so glorious might not attract the average
person without so fascinating a story. There have been more brilliant stories more brilliantly told. Dorothy Donnelly who adapted it
did not attempt to make the book sparkle. She evidently felt--and
wisely--that hers was a job. The job of subduing the story to such
an extent that it merely <u>told</u> the music. Telling the music meant
simplicity. And the life of the composer, Franz Shubert, needed
only simplicity. Any attempt at brilliancy would have fallen as flatly
as did the aforesaid "comedy." And would have lessened the effect
of the music. As it is, the music heightened the story because the
music is told via the composer's simple love story. The story of a
composer who writes his music to tell his love to his beloved.

And the cast has at least two voices. Bertram Peacock was
Schubert and Howard Marsh was the Schober. One had the awkward-
ness and the other the dash. And they sang! Olga Cook took a
daring step when she went from vaudeville to this role but she gave
a satisfactory account of herself. A great many other small "bits"
but no one mattered very much excepting Zoe Barnett.

> --S. Jay Kaufman in <u>The New</u>
> <u>York Dramatic Mirror</u>, October
> 8, 1921, page 520.

* * *

After seasons and seasons of musical scores containing nothing
but lethargic blues and steals on previous song-hits which weren't
worth stealing in the first place, the music in <u>Blossom Time</u> makes
you want to lean over and cry on the person sitting next to you.
You suddenly remember the ideals with which you started out in life,
how you were going to be a great and good man and pat little children

on the head from your victoria as you drove through the streets.
And here you are, a worthless ne'er-do-well, in fact a wastrel, already past your prime, with nothing left but the faint pink in the
clouds where the sun has set. Ah, happy, happy, golden days!

To be sure, it is Franz Schubert's music which does all this
to you, Franz Schubert's melodies frankly adapted by Sigmund Romberg for use in a play built around an incident in the life of the composer himself. So you needn't feel ashamed of breaking down. It
is perfectly good form to be affected by Franz Schubert. And, although I am one of those to whom the Duncan Sisters represent the
highest point yet reached in American music, I think I am safe in
saying that Mr. Romberg's handling of this very difficult task will
give a minimum of offense to Schubert lovers. And the orchestra,
under the direction of Oscar Radin, must surely be satisfactory to
even the most offensive musical experts.

It might be well, in the interests of accuracy, to add that
Blossom Time is acted quite as badly, for the most part, as any
grand opera, but so long as Olga Cook, Bertram Peacock and Howard
Marsh sing every now and then, they don't have to act well.
                              --Robert C. Benchley in Life (Octo-
                                 ber 20, 1921), page 18.

THE BLUE FLAME (George V. Hobart and John Willard; Shubert
       Theatre, March 15, 1920)

What a night! The most terrible play within the memory of
the writer has served to introduce Theda Bara to the spoken stage.
All of Broadway and Fort Lee turned out for the occasion. They
came to see what the reputedly greatest vampire of the screen would
do on the stage. They remained to laugh long and hilariously at
the preposterous situations, the Fourteenth Street dialogue, the crude
scenes and the absurdly bad acting of the star.

It was indeed one of those rare occasions when a play is so
hopeless that it is funny. The audience, alert to the crude and ridiculous impossibilities of it ten minutes after the curtain rose, burst
out unrestrainedly at the lines delivered with defiant seriousness by
Miss Bara. And it waited to the bitter end to see how much worse
the play could become.

The reaction of the audience it is reasonable to expect, came
later. Then it must have occurred to all who witnessed the awful
thing that an appalling waste of time had been endured. To see a
crude actress, no matter how famous she is in the films, unfamiliar
with the rudiments of dramatic art, lacking any knowledge even of
the uses of the voice for emotional moments, and possessing only the

slightest appeal in her personality, strutting about extravagantly in a series of maudlin episodes is not really worth fifteen minutes time of any intelligent man or woman.

George V. Hobart shamelessly added his name to the play. He has probably reached such a state of affluence that he does not care. But he should care. He should at least have respect for his public—a public that never in its most primitive days witnessed such a rotten play as The Blue Flame. Even the old Bowery and Fourteenth Street melodramas were more convincing, more true to life, more skilfully written. They never handicapped their players even in their wildest moments as The Blue Flame handicapped Donald Gallaher and Alan Dinehart. How Messrs Gallaher and Dinehart can maintain a serious mien with the dialogue that they utter is in itself a mystery.

Mr. Woods comes out of the enterprise with profit. His good sense of showmanship may bring enormous returns. Reports have straggled in from distant points that riots were held in the vicinity of the stage doors where Theda was playing, so anxious were people to catch a glimpse of her. Such people naturally will pay—at times—to see her "act." In addition, Mr. Woods will collect a handsome sum from the motion picture rights.

Miss Bara is given an opportunity in the play to show a two-sided character—a kind and virtuous girl who does settlement work and loves an atheistic scientist in spite of himself, and a vampire who is the inspiration for countless crimes and degradations. When a flash of lightning strikes her dead in the laboratory of her scientific friend the latter restores her to life. But her soul eludes him. It goes, looking for all the world like a molar tooth, straight up to the top of the Shubert Theater.

And then the vamping begins. Theda without her soul goes from bad to worse. She abuses her husband, strikes her old servants, sniffs cocaine, kills one of her lovers to get his money and finally winds up in Chinatown where she sells a blue diamond to a tong leader. But it has all been a dream. The atheist wakes up from his nightmare and renounces his attitude of unbelief. And Theda is again the kind and virtuous girl of the opening scene.

Miss Bara's every move and gesture were studied and mechanical. But she might have held the interest and kept submerged the risibilities of the audience had she been a convincing vampire. She lacked color and appeal and physical charm. To compare her for a moment with Dorothy Dalton in Aphrodite or Geraldine Farrar in Zaza or Mary Garden in Thaïs will give you a realization of the futility of her vampire pose. Donald Gallaher gave a good sketch of a dope fiend, and Henry Herbert sang the lines of the Chinese tong leader eloquently.

—Louis R. Reid in The New York
Dramatic Mirror (March 20, 1920),
page 520.

BROADWAY (Philip Dunning and George Abbott; Broadhurst Theatre,
    September 16, 1926)

    We tried to review Broadway in our last issue, but didn't have
space enough. And now that we have plenty of space, all that we
can say is that it is a swell show.

    There has been a lot written about Broadway already and there
probably will be a lot more. There will also probably be a lot more
written like Broadway. Managers and playwrights are the most
broad-minded people in the world. They have just as soon have it
said that their play is like Broadway if their box-office statement is
also like Broadway's.

    But in case you don't happen to have read a story a day about
this first real hit of the new season, let us put it in the records
that it is as perfect a piece of direction (by the authors, Philip Dunning and George Abbott) and of casting (presumably by the producer,
Jed Harris) as we have ever seen. From Lee Tracy as the young
hoofer who is "first the artist, then the human being," down to the
waiter who jingles small change in his pockets as he walks, it is a
beautiful job. If we started mentioning names, we'd get 'way over
into the next column, for there are about twenty-five people in the
cast, including as darling a bunch of gangsters as ever wore "smok-
ings." So we will let it go at saying that this epic of night-club
life has made us reconsider our threatened retirement into the Bide-
a-Wee Home for Critics; for we know now that it was not old age
that made us cold toward the other shows of the season, but simply
that the other shows were bad.
                            --Robert C. Benchley in Life (Oc-
                                tober 14, 1926), page 23.

                        *   *   *

    The first overwhelming success of the season burst upon us on
the night of Thursday the sixteenth in Broadway, by Philip Dunning
and George Abbott, at the Broadhurst Theatre. I notice that it is
described on the program merely as "a play." I should diagnose it
as a comedy with a tragic, swashbuckling secondary plot. The sub-
plot is a chronicle of Tabloidia, the land of the Big Gunmen. It
tells how Steve Crandall shot Scar Edwards in the back, for economic reasons, and how Scar's girls repaid him. While in its main
outlines this portion of the play is a little stereotyped, so beautifully
is it told, and with so little hysteria, that its familiar contour only
impresses the observer after study.

    The main plot concerns the love affair of the hoofer of a Broad-
way dance palace (Lee Tracy) with one of the girls in the place
(Sylvia Field). It is told with poignancy, with humor and in a ver-
nacular which never falters. The action takes place in the private

party room of the joint which is also used as an auxiliary dressing
room for the performers. There is a charming love scene played by
the hero in his B.V.D.'s, a fact of which he is entirely unconscious,
and in it he threatens to spank the heroine if she doesn't behave
herself, which is not quite a sample of the authenticity of the dialogue. Perhaps the "Pagliacci" possibilities of exits into the cabaret
in dance formation are a little overdone; I guess not.

      The plot fuses in a second-act climax of gigantic tension, and
if I weren't irresponsible with enthusiasm that's a phrase you wouldn't
have found on me dead.

      For the direction of the play, which was by the authors, I
can think of no meaner adjective than faultless. That same word
might almost do duty for the performances of the cast.

      Lee Tracy, who first came to my notice as the brother in The
Show-Off, a role as different from his present one as possible,
achieved the greatest personal triumph and deserved it; though Miss
Field and Robert Gleckler, as Steve Crandall, did superlatively good
work.

      Broadway has the vibrant, Elizabethan quality which I believe
accountable for the success of Lulu Belle and The Shanghai Gesture;
like them it explores a strange and fascinating world, it has their
sensational romanticism; and yet it omits the worse features of both.
It would take an expert prig to find anything objectionable in Broadway.

      I'm afraid I'll have to tell you that Broadway is compulsory.
                        --Charles Brackett in The New
                          Yorker (September 25, 1926),
                          page 30.

BURLESQUE (George Mankin Watters and Arthur Hopkins; Plymouth
      Theatre, September 1, 1927)

      The dams which theatrical managers have erected for many
years against plays about stage characters have been efficiently
dynamited and the flood is now upon us. It started last year with
Jed Harris's production of Broadway and Kenyon Nicholson's play,
The Barker. The first dealt with cabaret performers, bootleggers
and highjackers, the second with the private existence of tent-show
people. And now comes Arthur Hopkins as producer and co-author
with George Mankin Watters, of Burlesque a play dealing with the
intimate lives of performers on the small-time circuit. Because of
the current fad, and also because of Mr. Hopkins's reputation as a
producer, Burlesque was heralded many weeks before its appearance

in New York as this season's successor to <u>Broadway</u>. Yet as facts
stand, it has almost nothing in common with <u>Broadway</u>. It is a
sentimental play whereas <u>Broadway</u> was purely melodrama.

Probably the advance heralding had much to do with the disappointment of the first-night critics. They came prepared for salt,
and were handed sugar. They looked for melodrama and found only
pathos and characterization. And so it happened that most of the
early reviews carried the warning that this was not, after all, another <u>Broadway</u>; with a natural inference that it was not as good as
<u>Broadway</u>. That, I believe, is much too harsh a statement of the
case.

<u>Burlesque</u> is essentially a very simple story, quite simply told,
and largely dependent for its theatrical interest on the supposed
glimpse it furnishes into a life far different from that of the audience. Bonny, the leading lady of the Parisian Widows, is married
to Skid, the leading comedian of the same traveling company. Skid's
work attracts the attention of a theatrical scout who offers him the
comic lead in a big Broadway production. This offer Skid accepts.
The first act closes with an affecting farewell, modified by the appearance of a simple, straightforward cattle man from the West, who
has become Bonny's devoted, though distant, admirer. In the second
act you see the result of sudden success on Skid's character. New
York and a big salary prove too much for him. Bonny, after every
effort to reclaim him by long distance, has divorced him and come to
New York with the intention of marrying Harvey Howell, the cattle
man. Her real love, however, is still for Skid, and when they all
meet in her apartment, there results a curious scene in which the
lives of three people are shattered by the false pride of Bonny and
Skid.

In the last act Skid has been fired from the New York production, and after being reduced to the lowest straits is given his
last chance in a new out-of-town show. But he is apparently beyond
all reclamation until Bonny, yielding to the frantic appeals of the
manager, comes to him at the last minute to try and put him on his
feet. The concluding scenes of the play are supposed to be numbers in the burlesque show itself, in which we hear the promise of
Bonny, whispered between the steps of a routine number, to come
back once more to Skid.

Obviously a play of this character must be handled with the
utmost skill to convey a complete sense of reality--skill in direction,
staging and acting. Of the staging of <u>Burlesque</u> there can be no
complaint. Arthur Hopkins is nothing if not thoroughgoing in his
attention to detail. But his direction is rather famous for following a
slow pace. In the kind of scene where two young people are facing
each other with breaking hearts across a gulf of misunderstanding,
Mr. Hopkins has a genius for extracting the last ounce of pathos.
But to achieve a full effect, such scenes ought to be set in a con-

trasting mood of quick, spontaneous action. It is in the lack of such
a contrast, I believe, that Burlesque falls short of its full possibilities. The play grows oversweet at times. Of course the lines themselves as well as the slow pace contribute to this. There are too
many long and unbroken speeches which give quite unnecessarily
a feeling of talkiness.

The acting in general is excellent, with Hal Skelly, as Skid,
and Ralph Theadore, as Harvey Howell, the chief luminaries. Mr.
Skelly's performance is quite as good within its own outlines as that
of Lee Tracy in Broadway. Mr. Theadore makes the rather difficult
and sentimental character of the cattle man utterly believable and interesting. Unfortunately for the effect of the play as a whole,
Barbara Stanwyck is not quite so well cast as Bonny. It so happens
that she has most of the difficult and long speeches, and her delivery of them lacks the variety and incisiveness which might bring
them to life. She is much at her best in the slower scenes of the
second act. Burlesque, as a whole, is fair to middling entertainment,
the amount of glamour you find in it being dependent largely upon
your own feeling about stage characters.

--Richard Dana Skinner in The
Commonweal, Vol. 6, No. 21
(September 28, 1927), pages 500-
501.

* * *

The first Arthur Hopkins production of the season is Burlesque,
by George Manker Watters and Mr. Hopkins himself. Here is another
play about show folks. Broadway probably precipitated this recent
craze for letting the public into the secrets of the dressing-room,
though The Barker was written before Broadway saw the footlights.
But unless I am mistaken, the first of this species of play (in recent
times, at least) was Knowles Entrikin's The Small Timers, first seen
at the Beechwood Theater, Scarborough, three years ago, and then
put on, less skilfully, for a short run at the Punch and Judy Theater,
New York. The authors of The Small Timers, Broadway, The Barker,
and Burlesque, each in his own way, seem rather too anxious to de-
pict the simple-hearted troupers as slangy but picturesque denizens
of a world in which everyone at the proper moment turns out to have
a heart of gold. Mr. Entrikin's and Mr. Nicholson's plays, however,
are in this respect not quite so conventional as the other two.

Burlesque shows us an attractive girl whose husband is a successful "comic," a song-and-dance man, but without ambition. He is
offered the chance of a lifetime in New York, is forced by his wife to
accept it, and leaves the little girl sobbing her pathetic farewell.
After a short period of great popularity on Broadway he takes to
drink and a few other conventional vices, and is shortly down and
out. At the right moment, just before his wife has secured a divorce
from him in order to marry a wealthy Westerner, she is summoned to

New York, makes her husband behave himself, and promises to return
to him. Presumably all is well again. All of which could indeed happen, only I think that it doesn't. Skid would actually try to reform, and he would ask Bonny to help him, for if the dramatists
were in earnest about the Skid they have shown us, we must believe
him an incompetent man, even if he is an amusing comedian. But to
show him a permanent failure would not make so pretty a play.

The trouble with Burlesque is that it is composed largely of
theatrical elements: there is too much "theatre" and not enough
truth. This is seen especially in the three scenes actually shown to
the audience from the show in which Skid finally appears: these are
padding, pure and simple. They are motivated by nothing but a
desire to give the audience some songs and dances and bright costumes. In The Small Timers on the other hand, it was necessary to
show us the young boy and girl actually performing, because their
talent or want of it was the point of the play. Mr. Entrikin's "hero"
was not an actor at all, but a rank amateur; this had to be shown,
and when it was shown we believed it. But the "lead" in Burlesque
is said to have been good enough to bring to New York at a salary
of $500 a week. We see him doing the thing for which he received
this money. He is not convincing, because he so obviously is not a
$500 actor, and all we say after we see his stunts is that he is
getting at least $300 too much.

In treating anything so theatrical as the theatre, a dramatist
must, I think, go out of his way to avoid theatricality. This is just
what Messrs. Hopkins and Watters have not done.

--Barrett H. Clark in The Drama,
Vol. 18, No. 2 (November 1927),
page 39.

THE BUTTER-AND-EGG MAN (George S. Kaufman; Longacre Theatre,
September 23, 1925)

One of the quick successes of the year seems to be G. S. Kaufman's The Butter-and-Egg Man, with Gregory Kelly as the sucker in
question. There is no reason that we can see why it shouldn't be a
success. An evening full of snappy retorts in that most humorous
of all jargons, the language of Broadway, a sure and skilful handling
of business tactics as sudden and questionable as those in Turn to
the Right, by far the best performance that Mr. Kelly has ever given
to our knowledge, which is no faint praise, and a supporting cast of
runners-up, including Lucille Webster, Sylvia Field, Robert Middlemass and Denman Maley. All this, added to the fact that most of the
general public who are not enough on the inside of the theatrical
mart to understand all of its shoptalk are, like Mr. Kaufman's hero,
consumed by an inexplicable desire to make believe that they under-

stand it, would seem to indicate a happy New Year for the The
Butter-and-Egg Man.

                            --Robert C. Benchley in Life
                              (October 15, 1925), page 18.

                              *   *   *

        Last but not least we found The Butter-and-Egg Man a grand
show, especially in the work of Lucille Webster, Robert Middlemass,
and Denman Maley. In the title role Gregory Kelly gave a type performance of the sort he has succeeded in capitalizing admirably.
Since the piece, from the title on through, is concerned with the inside of Broadway, a word of explanation is necessary. A "butter
and egg man" in the parlance of Broadway is "a sap with money"
from the provinces--the sort that falls prey to shady theatrical producers and gold digging chorus girls. The comedy concerns itself
with the trials of Peter Jones who comes to Broadway from Chillicothe,
Ohio, with $20,000, to break into what he calls "the theatrical game."
Woven through it runs the thin but necessary (for box office pur-
poses) romance of Mr. Jones and a stenographer. Miss Webster is
nothing short of superb as the female ex-juggler who keeps throwing
cold water on the whole business, and Mr. Maley as the half witted
hotel clerk who also wants to take a fling at "the theatrical game"
provides the most perfect moron we have ever seen on the stage.

                              --Louis Bromfield in The Bookman,
                                Vol. 62, No. 4 (December 1925),
                                page 480.

CAESAR AND CLEOPATRA (George Bernard Show; Guild Theatre,
       April 13, 1925)

        As openers for its new theatre, the Guild lays down Caesar
and Cleopatra, and we accept them as good here. We doubt that they
can be beaten.

        If we were just starting out on the job of reviewing plays, we
should try to tell why we like Caesar and Cleopatra. We would give
Shaw a good word or two on his dialogue and effects, and would do
a bit of analytical work by showing just where he does and where he
does not adhere to the unities. The article would end up with a summary in which we would decide that the play is swell. Being one of
the older boys in the game, we will simply begin with this summary
and let it go at that. At no time does a reviewer look so silly as
when he is praising Shaw--unless it is when he is knocking him.

        There is one thing, however, that we do feel qualified to take
a flying boot at. And that is this prologue business. Shaw has been
bored too much himself not to realize that the best prologue in the

world, recited at length in front of the curtain, is dull and tiresome.
It can't be done. If it could, Mr. Albert Bruning could probably do
it.

So, if you will take a tip from us, you will arrive at Caesar
and Cleopatra about 8:10, just in time to miss the prologue and wait
a few minutes at the head of the aisle until they will seat you for
the regular bill. The show itself starts at 8:15, which is none too
early.

The production is beautiful, and the cast a fitting one. Miss
Helen Hayes is probably the first Cleopatra who has fulfilled the
specifications in the blueprints, a slightly bewildered flapper queen.
We saw Forbes-Robertson play Caesar before, but we have forgotten
who played Cleopatra. We shall not forget Miss Hayes.

Lionel Atwill, aside from being an impressive Caesar pictorially,
has dropped most of his ham-actorisms, and those that he still re-
tains are not particularly out of keeping with the imperial purple.
For the first time since his early apperance in this country in The
Wild Duck and Eve's Daughter (when he was one of our favorite
actors), he seems to have settled back into a quiet, humorous vein
which is much more becoming. Let us hope that he doesn't fall in
with Mr. Belasco again.

Mr. Henry Travers as Britannus, the slave from the right-
little-tight-little island, is grand and, of course, has some of the
tastiest nut-meats in the play to dispense. Here, however, our enjoyment of Shaw's dirty cracks at his countrymen is again hampered
by the excessive enjoyment of the same lines by those in the audience
who are anxious to be counted among the wise ones who know what's
Shaw. The lines are funny, but they can't be as funny as all that,
even with Mr. Travers reading them.

The Guild's new theatre is just what it should be, and we have
a warm glow of anticipation of good things to come there. Sitting
back in the commodious pit, with its high white walls running into
the rich curtain, one experiences a sort of sensuous enjoyment like
the kick derived from holding a cool metal cigarette-case or a finely-
wrought jewel-box tightly in the hand. No matter what the play, it
can not help being enhanced and sharpened by this setting. It is
good to know that there is always the Theatre Guild.

--Robert C. Benchley in Life
(April 30, 1925), page 20.

THE CAT AND THE CANARY (John Willard; National Theatre, Febru-
     ary 7, 1922)

It has been a long time since we have clutched in terror at the

person beside us in the theatre. Certainly not since The Bat. But
at the conclusion of the performance of The Cat and the Canary the
young lady on our right complained to her escort that her entire
left arm was lacerated from repeated assaults by some man. She
couldn't remember when these assaults had occurred, having been in
such a state of nervous depletion herself, and if her young man had
got at all fresh, we could have shown him the places on our right
arm where she had been clutching at us.

Mr. Kilbourn Gordon has chosen for his second offering as a
producer a certified Grade A thriller, in which maniacs and voodoo
women and other things which are nameless glide in and out of the
rooms of an old house, while long, bony hands reach out from the
walls and clutch at people sleeping in bed or drag them noiselessly
into the plastering. There is not quite such a variety of horror as
there is in The Bat, but what there is makes most of The Bat seem
like a dramatization of Little Women. And there is not the disturbing
presence of May Vokes to turn the thing into a children's entertainment at regular intervals. (We warned the producers of The Bat
against May Vokes' comic relief when the play opened, but they would
have their own way and, as a result of their pig-headedness, their
show has run only a year and a half so far.)

Furthermore, The Cat and the Canary contains one or two
characters for which John Willard, the author, is indebted to no one
else, an item worthy of note in these days when a character which
has been popular in one play is usually taken bodily by the author
of the next play of a similar nature. Henry Hull, as the unheroic
hero, does a bit of comedy work which should make it happily impossible for him ever to go back again to ranting through opium-dens
or the aspirate defiance of crooked financiers.
                              --Robert C. Benchley in Life
                                (March 2, 1922), page 18.

CHICAGO (Maurine Watkins; Music Box Theatre, December 30, 1926)

If Chicago is to be a criterion, the products of Professor
Baker's course at Yale will differ from those of his Harvard classes
in the stimulating virility which is the traditional characteristic of all
New Haven products. Chicago is a he-man's play--written by a woman, Miss Maurine Watkins. And it is a devastating piece of sanitary
satire.

In it about ten good American characteristics are subjected to
as thorough a basting as has been given to anything in our memory.
Miss Watkins is merciless in the broad welts of slapstick kidding
which she lays across the back of our national sentimentality, hypocrisy, tabloid-fed pruriency and everything else ending in "y." And

over it all is a disclosure, for the first time, of the craze for publicity which furnishes the motive power for nine-tenths of our individual activities. Sometimes it seems as if she were laying it on a
bit too thickly, but such a thing is probably impossible.

There are, it is true, an unfortunate number of gaglines when
the same effect could have been had by sticking to the truth. Some
of them are inexcusable in a play as important as this, as, for instance, when the Judge asks if there is any lady who would prefer
to leave the courtroom and the defendant makes a lunge for the door.
But it is probably these touches which will endear the play to those
who need it most, and almost any ruse may legitimately be employed
to bring it before as many Americans as possible. It would not be
surprising if Chicago, together with the inevitable imitations of it
which will spring up from now on, played a very important part in
the gigantic task of de-bunking America.

And, incidentally, Miss Francine Larrimore, having cooled in
her obvious enjoyment of the joke of the thing, now makes a practically perfect Roxie.

                              --Robert C. Benchley in Life
                                 (January 20, 1927), page 19.

                         *   *   *

At first sight Maurine Watkins' Chicago looks pretty bad. It
is a crude and incredibly raucous melodrama of crime. It is Barrie's
Legend of Leonora jazzed up to the key of the tabloids. This play
shows how a flashy and unscrupulous woman and a hard-boiled lawyer
so impose upon the public and the jury that they come through a
murder trial not only free of conviction, but as heroes in the public
estimation. The play shrieks aloud. It appeals with all the obvious
blatancy of the yellow press it satirizes; it is a gross caricature of
press and bar, the machinery of the law and the idiotic complacency
and ignorance of the Great American Public.

Yet it is a magnificent thing in its way. Here is a melodrama
played fortissimo throughout. Without sympathetic characters, without suspense, and without a love story, it romps along, absorbs
you by its noise and its garish appeal to your obscene sense of humor over our whole system of trying cases not on their own merits,
but on the sex-appeal of the prisoner at the bar.

Incredible as it is--in detail--there emerges ultimately the notion that this is what actually happens every day in our fair land.
(Another play for the censor; here is a playwright who shows that
murder, even when admitted, goes unpunished; that lawyers are
crooks, that judges are dozing simpletons; and that the law is a
farce.)

I have a notion that Chicago was originally written as a serious

drama, with carefully prepared motivation and modulated climaxes.
It has turned out something quite different. But there is a new
note here, Rabelaisian, Aristophanic. There is a laughter and bit-
terness and a wholly admirable sense of ironic criticism. The play
has a point that pricks.

I could not help comparing it with Broadway, another first-
rate bit of playwriting; there is no point to that show at all.
                              --Barrett H. Clark in The Drama,
                              Vol. 17, No. 7 (April 1927),
                              page 200.

THE CIRCLE (Somerset Maugham; Selwyn Theatre, September 12,
   1921)

     There isn't much that can be said in the face of so satisfying
a performance as The Circle. The cast alone, including John Drew,
Mrs. Leslie Carter, Ernest Lawford, Estelle Winwood and John Halliday, would make any play a good risk as an investment, but in con-
junction with Somerset Maugham's comedy, in which one delicious
situation follows another just as fast as the characters can get on
and off the stage, it simply becomes a matter of trying to remember
when you have ever seen anything more this season for fear of an
anti-climax. It would be good to see The Circle and then go into
the country for the winter with your enthusiasm for the theatre thus
refreshed.
                              --Robert C. Benchley in Life
                              (September 29, 1921), page 18.

                    *   *   *

     One has always had the impression that Somerset Maugham is
a novelist who, now and then, tosses off a play for the fun of it.
He has always seemed to turn to the stage for his recreation; and
he has found it congenial play; he has always had a good time. His
comedies have the flash and whir of a good game of tennis on a
sunny day. The Circle is as airy and irresponsible as anything he
has ever done for the stage, but there is nothing offhand about it.
It was written by the author of The Moon and Sixpence and Of Human Bondage, not by the author of Mrs. Dot and Jack Straw. There
are times when there is a note of wistfulness in the banter, and that
is one of the reasons why it is such excellent banter. Side by side
in the play are two love stories, and they are just alike. We see
the beginning of one and the end of the other. All for love, Lady
Kitty Champion-Cheney, in her youth, threw over husband and position and ran away to the far places. All for love Elizabeth Champion-
Cheney is on the point of doing the same thing. Lady Kitty, after
thirty years, is not the pale, frail lady of romance whom Elizabeth

had expected to see. She is rather a flashy and frivolous poseur
with dyed hair and a soul as thickly rouged as her face. The once
dashing Lord Porteous is a soggy old chap, very bored, who has
trouble with his false teeth. Their life of love--among the outcasts--
has robbed them of everything fine. Even the love for which they
gaily lost the world has withered long since. They are as yappy
with each other as they would be if they were respectably married.
Elizabeth, with dismay, realizes what folly it would be to fly away
with her penniless lover to his rubber farm in the Federated Malay
States. And then she goes right ahead and flies away with him.
It is one of those rare plays which does not end, for you, when the
final curtain comes down. You enjoy it thoroughly while it is going
on; but next morning you like it better still and, curiously enough,
for entirely different reasons.

> --Kenneth Andrews in The Book-
> man, Vol. 54, No. 3 (November
> 1921), page 232.

THE COCOANUTS (Music and Lyrics by Irving Berlin, Book by
    George S. Kaufman; Lyric Theatre, December 8, 1925)

        Which brings us to the new vehicle (a station-wagon is neces-
sary) for the Marx Brothers, whom we may have mentioned last season as being mildly amusing. The Cocoanuts had much the same effect on us as last year's I'll Marx She Marx, except that this time
we made provision against falling into the aisle by sitting in the second seat from the end. Mr. Groucho Marx, in collaboration with
G.S. Kaufman, delivers a series of magnificent wheezes, nine out of
every nine and a half of which landed full on that tender spot between our eyes, and the sensuous Harpo completed the knockout without saying a word. Chico, the Annie Oakley of the piano, is not
without his lighter side, either, and all in all, the effect is such that
it is impossible to keep from smiling now and then. The chief difficulty, after finally getting a seat, will be to keep sitting upright
in it.

> --Robert C. Benchley in Life (Janu-
> ary 7, 1926), page 20.

A CONNECTICUT YANKEE (Book by Herbert Fields, adapted from
    Mark Twain, Music by Richard Rodgers, Lyrics by Lorenz Hart;
    Vanderbilt Theatre, November 3, 1927)

        There seem to be two divisions of musical comedy endeavor at
present--the shows written by the Fields, Rodgers and Hart combination, and all the others. Their present opus, A Connecticut Yankee--

a modernized and musicalized version of the Mark Twain book--is
another in the noteworthy series of accomplishments to the credit of
these young men. With a very pleasant cast consisting of Williams
Gaxton and Norris, Constance Carpenter and June Cochrane, and
with what is perhaps the loveliest musical comedy song in recent
years ("My Heart Stood Still"), A Connecticut Yankee shapes up as
one of the show-pieces of the year.

                              --Robert C. Benchley in Life
                                (November 24, 1927), page 23.

THE CONSTANT NYMPH (Margaret Kennedy and Basil Dean; Selwyn
    Theatre, December 9, 1926)

    The Constant Nymph, Margaret Kennedy and Basil Dean's play
from Miss Kennedy's novel, has come to the Selwyn Theatre after
having achieved an overwhelming success in London with another
cast. It proves to be a lovely, tender, humorous, tragic play, badly directed and disastrously housed.

    Were it not for the emergence, despite obstacles, of what I
believe managers like to call a "big" love story, The Constant Nymph
would be a lost play. Some almost operatic quality is required to
fill the enormous settings and the big theatre. The Constant Nymph
proves to have such a quality, but much of the play that is too
precious to be wasted goes wandering off into vast reaches of empti-
ness, never to make contact with the eager but faraway audience.

    The first act, which sketches in the background of the childish
love of Teresa (Beatrix Thomson) for Lewis Dodd (Glenn Anders) in
the mad, haphazard, musical household of Teresa's father, is particularly wronged, for it is an intimate act and one could get as much
sense of intimacy out of a performance by a flea circus at the Hippo-
drome. Not only is the set enormous but everyone plays as far back
on it as is possible without actually adhering to the painted Tyrol of
the backdrop.

    Again, the second act, which shows Lewis Dodd married to
Florence Churchill (Lotus Robb) should take one into Florence's per-
snickety home, and the arty musical evening she has maneuvered with
great care, and it is thwarted by the same conditions. Before this
act is over, however, the sensitive and beautiful and "big" performance of Miss Thomson makes itself felt and The Constant Nymph possesses its audience.

    The flight of Teresa with Lewis and her death in the dingy,
shady, boarding house in Brussels are heartbreaking, and a good,
thorough-going heartbreak can discount space.

Beatrix Thomson, a young English actress, is an incredibly lucky discovery for the producers. She realizes Teresa fully, combining childishness with strength, humor with poignancy.

Glenn Anders makes rather a clumsy job of Lewis Dodd. The script placed in the hands of Lotus Robb calls for an unmitigated shrew, and there seems to have been nothing for her to do about it but provide one. Helen Chandler as Paulina and Flora Sheffield as Antonia were memorably excellent.

See The Constant Nymph by all means, but have seats in one of the first six rows or wait till it moves to a smaller theatre.
                                    --Charles Brackett in The New
                                      Yorker (December 18, 1926),
                                      page 33.

* * *

After a great deal of ballyhoo Margaret Kennedy's famous book The Constant Nymph at last appeared as a play, only to find the critics and public much divided over it. There were those who liked it and those who didn't. For ourself we found much good and some bad in the production, which after all might well have been expected. The Constant Nymph must have been no easy thing to dramatize. In the first place, a play creates or is supposed to create in its opening act an atmosphere that thereafter remains the keynote of the piece. Naturally, when one is jumped from Sanger's Circus in the Tyrol to the music room of a London home, from there to a concert hall, and finally to a bawdy house in Brussels, the continuity of the play is apt to become somewhat confused. It is not only the locale that changes but the characters as well. Antonia, from being a naughty little girl, "no better than she should be," is metamorphosed into a respectable young matron; Florence Churchill develops a temper conspicuous for its absence before; and even the famous Tessa changes from a nymph-like creature all airs and whimsies to a pathetic drudge-like little soul not unlike June Walker's interpretation of the girl in The Glass Slipper a year ago. The fun and naive sophistication, if there is such a phrase, of Sanger's Circus fails entirely to come off. The part showing this musical and temperamental family at home in the Tyrol is merely confusing, and we had much difficulty in understanding the lines. In the novel it is all quite convincing and logical, but the stage is after all limited in ways that a book need never be. There are some lovely scenes showing Tessa's awakening love for Lewis Dodd, and her death in the pension at Brussels is as poignant a thing as the stage has had to offer this year. Beatrix Thomson made a beautiful role of Tessa. She was brought over from England after the producers had sought diligently here for someone adequate to fill the part, and after some thought we agree with them. We know of nobody on the American stage who could do it half so well. We wish they had taken as much care with the part of Lewis Dodd. Glenn Anders, to whom it was handed, makes his selfish musician a

thoroughly unconvincing affair. You may like the play or you may
not. It is neither all good nor all bad. What is all bad, though, is
the singing which interlards the first act. It must have contributed
much to the death of the musical Sanger in his room offstage.

> --Larry Barretto in The Bookman,
> Vol. 65, No. 1 (March 1927),
> pages 71-72.

THE CONSTANT WIFE (Somerset Maugham; Elliott Theatre, November
29, 1926)

If, at this late date, there should be any doubt as to the
truth of the old saying that blood (unlike the daisies) will tell, it
can easily be dispelled by a visit to the Maxine Elliott Theatre, where
Ethel Barrymore is playing in Somerset Maugham's The Constant Wife.

If ever there was a patrician performance, here it is. All the
Barrymores and Drews that have ever graced the theatre are con-
tributors to each tilt of the chin, and they have every reason to be
proud of their contribution, for never have we seen a chin tilted
with such distinction.

This does not mean that Miss Barrymore's comedy methods are
those of Colley Cibber and his age. They are, in fact, highly
modern and informal. When, explaining a knee-disorder of her rival,
she says: "It slips," the delivery and intonation are indubitably
those of 1926 and yet in the background stands the shade of some
Katharine ready to emerge if the occasion should demand.

Mr. Maugham's play, while far from perfect, has a great many
lines of high comedy and not a few of wisdom. It should be the
despair of American playwrights to hear what these English can do
with one word in the structure of comedy. When Mabel Terry-Lewis
(another shining example of the existence of a stage aristocracy) remarks on husbands who are "systematically" unfaithful, Mr. Maugham
has Miss Barrymore ask if "systematically" is not a rather grim word
to use. Or again, when it has been suggested that an unfaithful
husband makes his wife ridiculous, it is Miss Terry-Lewis who is
allowed the remark: "If every unfaithful husband made his wife
ridiculous there would be a great deal more merriment in the world
than there is to-day." By the use of these two words, "grim" and
"merriment," Mr. Maugham has transformed two lines which might
otherwise have been just lines into delectable comedy. It is very
discouraging to those of us who would never have thought of using
those words in a hundred years. It is a gift that even the most
humble English writers seem to have, and something ought to be
done about it.

> --Robert C. Benchley in Life (De-
> cember 16, 1926), page 19.

* * *

The other foreign play was Somerset Maugham's The Constant
Wife, another Charles Frohman production under the directorship of
Gilbert Miller. Ethel Barrymore played the leading role. As usual,
Mr. Maugham introduces us to a set of well-to-do "upper-class" English people, not very interesting in themselves but in this instance,
neatly and cleverly involved in an absorbing situation. The Constant
Wife is a woman of thirty-five endowed with a Shavian and almost incredible clairvoyance. Constance and her husband have been married
for some years, and get along remarkably well; but they are no
longer in love with each other. The husband has for some time been
involved in an affair with a friend of the family, and as the play
opens a former suitor of Constance's turns up. But the relationship
between these two is quite platonic until the very end of the play,
when Constance, after having earned her living and paid her husband for board and room, walks out with the ex-suitor, intending to
spend six weeks with him on the Continent, after which she will return home.

The point of the play is that Constance sees the situation from
every possible angle, and with a wholly unanswerable logic. Mr.
Maugham has put on Bernard Shaw's "normal" spectacles, and en-
visaged (through his heroine) the whole affair from a reasonable viewpoint. But Constance is a bit too logical. It is hardly credible that
any human being should be so practical and so wise. Nothing ruffles
her complacence, nothing surprises her, nothing is too much for her.
I fear she is rather a projection of the dramatist's logic than a human
being. Yet she is made up of a thousand human qualities.

Sociologically speaking, The Constant Wife is dreadfully im-
moral. The dramatist has so little regard for the accepted laws of
morality that he shows us a woman who dares to live in sin with a
man, and defend herself on the ground that she has paid her husband for board and lodging! And the husband actually wants her
back after her six weeks' jaunt! She is not unhappy, and no just
vengeancy is even hinted at. Dear, dear, what are we coming to?
If our dramatists take to being reasonable and true and logical, regardless of the morals of society, what will become of the old-time
object lesson?

> --Barrett H. Clark, in The Drama,
> Vol. 17, No. 4 (January 1927),
> pages 105-106.

COQUETTE (George Abbott and Ann Preston Bridgers; Maxine El-
    liott Theatre, November 8, 1927)

George Abbott and Ann Preston Bridgers have fashioned two

acts of a memorably poignant and sensitive play from material originally suggested by Miss Bridgers, and have wandered into the by-
paths of unnecessary plot and contriving for a third act, which is
held together only by the unforgettable playing of one of the pre-
mier artists of our theatre, Helen Hayes. I cannot share the general unrestrained enthusiasm for the play as a whole, nor, on the
other hand, can I find words adequate to describe the apparently
fragile yet strong and enduring artistry of Miss Hayes. Her growth
as an actress in the last two years has been an event almost un-
paralleled in the modern theatre, springing, as it most certainly
does, not from the mere chance of a good vehicle's having come her
way but from a sort of inner flame.

The story of Coquette is woven from the antique chivalry, the
primitive aristocracy and the over-protected womanhood of the South.
Dr. Besant's daughter, Norma, comes before us as one of those
dainty flowers whose instinct for innocent flirtation has been nour-
ished from generations back in the hothouse of a land of soft-voiced
troubadours. She meets Michael Jeffery, a young man of hot blood,
careless speech and unpretentious ancestry. Dr. Besant tries to
drive him from the house. Fired by this opposition and the first
real love of her life, Norma gives herself to him. Michael is beset
by remorse, and wants to marry her at once. She agrees, of course,
but her father interferes again. Michael in his anger blurts out the
entire truth, and Dr. Besant, following him from the house, shoots
him, actuated by the blind conviction that in doing so he is defend-
ing his daughter's honor.

The last act is then given over to the day of Dr. Besant's
trial for murder. His only defense is the unwritten law; his only
chance of acquittal depends on the required testimony of his daughter that Michael Jeffery had attempted unsuccessfully to dishonor
her. As the play now stands, the fact that she is to have a child
by Michael is supposed to invalidate her father's case. In her dilemma, and rather than appear on the stand, Norma kills herself--
thinking, in her bewilderment and torture of mind, that she will
thus save her father's life. The motivation of this scene becomes
utterly confused and artificial. The natural sequence to the first
two acts would be a much simpler, but no less tragic, dilemma for
Norma--the choice between saving her father's life by false testimony
that Michael had taken her against her will, and saving the memory
of the man she loved by admitting what actually happened. Whether
or not her escape, under these conditions, would have meant suicide
would have depended entirely on the authors' conception of her character. Either alternative would have meant a life of never-ending
tragic memory. Would she, or would she not, have had the courage
to face such a life?

I suspect that the authors found suicide a more conclusive
final curtain, and that, to this end, they manufactured the round-
about and seemingly false notion that only Norma's proved innocence

could save her father. This, they may have thought, would give
Norma's death a touch of heroic self-sacrifice. But, like everything
artificial in fiction or the theatre, its effect upon the last act of the
play is disturbing. The strain of simple emotion is broken. A sense
of insincerity invades the play, and there remains only the exquisite
manner in which Miss Hayes portrays Norma's mental conflict, and
her touching farewell to her father before going out to her death.

Any attempt to justify or to elevate suicide in the theatre
must inevitably fail, as this fails. It is far better to have the stark
brutality of an Ibsen, and permit a suicide, as in Hedda, to be its
own conclusive comment on character. Perhaps it is a poor box-
office formula, but it has at least the merit of artistic integrity.

Of Miss Hayes's performance through every gradation of mood,
from her devastating innocence in the first act, through the blind
love that carries her away, to the climax of appalling tragedy when
she waits for and finally receives the word of Michael's death, there
is but one statement to be made--it is the nearest approach to perfection we are likely to see in many a long year. The entire cast,
under the direction of George Abbott, achieves a fine distinction,
surmounting, among other things, the difficult task of simulating a
southern accent without the least appearance of effort or exaggeration. But the one performance which rivals that of Miss Hayes is
Elliot Cabot's as Michael. In the second-act quarrel with Dr. Besant
he reaches a restrained and virile power as rare as it is refreshing.
The staging, to the last detail, breathes, so Southerners tell me, the
true spirit of a small town of the South. For its first two acts there
is no play in New York at present which can be said to approach
Coquette. Thereafter, it must regrettably be written, it stumbles
badly in the quagmire of contrivance.

> --Richard Dana Skinner in The Com-
> monweal, Vol. 7, No. 4 (November
> 30, 1927), page 760.

* * *

It is perhaps just as well that this department was forced to
suspend operations for a week, while the bouncing Christmas Number was hurtling off the presses; otherwise we might have been im-
moderate in our praise of Helen Hayes in Coquette. Now, in the cool
of the evening, we will merely say that it is the best thing in town.

There is little that can be written of Miss Hayes' performance,
except that it is perfect. The combination of George Abbott and Jed
Harris which resulted in Broadway has again brought forth a masterpiece of casting and direction. The play which Miss Bridgers and
Mr. Abbott wrote has been put into the hands of people who evidently were born for the rôles (to mention the good performances
would be to name the cast, beginning with Elliot Cabot), and these
people have been guided by a master hand. It is hard to tell where

the script ends and the direction begins, but if for no other reason
than for the thrilling synchronization of comedy and tragedy toward
the end, the play should come in for its share of the general huzzaing.

If we had written last week about Coquette we should have let
ourself go more.

--Robert C. Benchley in Life
(December 8, 1927), page 21.

THE CRADLE SONG (Gregorio and Maria Martinez Sierra, translated
by John Garrett Underhill; Civic Repertory Theatre, January
24, 1927)

The Civil Repertory Theatre presented as one of its midwinter
offerings The Cradle Song, written by that same Martinez Sierra
whose Romantic Young Lady was presented last year at the Neighborhood Playhouse. Critics generally went quite made over The Cradle
Song. It was deemed one of the most perfect bits that has ever
been brought to our stage. "Bits" is right, for The Cradle Song
is but a fragment of a play. What there is in this story of convent
life is done with understanding and sympathy, but actually there is
no story at all. That a baby should be adopted by a community of
nuns, reared by them and eventually married with their approval to
a worthy young man, is very nice and does credit to the feelings of
the sisters, but it is not quite plot enough on which to base a play.
But since we appear to be the only dissenting voice we shall let it
go at that. At any rate, the direction and producing were interesting.

--Larry Barretto in The Bookman,
Vol. 65, No. 2 (April 1927),
pages 207-208.

CRAIG'S WIFE (George Kelly; Morosco Theatre, October 12, 1925)

There isn't much doubt in this department about George Kelly's
American ranking as a playwright. He is easily in the first three,
and don't ask us who the other two are. We rest our case with
The Torch Bearers, The Show-Off and Craig's Wife.

In Craig's Wife Mr. Kelly turns from comedy to the serious
business of life, and its first two acts are real playwriting if ever
we saw it. As in The Torch Bearers, he has a bad, bad attack of
third-act Messiah-trouble, causing him to suspend all operations while
his hero stands in the doorway and gives a short talk on the lesson
for the day. But this third-act slump may well be forgiven in the

thrill of the final curtain, which, descending at half-speed, held the
audience motionless and silent in their seats until it had touched the
stage. It was one of the big moments in our theatre-going career.

What might be considered a minor theme, the house-fetish of
a neurotically tidy woman, is developed by the compact and intensive
pressure of Mr. Kelly's treatment into a major tragedy of Ibsen-like
proportions. Mrs. Craig's house becomes a Geist, a heavy-menacing
Presence, and Chrystal Herne's magnificent performance makes the
whole thing an unforgettable experience. And we hope that we are
not crediting the direction (Mr. Kelly's, and well-nigh perfect it is)
with too much subtlety when we suspect that the uncomfortable atmosphere of Mrs. Craig's house was deliberately heightened by having all the characters wear rubber-heels which squeaked whenever
they walked across the polished floor. Please say that this was in-
tentional, Mr. Kelly.

> --Robert C. Benchley in _Life_ (No-
> vember 5, 1925), page 22.

* * *

George Kelly, the author of _The Show-Off_, has turned his attention from group portraiture to that of a selfish woman. His new
play, _Craig's Wife_, is an honest, at times a brilliant thrust at the
woman whose marriage instinct is limited to the security which it
gives her life and to the visible property which is the symbol of
that security. It is not, unfortunately, one of those plays which,
given its characters, seems to work out its own conclusion. The
author steps too frequently before the footlights, in the person of
one or another of his characters, to explain what is happening or
about to happen. This effect comes more from faulty construction
than from the necessities of the story. It might have been avoided.

You have here a wife who is determined to feather her own
nest. She sets about it by various subtle means--by being cold or
disagreeable to Walter Craig's old friends, by gaining complete
dominion over his every action, by making her house a domestic god,
perfect in every surface detail, never to be defiled by cigarette
ashes, misplaced ornaments, or even by flowers "because the petals
fall all over the rugs." One gathers she has reacted from a mother
who always gave into others and suffered for her weakness. If the
delight or derision with which the audience greets each new evidence
of Mrs. Craig's implacable character be any criterion, this country
of ours must be overridden with such women. You can almost hear
them breathing "just like Mrs. So-and-so." The awakening and final
revolt of Walter Craig become a source of popular joy. There can be
little doubt that Mr. Kelly strikes near home--in fact, just next door!
(There may even be some honest enough to accept the tale the mirror
tells!)

Chrystal Herne has given a minutely perfect portrayal of Mrs.

Craig--the suave manner, the icy loftiness, the metallic obstinacy, the fluttering meticulousness, the piercing sarcasm. It is altogether an admirable piece of acting. Charles Trowbridge is equally effective as the husband, and Josephine Hull makes the rôle of a sentimental, middle-aged, flower-loving and neighborly widow memorable. Acting, direction, and the broad lines of characterization combine to make this an exceptional play.

But its one great defect rankles none the less. There is no real suspense. The author gives a complete outline of Mrs. Craig's character, in the first act. Nothing is left to development or later discovery. And to make the points clearer, Mrs. Craig is made far too conscious of what she is doing. If she knew half as much about the hidden springs of her selfish actions as the author would indicate, she could not live in the same house with herself for one day. The worst of characters nearly always discovers an imaginary excuse for gross selfishness. Mrs. Craig calls herself a spade--which is hardly credible. Of course she is admittedly digging for her own ends--but even the blackest spade would probably call itself a garden implement. The Show-Off had no such structural weakness. Its hero was serenely unconscious of his own bombast. For that reason it was a better play. But the theme of Craig's Wife is deeper, nearer the core of real human difficulties. That is why its inherent interest surmounts even obvious defects. It does, however, leave you with one curious question. Why does Walter Craig meet his problem by not meeting it? He simply withdraws from the house. Is this a real surging of manhood--or just an escape. To me it had the aspect of an unfinished play--or if not, then one with a very futile last gesture. (Note: Why not a revival of The Taming of the Shrew?)
--Richard Dana Skinner in The
Commonweal, Vol. 2, No. 26 (No-
vember 4, 1925), pages 650-651.

* * *

We can also heartily approve of Craig's Wife, which brings our favorite Chrystal Herne back to Broadway. This play, thanks be, is described as a drama, in distinction to most productions which are labeled comedies unless sudden and violent death meets the actors in the last act. We have not detected any intense yearning on the part of the public for comedies only, but apparently the managers think they are a requisite to success. This is a piece in which Miss Herne plays a wife who loves her house better than her husband, her polished floors better than the flowers that fall on them, and she extracts every bit of value from the rôle. That she is a part of every woman was evidenced by the uproarious way in which husbands discussed the play during intermissions and the insistent way in which the wives ignored it. We can think of no actress at the moment who plays a subtle rôle in so polished a manner as Miss Herne, with the exception of Clare Eames, and she unfortunately was seen only for a flashing space in Lucky Sam McCarver. Sidney

Howard, the author, also wrote They Knew What They Wanted. In
this case the public knew what it didn't want and Lucky Sam de-
parted after the briefest of runs.

--Larry Barretto in The Bookman,
Vol. 62, No. 5 (January 1925),
page 596.

THE CRIMINAL CODE (Martin Flavin; National Theatre, October 2,
      1929)

      Martin Flavin's first bow to New York was through a serious
and mordant play called Children of the Moon. It did not score a
commercial success, but has remained deeply engraved on the minds
of steady theatregoers as a work of considerable distinction. It
dealt with the power of a selfish mother to distort the minds of those
about her. The Criminal Code is quite understandable as a successor to Children of the Moon--utterly different in theme but displaying
the same qualities of mind of the author. It is a play dealing with
mental states and the distortions wrought through environment.

      If you happen to have seen, many years ago, Galsworthy's play
called Justice, you will have a good general impression of the type
of play to which The Criminal Code belongs. It jumps right into the
middle of that vicious circle surrounding the criminal mind, and in-
terprets the circle to you in terms of a young man wrongly con-
victed of second-degree murder. A prologue in the district attorney's
office gives the first tragic premise--a lonely boy who defends a
street walker from insults and in doing so accidentally kills the scion
of a rich family. Robert Graham has nothing of the criminal in him--
nothing, that is, beyond the normal human mixture of good and bad,
with the bad under reasonably safe control. A good criminal lawyer
could have secured a prompt acquittal. But Graham's employers
lend him the services of their business attorney, a man as unfamiliar
with criminal practice as a new-born babe. Martin Brady, the district attorney, faced by an approaching election, sets out to get,
and does get, a conviction. Several years later, Brady is made
warden of the state's prison where Graham is still serving his term.
It is at this point that drama begins to stalk the stage.

      Mr. Flavin has used many devices to heighten the points of
his story--an interesting prison doctor to interpret Graham to us,
Brady's daughter to warm the stone-grey prison into a place for romance, and a series of well-drawn cross-section types within the
walls, men who prey upon Graham's imagination in one way or another
as the heavy years roll by. Drama quickly deepens into melodrama
when the criminal code dictates that one of the inmates, a squealer,
shall pay for his cowardice with his life. Graham has the bad luck
to know who did the killing. He is offered every inducement to tell,

but, bound himself by the code of loyalty within the walls, remains
silent. He is put in the dungeon and tortured. He does not know
that the warden has his parole ready, nor that Brady, moved at
last by the discovery that his daughter is in love with Graham (who
has acted as the family chauffeur) is ready to forego forcing a confession. Crazed by hunger, torture and the phantoms conjured in
his brain through long years, Graham murders the man who has tortured him, not knowing that this same man has now come to set him
free. The irony of the "bad break." Too late. Like the tolling of
an old cracked bell--too late, too late.

It is a play that holds and fascinates with grim determination.
It is a play abounding with pity, understanding and a fine indignation at the rigidity of human legal codes, at the clanking, crushing
machinery of the law driven by the unselfish actions of small-minded
men. But it is not, in spite of all this, a great play. It has too
many glaring defects, especially as seen in retrospect. The "bad
breaks" are too often of the author's own making--happenings that
are not really inherent in any of the situations. At other times,
sheer coincidence plays too big a part. And in the final episodes,
it is always painfully evident that Robert's confession is not the only
way in which the prison murderer might be brought to justice. The
warden, already somewhat conscience-stricken at the part he played
earlier in Robert's life, would, one feels, have exhausted all the detective talents of the state before throwing the boy in the dungeon
or trying to make him turn traitor to his fellow-prisoners. No real
effort is ever made to discover the identity of the murderer except
through Robert. In other words, one feels that Mr. Flavin saw his
ending before he began his play, and allowed nothing to stand in
its way. The play thus suffers badly from forced situations, and
also from patent theatricality.

Albert R. Johnson's settings for this play deserve special mention. By the use of a grey curtain and a half a dozen other well-
chosen devices, he does as much through scenery to heighten the
dismal gloom as the story of the play itself. Arthur Byron as Martin
Brady, district attorney and later warden, gives one of those amazingly natural performances which establish him in a special niche
among character actors. Anita Kerry as his daughter, Ethel Grif-
fies as his nervous sister, William Franklin as the squealer and Walter
Kingsford as the doctor all contribute bits of rarely restrained and
affective work. There is not a bad piece of casting in the play, and
William Harris, producer, contributes also an excellent example of
stage direction.

> --Richard Dana Skinner in The Com-
> monweal, Vol. 11, No. 4 (Novem-
> ber 27, 1929), page 115.

* * *

Another established playwright, Martin Flavin, has just shown

us a new aspect of his talent: The Criminal Code, the latest produced work of the author of Children of the Moon. Mr. Flavin first
attracted our notice with the play just mentioned: a somber, well-
written but not particularly significant work. His next was Lady of
the Rose, a failure, but a far more interesting play than his first.
A season or two ago he proved in Service for Two that he could
write an amazingly ingenious French farce, though that play was
also a failure. Besides The Criminal Code, I have read in all at
least three more Flavin plays that are as yet unproduced.

The Criminal Code is undeniably Galsworthian in its technique
and viewpoint. It reveals in several short scenes what may happen
to a man who is morally innocent of crime, but legally guilty. A
youth has killed a man who, he had reason to think, was about to
attack him. Both were drunk at the time. Falling into the hands
of a district attorney who is at once a decent fellow and a tool of
the political machine, he is sent up for ten years. After six he
breaks down, is given a job as chauffeur to the warden (the ex-
district attorney) and falling in love with the warden's daughter,
becomes a new man. At the moment when he has high hopes of a
pardon, he becomes involved in a prison plot, and acting on the
ethical code of the men "inside," he commits murder. Admitting it,
he is left to face the consequences.

A somber, almost wholly unsentimental play, honest, straightforward, compelling. But it would have been doubly so had Mr.
Flavin been able to make out a better case. First the boy was given
a hopelessly inadequate defence; second, the very man who prose-
cuted him was made warden of the jail to which the lad was sent;
and there are a couple of other cases of coincidence. Emotionally
we want to believe everything in order that the thesis promulgated
by the playwright shall seem absolutely flawless, but one's logic will
intervene occasionally.

Galsworthy would, I think, have avoided these minor mistakes,
but on the other hand he would have suffused his play with an over-
insistent note of pity and irony instead of allowing the audience to
draw upon their own sense of the fitness or unfitness of things. In
other words, Mr. Flavin has been able to let the case carry its own
implications.

> --Barrett H. Clark in The Drama,
> Vol. 20, No. 2 (November 1929),
> pages 41 and 63.

DADDY'S GONE A-HUNTING (Zoë Akins; Plymouth Theatre, August
     31, 1921)

In Zoë Akins' best play to date, Marjorie Rambeau has her best

opportunity to date, and the combination spells something very like
success. Miss Akins' ability as a playwright has grown by leaps and
bounds since <u>Declassée</u>.

The story relates the sad affairs of Edith Fields. Her husband
has been studying art abroad for a year, and when he returns she
finds him grown cold to her and preferring rather the lurid type of
woman who has chosen to seek him out. In despair, she accepts the
offer of another man who is in love with her, and goes to live in
an expensive apartment at his expense. But it is her husband she
still loves, and the end of the play finds her leaving her lover and
not knowing what she is to do for the rest of time.

It is a bit morbid, perhaps, but intensely moving. Staged
with the customary Arthur Hopkins skill, it seems almost too real to
watch with equanimity. This effect is heightened by exceptional
playing. Miss Rambeau has never done such brilliant work before.
Frank Conroy as the husband also presents an unforgettable portrait,
and Lee Baker plays the other man faultlessly.

--H.K. Wheat in <u>The New York
Dramatic Mirror</u>, September 10,
1921, page 376.

DAISY MAYME (George Kelly; The Playhouse, October 25, 1926)

In <u>Daisy Mayme</u> the author of <u>The Show-Off</u> and <u>Craig's Wife</u>
has done something as different as possible from <u>On Approval</u>. Here
we have the great American middle class with a vengeance. Its
foibles, weaknesses, vulgarities, and virtues are held up and exposed
quite pitilessly to Mr. Kelly's sharp scalpel. He does a good deal of
trimming and slicing too before the play is over. If Cliff Mettinger
had not made money, the mercenary and generally unpleasant instincts of his relatives might never have been shown up; but he
had made it and in consequence two sisters, a niece, and the niece's
fiancé all settled down on him, sure that the pickings would be good.
They made somewhat of a bluff about offering something in return
for what they were about to receive, such as cooking dinner for him
on his return from a trip, running a dust cloth hurriedly around the
window sills, and so forth, but it didn't fool Daisy Mayme Plunkett
for a minute. This person, who had been invited to spend a week
by another and favorite niece, promptly made up her mind to expose
the whole crew of them. She did it so well that before her visit,
slightly extended, was over she had routed them all and had become
the fiancée of the opulent Cliff. Certainly they needed to be exposed, but on analysis Daisy Mayme's methods were not so very nice.
She opened her campaign by calling these genteel ladies by their
first names; she met "refinement" with vulgarity; she outraged their
sensibilities by pulling up shades and ordering the piano played in

a house of mourning. Social barriers meant nothing to Daisy--and
incidentally she cooked better than the sisters. Perhaps Cliff was
won through his stomach, or possibly he decided that one woman in
the house was preferable to two. At any rate he was a most phleg-
matic lover; his niece proposed for him, and the final curtain showed
him and Daisy sitting placidly several feet apart without so much as
a kiss to seal the bargain. Daisy Mayme is an admirably wrought
play, put together with much skill and understanding. Personally,
we did not happen to like it, but we were grateful that it provided
opportunities for excellent acting on the parts of Jessie Busley, Madge
Evans, and Josephine Hull.

> --Larry Barretto in The Bookman,
> Vol. 64, No. 5 (January 1927),
> pages 619-820.

                              * * *

     Ever since I saw The Show-Off I have believed that in George
Kelly we have one of the three or four most remarkable dramatists
our country has ever produced. Not even Craig's Wife--the last re-
cipient of the absurd Pulitzer award--could break my faith in Mr.
Kelly's genius. His new play, Daisy Mayme, is reassuring. Not so
brilliant as The Show-Off or so rightly resonant with the overtones
of life, it is no less a remarkably fine comedy. Without more than
the shred of a story, with no big moments, and with scarcely more
than a single emotional climax, it is compact with veracious observation. An old maid of forty comes into the home of a man about her
own age, teaches him how to handle his jealous and self-seeking relatives, proves to him that there is a lot of fun to be got out of life,
and in the end marries him. Eight human beings and an old-fashioned
parlor are quite enough for Mr. Kelly: he doesn't use a single detective, or even a revolver; there are no program notes to explain
what it's all about; I don't recall even a telephone. There is hardly
a word of profanity from start to finish, and no one robs, rapes,
or dies.

> --Barrett H. Clark in The Drama,
> Vol. 17, No. 3 (December 1926),
> page 74.

DANCING MOTHERS (Edgar Selwyn and Edmund Goulding; Booth
     Theatre, August 11, 1924)

     The new season opened with every one very dressy and very
warm at Dancing Mothers, a play so named probably because the only
mother in the cast couldn't dance. She essayed it once, it is true,
just to be riotous, but it evidently wasn't much of a success, for
when she came back to her table after her offstage try-out, the best
that her gentleman friend could do by way of reassurance to her

protestations of gaucherie was a remark that the tango is rather difficult at first. We have had those reassurances made to us too often
not to know that her attempt at being a "dancing mother" was probably more in the nature of a dancing behemoth.

Just a word, please, about those offstage dances. Like the
offstage battles in Shakespearean drama, they smack strongly of in-
efficiency. From what we are privileged to see of one corner of the
dance-floor or battlefield, with an occasional couple staggering into
view and out again, we are quite within our rights in judging that
the participants are not very good dancers or very good fighters,
as the case may be. In Dancing Mothers just the take-off is visible,
but the first few steps of the various couples as they pitch out into
the wings would indicate that the dance-floor, if viewed as a whole,
would look like the undulating surface of the "Helter Skelter" at
Coney Island.

That's all we wanted to say about offstage dances, and we hope
that we have offended no one, for we ourself live in the first glass
house on the right.

To return to the play under consideration, Dancing Mothers,
being the first play of the season, is the first to deal with the depravity of the Younger Generation by having the mother take up
drinking and smoking just to teach the youngsters a lesson. Counting the last two seasons, however, it ranks 211 chronologically.

When, in the first act, we sensed what it was all about, we
wrote out the following prophecy on a piece of paper which we folded
up and gave to an usher to hold until the curtain should descend.

"The first act will end with the following stage business:
Mother looks out window after departing daughter, ponders for a
minute, goes to telephone and calls up gay friend to arrange for
party that night, advances to table and significantly lights what is
obviously her first cigarette. (Quick Curtain.)"

Where we slipped up was in the speed of the curtain. It was
a slow curtain, as we might have known had we stopped to think.

As a matter of fact, although the play is built on as familiar
a pattern as a Ford sedan, it manages to swing along at a good pace
and, aided immeasurably by smooth performances by a cast which includes Helen Hayes, Mary Young, John Halliday and Henry Stephenson, makes you forget at times that you could be dictating it word
for word yourself as it goes along.

Too much praise can not be accorded the authors, Edgar Selwyn and Edmund Goulding, for fooling everybody at the end by having the mother really leave the family flat. Not since Nora Dolls
House stepped out has there been such a surprise ending. We are
just cynical enough to believe that there is an alternate ending all

written which is being seriously considered by the financial backers
and which may even now have been substituted, an ending in which
the mother, after leaving the room, bounces back and, embracing
her erring husband and daughter, says that it was all a joke and
that she did it only to frighten them.

Just one animadversion more, inspired by a speech in Dancing
Mothers, and then you may all go home if you will pass out quietly
so as not to disturb the other classes in the building. Mr. Halliday,
as the irresistible bachelor, is goaded to a very frank outburst in
which he says, in effect, that many men-about-town are accused of
chasing the ladies, when as a matter of fact it is the ladies who
pester them to death, much to their inconvenience and quite against
their wishes. This speech is greeted by thunderous and unquestionably heartfelt applause on the part of hundreds of chevaliers in
the audience. Ungallant as this tribute may seem at first, its spontaneity and sincerity indicate that there is a great latent unrest
smoldering beneath the dress-shirt fronts of the nation which needs
only the clarion-call of battle to stir it into revolt.

Now listen! We do not put this forward as our own feeling in
the matter; so don't write us any indignant letters. We merely indicate an ominous trend which must have been evident to every lady
who was present at the wildfire demonstration that night.
                              --Robert C. Benchley in Life (Au-
                              gust 28, 1924), page 18.

                              *   *   *

Coming down to the more or less serious drama, the eternal
problem of the younger generation and the older disports itself anew
in Dancing Mothers--one of those conventionally unconventional
plays that try so hard to be daring. Well cast and suavely directed,
this very probable hit repeats the story of the mother who sits at
home while husband and daughter frequent roof gardens, Philadelphia, and places even more sinister. The mother, according to
schedule, decides to follow their example and thus reform them--but
for once an alteration in the coiffure and the adoption of demonstra-
tive earrings do not bring about a family reunion on the sofa before
the gas log. Instead--and this is the one semi defiant twist--the
mother decides, after ample consideration, that the primrose path
may have something in it after all and departs for Europe under the
escort of the very agreeable villain, leaving husband and offspring
quite at a loss for words. The dialogue is often genuine. Mary
Young as the mother gives a performance of great mechanical excellence, the rest of the cast--which includes Helen Hayes, Henry
Stephenson, John Halliday, and Elsie Lawson--assist her nobly; but
for all the air of sham reality which the play possesses it never goes
deeper than the plaster.
                              --Stephen Vincent Benét in The
                              Bookman, Vol. 60, No. 2 (Octo-
                              ber 1924), page 211.

DEATH TAKES A HOLIDAY (Walter Ferris, from the Italian of Al-
  berto Casella; Ethel Barrymore Theatre, December 26, 1929)

      In Death Takes a Holiday, a piece from the Italian of Alberto
Casella, Death, off duty, knocks at the door of an Italian nobleman's
villa (here, the color and the lighting make a completely satisfying
harmony) and invites himself for the week-end under the style and
tide of His Serene Highness, Prince Sirki of Vitalba Alexandri, dis-
carding his conventional black robe for full military uniform--which
is the way stage princes always dress in private houses so that everyone will be sure they are princes and not just actors--and mingling
with the nobleman's mortal guests. It is Death's object, on his holiday, to experience human emotions, just to see what it feels like, and
it is practically no time before he has fallen in love with the leading
lady. She, lovely and ethereal, and a bit too good for any of the
other men in the cast, falls in love right back at him, and, in the
end, when Death must get back to the old grind, she follows him,
willingly, into the Great Beyond, where, we are led to suppose,
they marry and raise a large family of little illnesses.

      Philip Merivale, always a vastly entertaining actor, does him-
self more than proud in the rôle of the Grim Reaper. The play isn't,
unfortunately, as good as the idea behind it--something rather magnificent might have been got out of it--but Mr. Merivale's performance couldn't very well be better. He rises above it all and makes
a one-man show of it, which is worth a trip to Ethel Barrymore's
Theatre in any kind of weather to see.
                              --Ralph Barton in Life (January 24,
                                1930), page 20.

                          *   *   *

      This play, from the original Italian by Alberto Casella, has
been a long time in reaching the New York stage. For some years
Norman Geddes dreamed of producing it in truly imaginative style,
but was unable to get the necessary backing. The present adaptation is by Walter Ferris, the production by Lee Shubert, with Lawrence Marston directing and Rollo Wayne designing the setting. In
idea and in execution, it is an engaging fantasy, which manages to
present a novel thought with an unexpected sense of reality. It is
only in the closing moments of the last act that its fabric of invention grows thin and its central idea fails to mature completely.

      Imagine, if you can, a moment in time when Death, belonging
to the world of eternity, becomes curious to know why mortals fear
him and cling to life. Imagine, further, that to satisfy his curiosity
he decides to take a holiday and to assume for three days human
form and to subject himself to human appetites and emotions. During
the period of this holiday, nothing dies. The processes of decay
are halted. No leaves wither and fall. No accidents happen. It is

a sort of concentrated springtime. And during this springtime,
Death learns the meaning of human love. He begins to understand
at last why humans fear him, why they grow attached to familiar ob-
jects, and why the parting with loved ones seems unendurable. In
spite of this, Death remains puzzled to the end, for he knows eternal
is so much simpler than temporal life.

Obviously this idea offers endless possibilities in specific treatment. The particular plot selected to illustrate the idea is simple.
Death appears in semihuman but still forbidding form to Duke Lam-
bert just as he is arranging a house-party at his castle. Death reveals his plans to the petrified Duke, promising him that no harm
will come to any of his guests, unless the Duke reveals the identity
of his strange visitor. Death explains that he has recently "visited"
Prince Sirki (one of the guests expected that evening) and that the
Duke can let him masquerade as the missing Prince. By bringing
the lamp of illusion with him, Death can completely disguise his real
aspect and be free to move among unsuspecting humans. The one
thought he cannot bear is to have them shrink from him as they have
done through countless centuries.

Among the many guests is Grazia, daughter of the Princess of
San Luca--a fragile and lovely child. Death (alias Prince Sirki) falls
deeply in love with her. She is the only who who does not instinc-
tively fear him. In the end, when it is time for Death to end his
holiday, he once more strips himself of all illusion and asks Grazia
if she will go with him. She says she has know him from the first
in his true form--and departs with him.

Whether or not you regard this as a morbid tale depends on
how far you accept the author's premise that life at best is but a
transient and painful existence, compared to which eternal life should
be the mystic goal of all. Certainly in the detail of the plot and
action, much of the morbid sting is removed by many passages of
delicious comedy--Death's embarrassments in his first human contacts,
the sly double significance of everything he says, the contrasting
attitudes of the various characters as, all unsuspecting, they discuss life, love and eternity in Death's presence. Thanks to a beautiful performance by Philip Merivale, Death becomes, as the author
intended, quite an engaging and romantic figure, and not a little
pathetic withal. Yet ...

The conspicuous missing link in this chain of fantasy is, of
course, the absence of all concept of God in reference to eternal
life. There have been saints aplenty who have prayed for death as
the moment when the only true life would begin. But this is in the
positive terms of seeking the vision and the love of God. Either the
author or the adapter (it is quite impossible to tell which) has preferred to beg the question by a sort of vague doctrine of wish ful-
filment. Nor has he even partly compensated for this, as he might
easily have done, by making Death, in the last few moments of revela-

tion, a brilliant figure of deliverance, in contrast to man's everyday
sinister illusion. That is where invention fails in the last act. If
the audience could be, so to speak, let in on the secret, and permitted to see Death at the last as Grazia herself must have seen him,
then the author's idea would have reached full maturity, and one
would have felt almost ready to pity the other characters on the
stage, to whom Death still remained a symbol of horror.

Essentially, then, the idea of the play is at one with belief in
life as a brief pilgrimage, and Death as a revelation of higher life.
It simply does not go far enough--as if the author (or adapter) felt
a curious timidity in driving his thoughts to a triumphant conclusion.
Comedy and irony succeed in making it reasonably palatable, but not
in giving it the supreme note which it might have struck in the hands
of a poet with Dantesque vision and faith.

Rollo Wayne's setting of the great hall, with a vision of the
moon-drenched garden beyond, does much to create a believable
mood for this novel fantasy. Mr. Marston's direction is also smooth
and persuasive. Mr. Merivale's supporting cast is excellent. Frank
Greene, in particular, as a major in the Foreign Legion who has often
caught glimpses of Death, gives us a few moments of inspired simplicity. Rose Hobart as Grazia is utterly believable in her fragile
directness. Among all the recent plays which attempt to toy with
the supernatural, this one approaches nearest to successful illusion,
both in the possibilities of the script and in their realization. A
little more courage and it might have assumed genuine proportions
as a modern successor to the older morality plays.

> --Richard Dana Skinner in The
> Commonweal, Vol. 11, No. 13
> (January 29, 1930), page 369.

THE DESERT SONG (Music by Sigmund Romberg, Book by Otto Harbach, Oscar Hammerstein II and Frank Mandel; Casino Theatre,
November 30, 1926)

It was only a matter of time before the late Riff uprising became musical comedy material. It was musical comedy material while
it was still going on. Now Mr. Romberg has put music to it and Miss
Segal sings it and Eddie Buzzell does all that any one could do with
the jokes, and the net result is a show called The Desert Song.

The story concerns a mysterious Riff who is referred to in
whispers as "The Red Shadow" or "The Red Flash" or something because the only time that any one sees him is during the big song
numbers. Well, sir, you won't believe it, but "The Red Whirlwind"
is none other than Pierre Birabeau, dilettante son of old General
Birabeau, the very general who is tracking him down! And every

time "The Red Menace" wants to get a bite of home-cooking he rushes upstairs and changes from his red hood to natty juvenile togs and comes down as that good-for-nothing Pierre. How's that for a mix-up?

Things go on like this for quite a while, with Miss Segal singing some nice songs very prettily and a fine, strong male chorus booming out occasionally, with the result that the audience gets a very good evening for its money.

We have, as a matter of fact, been stalling along in the above paragraphs, trying to work in a gag about the "Riff in the lute," but the thing just can't be done. We might have made believe that the mountain pass where "The Red Whiz-bang" hid was called "The Lute" because of its resemblance to that instrument, but we should have been found out the minute any one went to the show, and it wouldn't have been worth it. So we'll just let the whole thing drop.

> --Robert C. Benchley in Life (December 16, 1926), page 19.

*   *   *

To one who found the much vaunted Student Prince and Countess Maritza wearisomely inane as to plot, The Desert Song came as a restorer of faith in the operetta as a form of entertainment. Here is good music wedded to a swiftly moving story. What is more, here is a cast whose members combine acting ability with real singing or, as in the case of Pearl Regay, with sinewy oriental dancing. Vivienne Segal and Robert Halliday make you willing to believe in the love story. Eddie Buzzell as the American reporter astray among the bold bad Riffs enlivens matters considerably. And a tall basso named Lyle Evans in his majestic rôle of harem lord reminded us of no less a person than Chaliapin. Scenes in mountain, desert, and harem give opportunity for beautiful settings. There is a chorus of good male voices, and a squad of energetic female steppers. What more can one ask?

> --Larry Barretto in The Bookman, Vol. 65, No. 1 (March 1927), pages 73-74.

DESIRE UNDER THE ELMS (Eugene O'Neill; Greenwich Village Theatre, November 11, 1924)

Given: An old husband, a young wife, a virile and contiguous young man. This triangle has long been the basis for one of the four great national jokes of France. In Russia they make tragedies out of it.

In America we do both. The subject has been taken by Eugene O'Neill and tortured into a terrific catastrophe with the title,
Desire Under the Elms. Sidney Howard has fashioned a fine comedy
from the same material and called it They Knew What They Wanted.
We rather think that, on the whole, Mr. Howard has done the better job, for his comedy has moments of great pathos, a necessary
thing for comedy, but Mr. O'Neill's tragedy has moments of unconscious comedy, a terrible thing for a tragedy.

Desire Under the Elms is, up to a certain point, one of the
finest things O'Neill has ever written. It shuts down over you with
its cold damp, until, in spite of the eight different varieties of New
England dialect (all wrong but one) which its characters speak, you
feel that you are a part of the rocky farm on which the scene is
laid and that you are never going to get in even to Boylston Center
again.

Then something happens, and Mr. O'Neill goes quite mad. It
is almost as if he were burlesquing his own tragedy. Like Hardy,
who, frenzied with the taste of heart's blood, has two-thirds of his
characters in The Return of the Native commit suicide by jumping
into a brook one after the other, O'Neill takes his people and has
them wallow in Weltschmerz until the chief protagonist can think of
nothing more terrible to do than threaten to turn all the cows loose.
Unless the cows should enter into the spirit of the thing and tear
moaning down the road, this would seem a rather flat manifestation
of tragedy. One pictures them rather as stopping a few feet away
from the barn and wondering meditatively what it was all about.

With his sudden access of energy, the author becomes positively phony in his theatrical repetition of catch-lines and "significant"
situations, and what was earlier in the evening a grand play ends in
a blaze of green fire with an imaginary orchestra playing "The Funeral March of a Marionette."

Mary Morris and Walter Huston, especially Miss Morris, are
worthy of the first half of the play, than which we can think of no
higher praise.

> --Robert C. Benchley in Life (De-
> cember 11, 1924), page 28.

* * *

In Eugene O'Neill's Desire Under the Elms there are displayed
the qualities that make O'Neill the first truth-teller of the modern
stage. Truth in art is less a matter of substance than of style,
less a quality of the body than of the soul. It is to O'Neill more
than to anyone else in America that we owe the resolute application
of truth to the ways of stage art. The task is a heroic one and it
has the disadvantage of most heroisms in that it demands of the
worker his last ounce of strength. When one is spending himself

daily beyond his powers there cannot be expected of him that grace
in action and poise in decision that are marks of less expensive endeavors. As a rule O'Neill's plays call for and receive his last
ounce of creative force. He never stints force and he seldom gives
a play to the world until sufficient force has been mustered to drive
it through to the final point of vision. And yet that economy that
is forced upon him, that New England husbanding and dealing of
resources, leave their marks in something spare and angular in his
work, in a falsetto note or a note of gruffness.

        Whatever faults there are in Desire Under the Elms are the
faults of great virtues. The author has driven through to hard
truth in the gnarled and twisted souls of his New England men and
women. The truth he seeks lies deeper than the surface of speech
and action. It uncovers the hidden motive, the haunting passion,
the skulking desire, that underlie the hard varnish of appearances.
As O'Neill presents his group on the New England farm each character becomes incandescent. In each there is a well spring of as-
piration. The elder brothers are lured by the adventure of the
chase for gold. The younger brother worships the memory of a
dead mother, the tired drudge who had never known rest until she
found it in the rocky hillside. The old man, the patriarch of the
tribe, is stirred by the last promptings of a passion that is confused with religious mania and the obsessions of greatness. And the
woman whom he brings home wants only a home, a piece of land to
call her own. Here we have the strands of which the play is woven.
These minor passions soon dwindle into the devastating sweep of
love of a middle aged woman and a boy. Not since John Webster
and the post-Elizabethans have we had such stark and unrelieved
horror as is released by the mad loves of this play.
                              --Thomas H. Dickinson in American
                                Review, Vol. 3, No. 2 (March-
                                April, 1925), pages 219-220.

DIAMOND LIL (Mae West; Royale Theatre, April 9, 1928)

        Miss Mae West in her own masterpiece, Diamond Lil, described
as "A New Drama of the Underworld," can be recommended warmly.
It is an irresistible piece of nonsense, costumed in the styles of
thirty years ago, and enlivened by a rendering of "Frankie and
Johnny" and the best incidental music of the period. The settings
are as lurid as the melodrama, which reaches its climax when Diamond
Lil covers the dead body of the rival she has stabbed by letting down
her hair and combing it, as the police break in. In London Nights
in the Gay Nineties, Shaw Desmond has raised the rather ingenuous
question: where are the ample bosoms of that time? He should see
Diamond Lil and discover what the corset could and can still do to

the female form.

--Ernest Boyd in The Bookman,
Vol. 67, No. 5 (July 1928), page
564.

* * *

Mae West won notoriety through her play Sex, and because
she chose to defy the police and bring the matter to an issue she
spent a couple of weeks in jail. This was last year, when the Pad-
lock Law was first invoked in New York City. At the time I rather
admired Miss West, and now that I have seen her and her new play
I feel sure she is not merely a publicity hound. She doesn't need
publicity: she can deliver the goods. Diamond Lil is a sincere
and immensely entertaining melodrama of the Bowery during the late
nineties. Because it is unpretentiously written it is nowhere near
so obvious as so mechanical a play ought, by rights, to be. The
story concerns a hardboiled denizen of the Bowery and the saloon-
keeping white slaver she is living with. Diamond Lil is a real character and most of the types surrounding her are convincing enough.
The play gives a vivid picture, while the mechanics of the plot are
no more grotesque than what we can find in almost any novel of
Dickens. Dickens! There's an idea. If I had more space I might
draw a parallel between Mae West and Charles Dickens. It would be
fun.

--Barrett H. Clark in The Drama,
Vol. 19, No. 1 (October 1928),
page 10.

THE DOVER ROAD (A.A. Milne; Bijou Theatre, December 23, 1921)

In The Dover Road Mr. Milne comes nearer being what we
have a right to expect of him than in any plan of his that has been
presented in this country. Like all the rest of them it stretches
rather thin in spots, but its humor is less conventional than that of
Mr. Pim, while between it and The Great Broxopp you could drive
a team of horses and still have room for the City of London in the
intervening space.

The first act, in particular, with its well-sustained air of
mystery and the graceful acting of Charles Cherry, is a delight, although it is in the second that Reginald Mason and Lyonel Watts
have their opportunity to make the thing even more hilarious, and
Miss Winifred Lenihan to prove that she knows how to be a worthy
Milne heroine. George Riddell is excellent in all three acts. Oh, and
there is the scene in the third act in which Molly Pearson reads aloud
from Gibbon which calls for several salvos. In short, The Dover

Road is very nice indeed, and it is to be hoped that the intelligent
company who play it will be occupied thus for some time to come.
                              --Robert C. Benchley in Life (Janu-
                              ary 12, 1922), page 18.

                         *   *   *

    Of the foreign authors, A.A. Milne's The Dover Road is one
unquestioned example of good comedy. Mr. Milne has a delightfully
irresponsible sense of humor that nevertheless reaches deep as does
true comedy always. One laughs to exhaustion and then pauses to
think. He has constructed an entire comedy on the idea that if one
stopped to reflect before eloping, one probably would not elope. It
is a slender idea but Mr. Milne knows how to dramatize it. The
Dover Road must be included in the plays worth seeing.
                              --Jack Crawford in The Drama,
                              Vol. 12, No. 6 (March 1922),
                              page 194.

DRACULA (Hamilton Deane and John Balderston, based on the novel
    by Bram Stoker; Fulton Theatre, October 5, 1927)

    Those who enjoy chilly spines will find in Dracula the same
kind of nervous agitation which tourists in Paris discover at the
Grand Guignol. Readers of Bram Stoker's novel of the same name
will recall that Dracula was a vampire gentleman who died some five
hundred years ago, but managed to maintain a sort of half-life
through the subsequent centuries by drinking human blood during
the nocturnal hours. When Dracula takes up his abode in a peace-
ful village and proceeds to drain the life-blood of two of its most
charming maidens, the father of the second victim summons the
famous scientist, Abraham Van Helsing, to solve the mystery. There
was probably never so much pure hokum thrown into three acts as
in this horrific tale. At one time Van Helsing repels Dracula by
waving a piece of wolf's-bane under his nose. Later he is able to con-
quer the vampire only by holding before him a packet containing the
Host. The needlessness of this particular touch is amply demonstrated later when Dracula is quite easily subdued by the sight of
the cross. Aside from this one slip in good judgment and good
taste, it is quite astonishing to see how successfully the authors and
the director have conveyed the sense of supernatural reality. If
the whole production had not been staged with expert care, it is
the kind of thing that would be laughed out of court at the first
hearing. Instead, it manages to hold its audience almost petrified
from first to last. From a purely theatrical viewpoint this is little
less than a stroke of genius.

    The dramatic version was written by Hamilton Deane and John

Balderston. The play is directed by Ira Hards. All three deserve
great credit for making the unreal seem painfully real. The baying
of frightened dogs, the howls of a maniac under the influence of
Dracula, the flying of bats, the mystery of dimmed lights and gauze
curtains, and all other familiar means to horror have been used to
step up the atmosphere of this play to a pitch of credibility. There
is no single element which cannot be analyzed in a perfectly matter-
of-fact way. The striking quality of the piece lies not in any one
of its elements, but in their masterly combination.

The actors have also contributed a very important share in
their deep earnestness, without which the play would simply become
a ridiculous situation. From Nedda Harrigan, as the mysteriously
hypnotized maid, to Bela Lugosi, as the evil Dracula, each of the
eight members of the cast gives an authentic and competent performance. This is particularly true of Edward Van Sloan as Professor
Van Helsing, of Bernard Jukes, as the maniac, and of Dorothy Peter-
son as Lucy Harker, the vampire's immediate victim. Dracula can
hardly be recommended as a health diet for jaded nerves, but as a
theatrical tour de force it is an outstanding achievement.

> --Richard Dana Skinner in The Com-
> monweal, Vol. 6, No. 24 (October
> 19, 1927), pages 584-585.

* * *

A horror play a bit overcharged with creeps but effective
enough in spots to spoil an afternoon for you.

> --Robert C. Benchley in Life (No-
> vember 3, 1927), page 22.

DULCY (George S. Kaufman and Marc Connelly; Frazee Theatre,
August 13, 1921)

The new season, long rumbling in the distance, has crashed
in on the New York district, striking about fifteen theatres in quick
succession. There was no insurance.

First in point of probable permanence among the new-comers
is Dulcy, a comedy by George S. Kaufman and Marc Connelly, built
around the Dulcy who has been dispensing genial conventionalities in
Franklin P. Adams' column in the N.Y. Tribune for several years.
For the benefit of those who do not read the Tribune, Dulcy may be
described as a young lady who, taking her cue from Gelett Burgess'
book of bromides, says something old almost every day in the manner
of one who makes an entirely fresh contribution to the American
golden treasury of words and phrases.

It was a daring mood in which Messrs. Connelly and Kaufman conceived the idea of having their heroine deal in frayed coversational currency, for it is a safe bet that at a Wednesday matinee there will not be three women in the house who will see anything amusing in Dulcy's saying that her books are her best friends or that she likes to visit New York but would hate to live there. The authors have avoided this danger which usually besets dispensers of esoteric truths by embodying their satire in a play so interesting, well-knit and amusing in its own right that Dulcy herself could stand up back some day and enjoy every minute of it.

In creating the rôle of Dulcy, Miss Lynn Fontanne joins Frank Bacon in the honor of having brought a new character to our stage. Her scene with the box of candy while one of her weekend guests is favoring with a piano selection is comedy as delicate and sure as any that we can find record of in the files of this department. Likewise, Howard Lindsay, with plentiful help from the authors in telling lines, makes the recital of the plot of his new movie an original and amusing scene. Gregory Kelly renders a small part effective and funny, in fact, everything but audible. Taken all together, Dulcy ought to be a hit for the simple reason that it is a good show, wholly aside from the "sifted few of matchless breed" to whom it will be an especial delight.

                        --Robert C. Benchley in Life (Sep-
                        tember 1, 1921), page 18.

*   *   *

Dulcy by George S. Kaufman and Marc Connelly is written with a bow of acknowledgment to Franklin P. Adams for the loan of the principal character. This might provide a text for some popular scientist or writer of syndicated uplift. It would be interesting to know what effect column conductors, as a class, have upon the country. For thousands the humorous column in the morning newspaper is a breakfast staple as indispensable as the poached egg or coffee. It is the mental pick-me-up of the nation. It is really more than that. The average American reads practically nothing but his newspaper, and he does not read much of that. He glances over the first page, skips to the sporting page to see what the home team did the day before, then turns to the column and reads it with absorption from top to bottom. And the spirit of the column is one of mockery. Thus thousands of good citizens go to their daily toil every morning, their native orthodoxy slightly tarnished by the impiety of their favorite column conductor.

It is just possible that this may have something to do with the general decline of hero worship among us, and the growing disposition to call attention to the flat feet of our national idols. It may have nothing whatever to do with it; but there can be no doubt that we live in a skeptical time. Broadway, ever sensitive to the changing mood, reflects this skepticism most vividly in the plays of the early

season. No less than five of them are definitely satirical in spirit,
and of these three devote themselves to the native culture. That is
quite astonishing. Satire has long been considered a lost art among
our playwrights and among our novelists as well. George Ade has
had a lonely time trying to keep it alive. If Broadway's receiving
apparatus is as well attuned as it has usually been, he is to have
company.

Dulcy is a breezy comment on the here and now, as up to the
minute as the column in this morning's newspaper, and in general
content it covers much the same ground. It is a haphazard sort of
play into which the authors have tossed a glittering array of bright
odds and ends, plucked at random from the life about us. This
lack of coherent dramatic plan at least has the virtue of leaving the
playwrights free to take a fling at whatever occurs to them. A number of things occur to them. As the evening goes on their fancy
moves in wider and wider circles until the play really becomes a
robust and rather sweeping satire of manners--one of the first and
one of the best to reach our stage in many seasons.

Dulcy is the effervescent young matron who goes in for all
the Movements, and who has a ready bromide for every human need.
Fresh from her Friday Afternoon Club, she comes in with her arms
full of flowers.

> Dulcy. Hello, everybody! Mm! It's cool in here, isn't it?
> You know, if there's any breeze going at all, we get it in
> this room. Well, Willie (to her brother) whom have you been
> doing? (She laughs at her own joke.)

Of course after that we can all imagine Dulcy. She naturally
insists on helping Gordie, her husband, in his extremely ticklish
business deal with C. Roger Forbes. Gordie makes pathetic attempts
to avoid being helped; but Dulcy knows her duty: she is his wife
and help-meet, and her place is at his side fighting the battle of
life shoulder to shoulder. She has invited Forbes and his wife and
daughter for the week-end, and has captured two tame tea lions from
the culture club to help entertain them.

> Gordon. But, Dulcy, Forbes isn't the kind of man that
> wants to be entertained--
>
> Dulcy. Leave Mr. Forbes to me, darling. Just wait. I've
> got a real surprise for you.
>
> Gordon (in alarm). Another surprise?

Her surprise is that she is going to arrange a match between
Angie, Forbes's daughter, and Vincent Leach, the famous scenario
writer. "If I fix it," she explains, "Mr. Forbes would be so grateful he'd have to give you more than 16-2/3 per cent of the combina-

tion." This is only one of the little helps she has thought of. For another she is going to see that Forbes has not one dull moment while he is a guest under her roof. He does not have a dull moment. Dulcy entertains him intensively. By morning he is a desperate, trapped soul. His little Angie has eloped. His wife has lied to him. He washes his hands of both of them, and of Dulcy's suppressed husband as well. But happily, during the night Angie has married Dulcy's brother Willie, instead of the movie person as she had intended. This arranges everything; and Dulcy gratefully accepts credit for it, reminding Forbes that captains of industry never understand women.

> --Kenneth Andrews in The Bookman,
> Vol. 54, No. 2 (October 1921),
> pages 144-146.

EARL CARROLL'S VANITIES OF 1923 (Lyrics and Music by Earl Carroll; Earl Carroll Theatre, July 5, 1923)

Anything involving Joe Cook robs us of whatever critical faculties we may possess, which therefore renders the following review of The Vanities of 1923 worthless. Unless you happen to believe, as we do, that Joe Cook should be the next President of the United States. He could be the entire Cabinet, too, with the aid of his genial assistant with the blond waterfall mustache.

Since we would rave about a biblical skit by Charles Rann Kennedy if it gave Joe Cook a chance to imitate three Hi-wayans, we are in no state of mind to pass on the actual value of Mr. Carroll's undeniably beautiful Vanities. They may be terrible, but we doubt it. At any rate, we distinctly remember laughing at times when Joe Cook was not on, and that is no small accomplishment for somebody.

The Cook act suffers considerably from being broken up into pieces in order to get it through the door from vaudeville, but it is still the same epoch-marking repudiation of all standards of sanity which have held civilization cowed for so many centuries (seven, I think it is, or possibly eight). You either like Joe Cook or you don't, but upon your feeling in the matter depends whether or not you shall marry my daughter.

On analysis (oh, just a little analysis, please) we find that the thesis, "Yes, we have no bananas," is a logical outgrowth of the Joe Cook philosophy. For many months Mr. Cook has been saying to his accomplice: "How's your uncle?" To which the reply is: "I have no uncle." "And how is he?" says Mr. Cook. "Oh, he's fine," is the transcendental answer.

Or again: "Those carrot-seeds you gave me yesterday haven't come up yet."

"Did you plant them?"

"No."

"That's funny. I certainly don't understand, then, why they haven't come up."

In this school of thought it will be seen that "Yes," when it means anything, means "No." And you can't get much farther than that on the road to Ultimate Truth.

Of course, none of this takes into consideration the fact that Joe Cook, aside from having one of the great minds of the age, can also really do the myriad tricks which he burlesques. He is an expert in all the lines that he kids, wherein he has it on several thousand of us kidders. We have seldom seen a greater exhibition of repression than in his act with the ball, on top of which he makes his way up an incline. The most difficult part of this trick, as he used to do it in vaudeville, was coming down a flight of steps on the other side, still mounted on top of the ball. In the present act, he makes believe that he can not do this, and never does it. He allows the audience to go away believing that it was too much for him, when, all the time, he had it in his power to win applause and send them home marvelling at his dexterity. We are not at all sure that, in addition to everything else, Joe Cook could not found a new religion.

Now that we have had a word about Joe Cook, let us turn to the rest of Mr. Carroll's show. There is an abundance of a certain type of comedy which always gets a laugh from us, viz., that furnished by elaborately but badly dressed assistants. Jimmie Duffy (who announces himself as Mr. Duffy of Gallagher and Shean) has a couple of lackeys in attendance on him who are remarkable specimens of the old-fashioned servant such as one seldom sees nowadays. Then Joe Cook (we are coming around to Joe Cook himself later) has his Blond Beast, and another who acts as a disinterested witness to his legerdemain, both very charming characters.

We must not forget Mr. J. Frank Leslie, who, wearing what is known as "full evening-dress," appears now and again before the curtain to give what is announced on the program as "Baritone Solo........J. Frank Leslie," or "Vocal Selection........J. Frank Leslie," none of which, however, is ever completed, owing to the interruption of a mysterious voice from back-stage yelling: "All right, Jack!" at which J. Frank Leslie takes a deep bow and retires, his vocal selection unfinished. Not exactly a new stunt, but one very, very dear to our heart.

As for Mr. Carroll's introduction of Miss (it is "Miss," isn't it?) Peggy Hopkins Joyce into his show, we can only say that it was probably a very good business move on his part, as there are a great many people who want to see her and Miss Joyce evidently

doesn't mind being seen. She is very pretty, and if she doesn't object to being placed on exhibition under the circumstances, it certainly is none of my business. She never got a nickel of mine.
                                    --Robert C. Benchley in Life (Au-
                                    gust 2, 1923), page 20.

                              *   *   *

     The new edition of The Ziegfeld Follies offers little that is
really new. Brooks John, Ann Pennington, and even Eddie Cantor
do not palliate the loss of Will Rogers and the charming Mary Eaton.
Earl Carroll wins in his Vanities. They are fresh, original and produced with a taste and lavishness that rivals and, in my opinion,
excels Mr. Ziegfeld. His music is good. His ballets are gorgeous.
His humorous sketches and specialties, even those which do not offer
the expert Mr. Cook, have a most unusual touch of drollery. Using
levels of blocks and stairs and a well lighted cyclorama, Mr. Carroll has simplified the background of a review and set off to advantage his rich if not heavy costuming. His star, Peggy Hopkins
Joyce, adds much personality, if not ability, to the show. All in
all, it is a most merry evening to be had at the Earl Carroll Theatre.
                                    --John Farrar in The Bookman, Vol.
                                    58, No. 1 (September 1923), page
                                    61.

EARL CARROLL'S VANITIES OF 1924 (Lyrics and Music by Earl Car-
     roll; Music Box Theatre, September 10, 1924)

     It is probably true that the new edition of the Vanities is no-
where near so good as last year's (Mr. Carroll's penalty for having
put on such a good first show), but on the opening night the fault
was not entirely Mr. Carroll's. The audience was at least twenty
per cent, to blame. It was what is known as "tough."

     A "tough" audience does not necessarily talk out of the corner
of its mouth or say, "Hully Gee!" A tough audience is one which
sits back and says to the performers: "Yea? Well, make me laugh if
you're so funny." In partial extenuation of its attitude it may be
said that it has usually paid eleven dollars or more a seat and has
a right to be a little skeptical. But no audience has a right to be
as downright belligerent as the one which placed itself in the way
of the Vanities on opening night. Much of the comedy did deserve
to be met with a dignified silence, but there were many quips which,
if given an even break, would at least have lived to see the sunrise,
yet which, under the influence of the grim reapers out front, shriv-
eled up immediately on being exposed to the air. For it is an in-
controvertible fact that a line, no matter how funny it is in the mind
of its parent, ceases to be funny even to him as soon as it is re-
jected by the receiving end.

We are not attempting to explain away the failure of much of
the old vaudeville humor in the Vanities to get across. We are not
attempting to offer an alibi for such gross violations of good taste
as Madame Tucker's song about the Prince of Wales. But Madame
Sophie did have some material which she had every right to expect
would go big, based on her many years' experience in going big,
and Joe Cook, our hero, has a very good case against the audience
for the murder of several ideas which, with a little sympathy from
some one, would have been as funny as anything he has ever done--
in other words, the funniest stuff in the world.

All this may sound like a very abstruse and filmy argument,
but we know it to be as tangible as if we had said that every one in
the audience was stone deaf. In the old days, when the stage was
at its zenith, we ourself worked for several audiences suffering
from the same anaesthesia as that one of Mr. Carroll's, and we know
what it feels like to face them, even with the magnificent material
that we had. Perhaps that is why our heart went out to the people
back-stage that night. They were up against an impossible job and
were not equipped for it.

On the other hand, we know how the audience felt. There
was some terrible stuff there. You can't blame people for not laughing if they don't feel like laughing. They are under no obligation
to the management or the performers. On the contrary. A situation like that is merely a combination of circumstances in which a
show which needs help from its audience runs into an audience which
is psychologically incapable of extending help. The result is unfortunate, that's all. For with considerable pruning and the insertion
of more material suited to Joe Cook and Sophie Tucker, the Vanities,
with its beauty and equipment, will be a one hundred per cent. better show than many which have flourished in the past at the Winter
Garden or the New Amsterdam.

--Robert C. Benchley in Life (October 2, 1924), page 20.

EARL CARROLL'S VANITIES OF 1925 (Music by Clarence Gaskill,
    dialogue by William A. Grew, additional sketches by Jimmie Duf-
    fy, Arthur "Bugs" Baer, Blanche Merrill, Julius Tannen, Les-
    ter Allen, Owen Murphy, Jay Gorney, and Bozeman Bulger;
    Earl Carroll Theatre, July 6, 1925)

In the Vanities, Earl Carroll has launched an excellent idea
which may fail only through the fault of the American public. He
has made a musical revue into a night club. The stage and the auditorium have been brought together and the orchestra has been placed
on the side of the theatre. There is a space cleared between the
stage and the audience for dancing before the performance and during

the intermissions and excellent music is provided. Over all this pre-
sides with exactly the proper verve and spontaneity Julius Tannen.
But the trouble lies with the self-conscious audience. It is afraid
to see itself dancing almost on the stage. It cannot get accustomed
to the beautiful girls who act as "hostesses." In short, it squirms
and shows every desire to look on, whereas the whole idea is to
participate. The revue itself is excellent entertainment and moves
rapidly, with excellent music, a multitude of pretty girls and handsome settings. It might also be added that it is a very funny show.
But the thing which impressed us most was the amount of money
represented. As Mr. Ziegfeld has grown parsimonious, Mr. Carroll
has become lavish, extravagantly so. It is the kind of performance
popularly associated with the idea of Babylon.

> --Louis Bromfield in The Bookman,
> Vol. 62, No. 1 (September 1925),
> page 70.

*   *   *

A formidable cast of comedians support the new Earl Carroll
Vanities--Joe Cook, Frank Tinney, and Julius Tannen vying together
to get laughs. The Vanities has not greatly changed since its last
edition. The intimate note prevails. You are told that this is a
night club, and ginger ale is served to prove it. There is the same
dancing by reluctant couples on the forestage during intermissions,
and various celebrities in the audience are introduced by the eagle
eyed Julius Tannen. We wonder what would happen if the Vanities
should run out of celebrities some evening; but perhaps a stock of
them is kept in reserve with the other theatrical properties. Some
of those who stood and took a bow seemed to us a little less than
celebrated, but at any rate the names were familiar. We thought
the settings and costumes of the Vanities a shade below perfect, but
we allow the show the most beautiful chorus that we have ever seen
anywhere, and at that we were practically sitting on the stage. The
average chorus needs perspective--a good deal of it.

Under the new dispensation revues are allowed to disrobe
their damsels until now one of the most vital reasons for visiting
Paris has been removed. It gives the visiting brethren the opportunity to see what a really beautiful body looks like, and doubtless
the Turkish baths and gymnasiums are profiting largely. That can
all be chalked up to credit, but if the girls of next year who pose
as powder puffs and pullets are anything less than completely lovely
they will have to be hurried back into silks again. A lady of our
acquaintance announced the other day that she never knew at a revue whether she was in a bathtub or a theatre. If the difference
is really so slight it should make bathing much more popular.

> --Larry Barretto in The Bookman,
> Vol. 63, No. 1 (March 1926),
> pages 79-80.

*   *   *

Certainly no one can accuse Mr. Earl Carroll of not trying to
get humor into his new Vanities. Could you pick out of a dream
three better comedians in their respective lines than Joe Cook, Julius Tannen and Frank Tinney? They represent practically fifty
per cent. of the laughs we have ever got in the theatre, and here
they are, all in one show.

Mr. Tannen has much the same things to do that he had in
the previous Vanities, to preside in his own personal manner over
Mr. Carroll's "night-club." Mr. Tinney, aside from a few minutes
of ill-advised reference to his homelife (and the fact that he does
this in black-face with white hands makes up for a lot), is the same
old Tinney, the very thought of whom gets us to laughing. And
Joe Cook--well, you know what we feel about Joe Cook. Suffice it
to say that in his straightforward explanation of the story beginning,
"Tweet, tweet, tweet, who has stolen my nest?" he has developed
an entirely new brand of stage humor, precarious as the blowing of
Tiffany glass, which he is not in the slightest danger of having
stolen from him because no one else could possibly do it. If you
are interested in new epochs, hear this story from Joe Cook.
                          --Robert C. Benchley in Life (Janu-
                          ary 28, 1926), page 18.

EARL CARROLL'S VANITIES OF 1926 (Lyrics and Music by
     Grace Henry and Morris Hamilton, Sketches by Stanley
     Rauh and William A. Grew; Earl Carroll Theatre, August
     24, 1926)

Mr. Carroll's Vanities has practically no satire, and, to our
way of thinking, not very good showmanship. There are one or two
sketches written by Kalmar and Ruby and acted by Dale and Smith
(nés Avon Comedy Four) which are very funny, and Julius Tannen,
in addition to his peripatetic (which Mr. Tannen may use if he likes)
banter, has a thrilling encounter with an indifferently trained seal
named "Pete" (who, on the opening night, escaped to take a well-
earned bow with Mr. Tannen), but, aside from these features, and
as occasional glimpse of Moran and Mack with new and only fair material, one does not laugh much at the Vanities, unless perhaps it is
in an elaborate number called "The Lament of Shakespeare," in which
Lady Macbeth appears in a costume by the Eureka Bracelet and Novelty Company, having evidently started on her sleep-walking from
the shower-bath instead of the Cawdor couch, and in which also
"Cleopatra" is rhymed with "flatter her."

There may also be a smile in the program note that Mr. Furlow
of the Otis Elevator Co. and Mr. Crowell of the Elevator Supplies
Co. "evinced a great personal interest in the successful construction
of the 'Orchestra-lift.' " These gentlemen must have felt well-repaid

in hearing the applause which greeted the elevation of several dozen chorus girls to a dizzy height from which they surveyed an enraptured audience. No show which has an elevator in it can ever be quite without merit for an American audience.

--Robert C. Benchley in <u>Life</u> (September 9, 1926), page 21.

* * *

The new edition of Mr. Carroll's <u>Vanities</u> is new chiefly in the presence of a little group of Britishers from the late <u>Charlot Revue</u> in London, headed by that appealing comedian, Mr. Herbert Mundin, and Miss Jessie Matthews.

The sketches which they have imported are good and bad. But even a bad English sketch has something worthy about it. You may not laugh at the lines but somewhere behind them you detect the functioning of a humorous mind and you have respect for them. You feel that the fault is partly with you and the rest of the audience that it falls flat. And no line delivered by Mr. Mundin can ever be quite without effect.

The rest of the show consists, as heretofore, of Mr. Julius Tannen, who is the only entertainer we know of who speaks three dialects at once (and how many more times do we have to plead for an act making use of his uncanny powers of mimicry?), and also Moran and Mack, again joined in dialectic union, thereby vitiating our tender paragraph on their separation a few weeks ago. And, although they hold their philosophic dialogues in new groves, they still are concerned over the early bird, the olive farm in Rome, and the irrefutable economic law governing the sale of pigs, which means that, for the seventeenth time by actual count, this representative of the press burst into small pieces with explosive appreciation.

--Robert C. Benchley in <u>Life</u> (February 3, 1927), page 19.

EARL CARROLL'S VANITIES OF 1928 (Book by Earl Carroll, Music by Grace Henry and Morris Hamilton; Earl Carroll Theatre, August 6, 1928)

There may be things about Mr. Earl Carroll's revues that you do not like, but he has always been one of the few producers who know where to go for plenty of comedy. Of course, there may also be things about his comedy that you do not like, but it is there, nevertheless, and somewhere in its abundance you ought to find a little sunshine, unless you are just an old crachity.

From certain complaints that have been filed by members of
the audience on the opening night of Mr. Carroll's new Vanities, we
gather that we got to laughing pretty loudly ourself. But that is
a way we have when W.C. Fields is up there. We have been doing
it ever since he used to play pool in pantomime, years ago in his
juggling days, and we don't see any way of stopping it at this late
date. And if people don't like the way we laugh they can leave the
theater. We won't.

In addition to Mr. Fields (pardon us while we laugh again)
there is that natural comic, Mr. Joe Frisco, who has practically
cured himself of stuttering without the slightest injury to his humor
and who gives an imitation of Helen Morgan riding her piano which
could go as it stands right into the Grand Street Follies. The famous pyrotechnic cigar is also in good working order, as are the
twinkling toes.

There didn't seem to be quite enough of the Dooleys, although
Miss Ray was there as the uneasy child and Gordon as an occasional
man with a beard. Probably what we really wanted was to have
Miss Dooley and Mr. Fields come on in an automobile, accompanied
by Fannie Brice and the mysterious little man in a long linen duster.
If we were ever to see that hallowed sight again we should probably
swoon. The human system can stand just so much ecstasy.

This will perhaps give you some idea of why we got to laughing at the Vanities. The reasons why we didn't get more excited
about some of the other features are less easy to enumerate. Mr.
Carroll has evidently spent a great deal of money on his production,
but perhaps he doesn't know how to shop as well as Mr. Ziegfeld or
Mr. White. Aside from one highly effective Machinery Ballet which
opens the second act (don't miss it by hanging around smoking too
long on the sidewalk), the effects are of the Christmas tree school
and designed to impress the infant eye. One curtain actually came
down with fireworks shooting out from it, probably the last word in
décor; at any rate it should be.

There are few tunes in the score of the Vanities which will
give you much bother during the fall, although Richard Bold does
very well with what he has and Miss Lillian Roth, another graduate
of the Texas Guinan Finishing School, puts quite a lot of something
into the numbers allotted to her. The young ladies of the ensemble
have been chosen with a clear and steady eye and their featured
leader, Dorothy ("The Most Beautiful Girl in the World") Knapp has
this year extended her activities to placing both hands on her hips
instead of only one, and, on another occasion, breaking into one or
two of the less intricate steps of a tango. In the big scene, showing
a cabin on the SS. "Paris," she decorates a bed so effectively that
one would be a fool to spend any time walking around on deck.
There were no beds like that on the "Paris" last February.

And, speaking of beds, several of the sketches have a distinct physical note to them; in fact, there are one or two cadenzas. But who cares? It's only make-believe, anyway.

A certain academic touch is given the proceedings at the close by the introduction of a series of college songs sung by young ladies who seem to be peeking through a movie-screen on which are being thrown scenes typical of the colleges themselves. Thus, while "Harvardiana" is being sung, a pretty shot of the confetti battle on Class Day is shown; for Yale there is a scene of some sort of revelry or other to the tune of what the program calls "Bula, Bula"; Princeton seems to be rowing in the picture thrown on to the "Canon Song March," and the big finale is allotted to the Navy with a song the title of which Mr. Carroll understood to be "Anchor's Weight." Having Harvard sympathies ourself, we are proud to note that the most applause from a typical Vanities first-night audience was for Princeton.

These random notes on the Vanities should not be taken as derogatory, for it is a generally satisfactory show, especially in the laughter department, and, aside from one or two raw moments, something that you can sit very comfortably through.

--Robert C. Benchley in Life (August 23, 1928), page 12.

EARL CARROLL'S VANITIES OF 1930 (Book by Earl Carroll, Music by Jay Gorney, E.Y. Harburg, Harold Arlen, and Ted Koehler; New Amsterdam Theatre, July 1, 1930)

Jimmie Savo and "The Most Beautiful Girls in the World" make this dirty show--funny and entertaining.

--Baird Leonard in Life (January 2, 1931), page 26.

EASY VIRTUE (Noel Coward; Empire Theatre, December 7, 1925)

We really are ashamed of letting Jane Cowl excite us into ignoring the fact that Easy Virtue is derived from The Second Mrs. Tanqueray and dozens of others. Imagine a dramatic critic of any standing at all not recognizing the Mrs. Tanqueray influence! Owing to Miss Cowl's compelling performance we thought that we were witnessing a new play, and all that we can say is that we have betrayed the trust that the readers of this page have placed in us.

We have, however, an additional excuse in the fact that Noel

Coward could write <u>Robinson Crusoe</u> and make it spin along like a
new plot. There is something essentially dramatic about Mr. Coward's
dialogue, thin as it may sound. And when thin dialogue <u>is</u> dramatic,
it is about fifty times more dramatic than the pregnant phrases of a
Sudermann. We have seen many a first-act curtain descending on a
scene of murder or betrayal that had not half the punch of the first-
act curtain to <u>Easy Virtue</u>, which leaves a party of small-talking
ladies and gentlemen simply going in to lunch.

Miss Cowl also has the advantage of being supported by one
of those practically perfect English casts, very few of whom one has
ever heard of before. And, after <u>Young Woodley</u> and <u>Easy Virtue</u>,
we wish to apologize to Basil Dean for anything we may have said in
the past about his direction, just in case it has given him any sleep-
less nights.

> --Robert C. Benchley in <u>Life</u> (De-
> cember 24, 1925), page 18.

* * *

One play that we had looked forward to seeing was <u>Easy Virtue</u>
by the prolific Noel Coward. We wonder whether Mr. Coward thinks
them up while shaving and writes them with his coffee. <u>Easy Vir-
tue</u> is all about a lady with a past who marries into a respectable
and dull English family. Of course it doesn't work out, and eventually, that is three months later, she disappears in the direction of
the Riviera or wherever it is that easy virtue finds congeniality.
Jane Cowl is charming as the naughty Larita and she is easy to
look at. Much of her anguish seems to come from being asked why
she is wearing a fur coat and why she isn't watching the tennis.
On this slight provocation she decides to leave her husband. The
characters are as metallic and inconsequential as Mr. Coward's characters always are. The first act runs pleasantly along like a Galsworthy novel, entertaining but with not much doing; the second act
begins to sag as the slim plot gathers headway; and the third is
fairly terrible. At that we liked it better than <u>The Vortex</u> which
we didn't like at all, and we predict that it will be nearly as successful. We borrow a word from Mr. Mencken in a recent issue of <u>The
Bookman</u> and elegantly exclaim, Bilge!

> --Larry Barretto in <u>The Bookman</u>,
> Vol. 62, No. 6 (February 1926),
> page 705.

ELMER GANTRY (Patrick Kearney, based on the novel by Sinclair
    Lewis; Playhouse Theatre, August 7, 1928)

The so-called "legitimate" theatrical season of 1928 and (if it's
lucky) 1929 opened in a highly inauspicious manner with a little peach

entitled Elmer Gantry. We were almost tempted to call the whole season off right then and there.

As those of you whose eyes and minds co-ordinate have already guessed, Elmer Gantry is based on Sinclair Lewis's novel of
the same name. Now, the novel itself was no marvel of subtlety,
but compared with the play it was written in code. The Elmer Gantry
of the play does everything but paint himself black on one side and
white on the other. We defy anyone to find a child small and stupid
enough (and there are some pretty small and pretty stupid children
barging about right now) not to understand, after the first four
minutes of the Reverend Gantry's dialogue, that he is just as nasty
a hypocrite as he can be. As for grown-ups, there is nothing much
left to do but make paper boats while the play is going on.

The delicacy of innuendo in this drama of the shameful shep-
herd may be detected in the scene where the Reverend Gantry is
discovered alone playing "Frankie and Johnnie" on the melodeon,
only to change quickly to "Nearer, My God, to Thee" when someone enters the room. You see, by this means the quick-witted ones
in the audience are given the tip-off that he really is carnal-minded
and only make-believing in his religious moods. And by the time he
has come in with a copy of what he says is the Christian Herald,
which is almost immediately held up to view as the Police Gazette,
the thing is practically an open secret. The whole play is like that.

The irritating thing about Elmer Gantry is that it is done with
the air of dropping a satirical bomb-shell in showing up religious
zealots as being really hypocritical sensualists. There evidently was
some idea of throwing the world into an uproar with this disclosure.
The fact that already three much better plays on the same subject
have been done in the past two years (two of them enhanced by the
presence of William A. Brady's daughter--so he must have seen
them) has not dampened the crusading spirit of the little band of
authors who are responsible for Elmer Gantry. By reducing the
thing to A, B, and possibly C, they have made unbelievable a theme
which originally possessed great dramatic power. If we ever see a
play about a lecherous preacher again, we shoot to kill. The fact
that Edward Pawley was able to give the character of Elmer any
semblance of life at all is a great tribute to his ability as an actor.
                                    --Robert C. Benchley in Life (Au-
                                    gust 30, 1928), page 12.

THE EMPEROR JONES (Eugene O'Neill; Neighbourhood Playhouse,
    November 1, 1920)

Since the relentless power of his Beyond the Horizon impressed
us last season, following upon the heels of a number of vastly prom-

ising one-act plays, we looked upon Eugene O'Neill as the one significant new force in our theater. So we are not surprised to find
his latest contribution, The Emperor Jones, produced by the Provincetown Players in Greenwich Village, to be the most interesting event
of our month in the theater.

The Emperor Jones is a study in fear. Jones is a negro ex-
Pullman porter who has drifted--a stowaway--to a "West Indian island
not yet self-determined by white marines." There the shell of shrewd-
ness and bluff he has acquired as porter quickly lifts him to the post
of emperor. He plays upon the credulities of his fellow blacks and
proceeds to squeeze his domain for all the wealth it will yield. Mr.
O'Neill's play opens with the sullen natives just breaking into rebellion.

From the hills comes the steady beat of a giant tom-tom, so
Emperor Jones starts coastward, his mind on the money he has placed
in a foreign bank for just this moment. At sunset he breaks into
the jungle, a bold adventurer with all the surface veneer of civilization. Mr. O'Neill's play follows the negro thru the trackless wilds
as night passes. Step by step, fear takes possession--primitive, un-
adulterated terror--personified by the dull, never ceasing beat, beat
of the distant tom-tom. The crust of civilization drops away as the
fear stricken black plunges madly thru the shadows. As dawn comes,
he staggers, a naked, broken creature, into the very camp of his
pursuers, where the natives complacently wait. He has completed
the terrorizing circle of his flight. Then and then only does the
sinister tom-tom cease.

The Emperor Jones is a thing of fragmentary scenes which
would tax the ingenuity of any theater. The Provincetown Players
gave it a clumsy and awkward presentation. Far be it from us to
quibble at the crudities of amateur production, however. At least,
they give a hearing to the worth while. And The Emperor Jones
brought forward a remarkable negro actor, Charles S. Gilpin, as
Jones. Gilpin played the black in Abraham Lincoln last year. Here
is about the best performance we have observed on the New York
stage all season.

Of the real worth of The Emperor Jones we grant unusual force
and originality. Really it is almost a dramatic monolog, altho vibrant
with accumulative suspense and with keen psychology of the primitive.
We admire Mr. O'Neill for his courage.

                    --Shadowland, Vol. 3, No. 5 (Janu-
                    ary 1921), page 57.

THE ENCHANTED COTTAGE (Sir Arthur Wing Pinero; Ritz Theatre,
    March 31, 1923)

In The Enchanted Cottage, Sir Arthur Wing Pinero, dressed in his customary faultless afternoon garb, has taken it into his head to fly. The result is not always graceful, and his wings at times get caught in his spats, but nevertheless, it was a good idea.

Before we say that we liked The Enchanted Cottage, we should perhaps warn our practical friends that we are still trembling with emotion from Mary Rose. This fact shows us up as fairly unreliable when it comes to matters involving that particular brand of sentiment. Therefore, Sir Arthur's story of the unprepossessing young couple who suddenly became beautiful in each other's sight through the magic of being in love, although to the rest of the world they still remained a neurotic young war-wreck and a very plain young woman, was bound to find a soft spot in us no matter how badly it was done. And unquestionably The Enchanted Cottage is pretty badly done in places.

It isn't necessarily the fault of the actors, although there is frequently the feeling that you are witnessing something done to raise money for a bust of Molière to be placed in the Assembly Hall. The author has written some of the stagiest, most literary-sounding sentences now to be heard in New York City, and there is a rather trying dream-scene which should have been handled by John Murray Anderson under the title of Courtship Through the Ages, or else not handled at all. And throughout there runs the metallic "tick-tock" of what is known as "a well-built play."

But Katharine Cornell and Noel Tearle, fortified by the inescapable poignancy of the idea of which they are the protagonists, made us forget most of the mechanism (especially after we had left the theatre and had become a prey to our own sentimental reflections) and, on the whole, we feel that we are a much better boy for having seen it.

                                        --Robert C. Benchley in Life (April
                                        19, 1923), page 18.

THE ENEMY (Channing Pollock; Times Square Theatre, October 20,
     1925)

After seeing this vastly press-agented play, to which its author, Channing Pollock, has apparently persuaded countless friends to come and be praiseful, I can only say--deliver the real workers for peace from some of the friends of peace! Unquestionably it is a sincere play, written under strong emotions of protest against the useless slaughter of war and against the enemy of blind hate which lies dormant in nearly everyone and becomes active under the least stimulus of mob or national spirit. But sincerely florid platitudes do not of themselves advance the cause of peace. And they do still less good when accompanied by muddled thinking.

Mr. Pollock, for example, has his favorite mouthpiece in the play draw an indictment against all the organizations which he holds responsible for fostering the enemy of hate, including even organized religious bodies--one of those destructive generalities which only demonstrate clearly that Mr. Pollock is a victim of his own creation. He has achieved a hatred of hate, to which you can trace most all of the well-meant fallacies in which the theme of his play abounds. His is not the solvent type of mind whose broad charity and understanding seek the good and the constructive in everything, select the helpful from the dangerous elements, and build from the material at hand a noble edifice. He would, if questioned closely, turn out to be one of those men who confuse suffering with evil, who weep copiously before the crosses of life and turn their heads before they have time to see its resurrection. This play would, I am sure, have been vastly different and more compelling if Mr. Pollock had had the illumination to call the enemy pride instead of hate--if for no other reason than that hate springs from pride and is a symptom rather than the disease itself.

The Enemy depressed me so greatly through its lack of insight, through its trite superficiality, and through its purely artificial construction, that it would not merit serious discussion except for the light it throws on so many similar efforts in every field--economics as well as the theatre, for example. We are experiencing a veritable surfeit of symptom reformers. They talk of brotherly love as if it could be generated by some patent form of auto-suggestion. Remembering, perhaps, the war-propaganda cartoons of a German family indulging in its morning hate, they would create an equally preposterous picture of American households indulging in morning love before breakfast. But almost never will they tell you that love flows forth like a great spontaneous stream, unconsciously and without effort, where pride has vanished, or that where there is no pride, you cannot discover hate.

If you want to see how true this is in a practical way, ask yourself why men settle their differences so readily in courts where once they used pistols. Does anyone really suppose it is merely because they are afraid of the law and its policemen--which they themselves have created? Is it not quite plainly because a court decision "saves the face" (i.e., the pride) of both parties? The same kind of disputes come up every day because the same kind of underlying pride is there--but the courts offer a safety valve for this pride which prevents its breaking out in gun play and physical slaughter, much as a drainage tube prevents death from an infected wound. Mr. Pollock would have done a far more constructive job if he had railed less at the fever and delirium of hate and had showered his eloquence on the need of international drainage tubes for the pus and poison of pride. But being concerned only with symptoms, he has utterly failed to see the disease.

Fay Bainter and the rest of the cast do as well as they can

with this emotional stuff, and lend it for the moment a certain theatrical reality. But they cannot do the impossible and raise it to the
power of drama, because the author has made them merely rhetorical
puppets who must say certain things at certain times because Mr.
Pollock wants these things said. I have no quarrel with Mr. Pollock's idea that the stage should be a sort of lay pulpit. Every
great dramatist has made his plays convey an eternal idea. The
trouble is with the idea Mr. Pollock is trying to preach. It is hard
to shed tears over the misery of men and nations unless you catch
a glimpse of why they are miserable. That is just what Mr. Pollock
forgot to tell.

> --Richard Dana Skinner in The
> Commonweal, Vol. 3, No. 6 (De-
> cember 16, 1925), page 160.

ESCAPE (John Galsworthy; Booth Theatre, October 26, 1927)

This play--reputed to be John Galsworthy's farewell to the
theatre--was given with considerable success in London. Winthrop
Ames, American producer-in-chief to Mr. Galsworthy, has given it
a splendid mounting and an exceedingly competent cast. In purely
theatrical terms, it is an exceedingly gripping story of the attempted
escape of a rather romantic convict, and of his ultimate voluntary
surrender when he finds what his concealment would cost one of
his generous protectors. In terms other than pure theatre, the
story suffers from the same false sentimentality with which Mr. Galsworthy garnished his well-remembered play, Old English.

In a prologue we see Matt Denant (Leslie Howard) rushing to
the defense of a street walker whom a plain clothes man has caught
plying her trade in Hyde Park. The detective accidentally hits his
head falling against a railing, and is killed. Denant, refusing to
run away, is arrested and sent up for manslaughter. The rest of
the ten episodes are taken up with his attempt at escape. The people he runs into are evidently intended to portray the gamut of human types. Of each type Mr. Galsworthy virtually asks the question
"If you were to meet an escaped convict, concerning whose imprison-
ment there might be some injustice, what would you do? Turn him
over to the authorities or speed him on his way?"

Some of the people the convict meets have a clear recollection
of the circumstances of his conviction, others are entirely ignorant
of them. But Mr. Galsworthy has so carefully engaged the sympathy of his audience for Matt Denant that the natural tendency is
to applaud his rescuers and to despise, as unthinking bigots, all
those who try to send him back to prison. This, I believe, is the
essential falsity of Mr. Galsworthy's technique. In Old English he
similarly engaged all the sympathy for an old reprobate and made all

his opponents stand forth as odious Puritans. This is a form of
literary special pleading which is just as vicious in its way as pretending that all heroes are angels with glowing wings, and all villains black monsters with cloven hoofs. To stick to purely literary
standards, it is a sin against the integrity of characterization. It
partakes of trickery and is essentially dishonest. The fact that
Mr. Galsworthy may conceal a great many truths of Christian charity
and forgiveness under this false mask does not make the mask any
truer. His method has more craft than craftsmanship.

Mr. Leslie Howard gives a surpassingly fine and sensitive portrayal of Denant. One feels it is a great good fortune to see an
actor of his ability in a part of greater substance than the ones he
has been languishing in for the last two years. Throughout the play,
indeed, Mr. Ames has done an admirable bit of casting. Nearly
every performer is worthy of some mention. But in the process of
forced selection, one can pick out particularly the engaging freshness of Frieda Inescort, the quiet understanding of Lawrence Han-
ray, and the brief moments of Henrietta Goodwin, as the girl in the
prologue. The scenic effects are all exceptionally fine.

> --Richard Dana Skinner in The
> Commonweal, Vol. 7, No. 2 (No-
> vember 16, 1927), pages 698-
> 699.

EXILES (James Joyce; Neighbourhood Theatre, February 19, 1925)

Taking the boat at Pier 52 for Capetown, we arrive, after a
rough trip, at the Neighborhood Playhouse, where James Joyce's
Exiles is on exhibition. We now understand why Mr. Joyce wrote
Ulysses in the incoherent style that he did. When he puts his words
together so that they make sense, as he has done in Exiles, they
sound just like ordinary writing. Very, very ordinary writing.

The idea behind the play is absorbing enough, and novel, in
a way. We don't quite know what it is, but it is pretty good. Four
people, some of them married, follow one another about telling what
"freedom" is in dull, sepulchral voices. There is always the Ibsen-
Strindberg atmosphere of "Lillian is dead in the next room." If you
are at all interested in Freedom (and almost every one is in an academic sort of way), there is food for passing meditation in Exiles.

But Joyce has couched his thoughts on the subject in worn-
out clichés, and paced his action to a chess-match, which, in con-
junction with as ham a set of performances as we have seen since
the seafaring days of Howard Kyle (here again excepting the heroine,
played by Phyllis Joyce), makes Exiles pretty close to zero in stimu-

lating drama and Grand Street much too far away to justify the taxi-
fare.
                              --Robert C. Benchley in Life
                              (March 12, 1925), page 20.

FATA MORGANA (Ernest Vajda, translated by James L.A. Burrell;
    Garrick Theatre, March 3, 1924)

    Occasionally, what with having to attend to our paper-route
and choir-rehearsals, we miss the opening night of a play. In this
event we see it later in the week, after reading the newspaper reviews. Even making allowances for what we know to be the low
boiling-point of several of the metropolitan critics, we are always a
little disappointed in a performance which we see after reading their
ebullitions in its favor. This, we have figured out, is only what
Kant calls "Human Nature."

    The same jolt is probably experienced by trusting readers of
this department who rush off to see something that we have recommended without reservation. The whole truth of the matter is that
no one should ever read reviews, except, of course, as one reads
this page, for an adventure in belles-lettres.

    All of which is a prelude to saying that we were a bit disap-
pointed in Fata Morgana, having seen it shortly after the encomiums
on it appeared. Viewed without any advance publicity, it would
doubtless have seemed more thrilling, but, prepared as we were for
something rather stupendous, there was a considerable let-down in
our plans for red-fire and snake-dancing after the performance.

    Not that we were unimpressed by the work of young Mr. Mor-
gan Farley, who has overnight turned from the eager over-acting of
high-school theatricals to a repressed and intelligent handling of a
rôle which would leave many a more seasoned actor flopping on the
beach. And not that Miss Emily Stevens did not endow the character of the susceptible matron with sufficient seductiveness and about
a roomful to spare. It was an interesting study of the ways of a
matron with a youth, embarrassing at times because it was so well
done, and full of little heart-breaking moments when Mr. Farley was
going through his concentrated Sturm und Drang, but not quite so
remarkable as we had been led to believe.

    And while we are on the subject of embarrassment at plays
which, like Fata Morgana, deal with the technique of sex, we here
go on record with our belief that the peak of discomfort and irritation is attained at a matinee performance where the audience is made
up of middle-aged matrons. Visiting drummers are supposed to be
the most lewd-minded audience in the world, but it has been our

experience that no congregation of men that you could assemble under one roof could match in giggling eagerness for salacity a matinee gathering of respectable American wives and mothers. It may be a nervous and mirthless reaction of offended modesty, this sniggering whenever sex is, however seriously, brought into play, but whatever it is that causes it, the fact remains that it is pretty fairly revolting. After one more matinee in the midst of the flower of American womanhood, we resign from the Gents' Chivalry Club and turn in our suit of shining armor.

> --Robert C. Benchley in Life
> (March 27, 1924), page 18.

* * *

Fata Morgana is most unusual. Essentially a tragic theme, it is written in the mood of comedy, and so adroitly written that you experience the emotions of tragedy even while you laugh. It is no small accomplishment to make an audience feel two diametrically opposed emotions simultaneously. Especially a New York audience. We incline to labels. It is only a few years ago that audiences refused to perceive the tragedy of Jimmy Caesar in John Ferguson because in the first act he had been a country bumpkin and a country bumpkin must be a comic figure. Our idea until recently seems to have been, "Comedy is comedy and tragedy is tragedy, and a character must be one or the other." It is heartening to observe at the Garrick the passing of this conception. It has come more slowly in the drama than in fiction, but it has come. Perhaps at last we are beginning to understand that life is not painted in stripes of black and white.

The Theatre Guild has cast and directed this exceptional play shrewdly. Even the parts that are caricatured--Orlando Daly as Gabriel Fay and Helen Westley as Rosalie, for example--are never quite out of the picture. Although Emily Stevens does not drain the part of the heroine of all its possibilities, she conveys the general idea of the character. But Morgan Farley--known heretofore merely as a sincere juvenile--plays the adolescent hero with vital significance. It is one of the important performances of the year, a year that has seen an unusual number of comparatively unknown actors give remarkable characterizations--Farley, Bartels in The Show-Off, Ann Harding in Tarnish, Ullrich Haupt in Queen Victoria, Alfred Lunt in Robert E. Lee and Outward Bound, Glenn Anders in Hell-Bent for Heaven, Donald Meek in The Potters, and Walter Huston in Mister Pitt--and several "big names" fail to live up to their bigness.

> --David Carb in The Bookman,
> Vol. 59, No. 3 (May 1924), pages
> 331-332.

FIFTY MILLION FRENCHMEN (Book by Herbert Fields, Music and Lyrics by Cole Porter; Lyric Theatre, November 27, 1929)

The opening night of <u>Fifty Million Frenchmen</u> was quite the
most brilliant and amusing party that has been given this season.
Everybody in the <u>world</u> was there--my dear, literally <u>every</u>body.
The old Lyric Theatre fairly quivered with orgueil to embrace so
many great names and belles faces within its portals.   The soirée
was indeed a gala one.

To begin with, the auditorium was draped with festoons of
pansies, and other seasonable flowers, suspended in mid-air by toy
balloons bearing likenesses of Mr. E. Ray Goetz.   The flags of all
nations outlined the boxes and balconies, and a small but costly "favor" was attached to the back of each seat.   The ushers were
dressed as characters from Mother Goose.   The smoke-room was
fitted out cunningly as an old-fashioned bar (only in fun, of course)
at which refreshments consisting of fruit cup, raisin-brown-bread-
and-frankfurter sandwiches and maple nut ice cream were served
throughout the evening.   The crush about the bar was, as you may
well imagine, positively suffocating.   Mr. Hermann Oelrichs and I
were so long in reaching it that we barely had time for half-a-dozen
fruit cups before the festivities began.

And by the festivities, I do not mean the show itself.   The
show was merely one of the many, many enjoyable incidents of the
evening.   First of all, before the show began, Mayor Walker and
Miss Elsa Maxwell staged a mock wedding in the lobby, which was
appropriately decorated with lilies-of-the-valley and black and blue
bunting.   Miss Maxwell wore a princess gown of ivory moiré and a
veil caught fetchingly over one ear with a cluster of orange blossoms.   The Mayor set off his conventional evening clothes with a
pair of tan shoes and was excruciatingly droll.

When the "wedding" was over, we all ducked for apples and
munched pop-corn balls and played Post Office until we thought our
sides would split with laughing.   We were glad enough to see Mr.
Vincent Astor, dressed in livery, appear in the doorway and announce, with a merry twinkle in his eye, that "Messieurs et mes-
dames sont servis!"   Then we all filed into the theatre to see the
show.

Of course, no one paid the slightest attention to seat stubs.
It was all so gay and carefree and we all knew each other so well
that we just sat down wherever we pleased.   I, for one, played
bridge all during the first scene with Miss Mary Brown Warburton
and the Prince and Princesse de Faucigny-Lucinge on a strapontin
placed in the aisle to give the theatre a French feeling.   Then I
moved over to Lady Mendl's ping-pong game in the left centre aisle.
It was like that.   Everyone did precisely as he liked.   At one point,
while the plot was being unfolded in a scene depicting the Ritz Bar
on the stage, Mr. William Rhinelander Stewart stepped down to the
footlights and stopped the show long enough to organize a little supper party with Miss Genevieve Tobin, Miss Betty Compton and Mr.

William Gaxton, who were for the moment on the stage, being members of the company.

At the end of the first act, Mr. Norman Bel Geddes' setting
representing the racetrack at Longechamps looked so comfortable and
so near, that a score of us, headed by that adorable cut-up, Mrs.
Fred Havemeyer, went up on the stage and sat in the grandstand
until the curtain came down. Being trapped, thus, behind the curtain, there wasn't anything for it but to stay backstage, so we went
into the dressing rooms and "made up" and appeared as "guests" in
the second act scenes in the lounge at the Hotel Claridge, Zelli's,
the Chateau Madrid, and whatnot.

It was in this way that I came to hear part of the show. And
very cute it was, too. All about Paris. I became deeply interested
in it before it was over. The music and lyrics are by Mr. Cole
Porter, who is about as clever at this sort of thing as they come.
I'd a little rather he'd forget his studies in zoology and geography.
I'm beginning to force laughs at the sex life of the armadillo in Lithu-
ania. But, I suppose, given my choice, I'd rather hear that than
songs about mother in Tennessee. However, the show has three
songs that I'd rather hear than eat: "Do You Want to See Paris?"
"Find Me a Primitive Man," and "I'm in Love." The last two are
magnificently put over by Miss Evelyn Hoey and there are few funnier comediennes than Miss Helen Broderick turned out to be.

On the whole, a good time was had by all.
                                        --Ralph Barton in Life (December
                                        20, 1929), page 20.

FINE AND DANDY (Book by Donald Ogden Stewart, Music by Kay
       Swift, Lyrics by Paul James; Erlanger's Theatre, September 23,
       1930)

It is never so easy to discover "what is wrong with the theatre" as when you strike an example of what is at least 90 percent
right with the theatre. In many years of theatre going, during
which poor plays and stupid plays have far outnumbered good ones,
and during which, especially, inane and routine musical comedies
have vastly outnumbered even the reasonably entertaining ones, I
cannot recall a production with more vivacity, pleasant nonsense,
clean fun and lightly tripping music than Fine and Dandy. Two-
thirds of it is a vehicle for Joe Cook--probably the most versatile
entertainer on the stage--and the rest is an outlet for the irrepressible Donald Ogden Stewart, who wrote the book and, in so doing,
showed what wonders can happen when real intelligence and wit are
applied to the business of being plausibly silly.

Let me make it clear that intelligence and a delicious sense of
the unexpected and incongruous have been applied to every part of
this undertaking. The wholly unusual settings, including the mechanical background of a drop forging plant, have been designed by Henry Dreyfus. The male chorus is supplemented by a few men of age
and portly build who contribute unexpectedly to the comedy and vastly relieve what is usually the strain of watching "gentlemen of the
ensemble." The ladies of that same aggregation are pleasing and individual and greatly assisted by an excellent group of Abbott dancers,
who can tap dance on their toes with inexhaustible ease. An excellent mechanical ballet is engineered by Eugene Von Grona, and
Charles Le Maire's costumes very happily combine brilliancy and
grace.

The principals, too, are as well and carefully chosen as if the
producers knew nothing of Joe Cook's single-handed prowess. The
tiny and fragile Nell O'Day--recalled, perhaps, for her part in Paul
Whiteman's screen review, King of Jazz--makes an eminently successful stage début, including a startlingly brilliant bit of "throw around"
dancing with the Tommy Atkins Sextet. Miss O'Day has an adequate
voice, a demure manner and surprising agility as a dancer. Eleanor
Powell, who frequently "stops the show," has certain qualities in
addition to looks and sprightliness which remind one, for no trace-
able reason, of Gertrude Lawrence. They are not the least alike
in feature nor in type of work. The resemblance comes through ability to project a personality without the least obvious effort. Joe
Wagstaff has a bit of the same quality as a juvenile, and John Ehrle's
voice more than makes up for the thankless part assigned to him.
Besides this group of major entertainers, there are innumerable character bits, such as the old man who eats his sandwich, injected for
no reason whatsoever, and for that very reason absurdly funny.

The trouble with most musical comedies (as one recognizes after
seeing Fine and Dandy) lies in the seriousness of routine approach.
One gathers that the book writers take themselves very seriously--
attempting to combine the routine plot, with its sobbing first-act curtain, and comedy relief in the form of one or two professional comedians. Donald Ogden Stewart is incapable of taking himself or his
work that seriously. You begin to suspect quite illogical nonsense
from the first two minutes on, and that is exactly what you get. The
same quiet unconcern about probabilities pervades Mr. Stewart's libretto that you find in any Gilbert and Sullivan work. You are not
asked to share any illusions of love or sorrow with the heroine. The
whole affair is carried off with that high exaggeration and solemn ab-
surdity which is only amusing when it is intended.

Fortunately the producing combination--Morris Green and Lewis
E. Gensler--enter into this spirit in every supporting detail, and Joe
Cook's many improvisations are all in the same mood. It is thus a
happy combination of viewpoints and abilities that brings this jam-
boree of nonsense to surprising importance as a standard of sheer

entertainment. Wit and satire join hands with slapstick with ex-
hilarating results. It must also be a surprise to the smut-mongers
of Broadway that a show of this sort can win its way to instant and
widely heralded success without resort either to nude displays or to
filthy jokes and implications. Fine and Dandy verges only once--
and that in a brief "before the curtain" interlude--on this trite
ground. By and large, it is probably the cleanest show of its kind
in recent years.

The program states "many nonsensical moments created by Joe
Cook." The truth is that Mr. Cook is a perpetual nonsensical moment. Whether as juggler, acrobat, dancer or grinning comedian,
he is the nearest approach we have to a one-man show. Yet, as I
say, Fine and Dandy manages easily to be more than a Joe Cook vehicle. It has just enough of everything never to grow tiresome or
lopsided. It is all for one and one for all.

> --Richard Dana Skinner in The
> Commonweal, Vol. 12, No. 23
> (October 8, 1930), pages 583-
> 584.

THE FIRST MRS. FRASER (St. John Ervine; Playhouse Theatre, December 28, 1929)

It has been a long time, now, since spats and teacups have
been imported in any quantity from England to our theatre, and, I
must say, it is a pleasant sensation to hear their squeak and tinkle
again in St. John Ervine's skillful, charming, Pinero-Jonesish, little
comedy, The First Mrs. Fraser, in which Grace George is given so
good a chance to remind us what a fine actress and director she is.

The play has to do with a little war between the first and second Mrs. Frasers, which, of course, the first Mrs. Fraser wins, and
Mr. comes back to mother and the boys--yes, on sober reflection, I
am quite sure the two English juveniles were meant to be boys.
The younger generation and the present deplorable state of civilization in general come in for a raking over the coals, but the tea
things are carried back and forth all evening in the most agreeable,
old-fashioned way, the talk is all very excellent, the situations delightfully thrilling, and the whole business is beautifully played--
especially by Miss George, A.E. Matthews, Lawrence Grossmith and
Carol Goodner.

> --Ralph Barton in Life (January
> 17, 1930), page 20.

THE FIRST YEAR (Frank Craven; Little Theatre, October 20, 1920)

Frank Craven is one of the most skilful actors on our stage--
possibly the most skilful. But in The First Year he also discloses
himself again (ten years ago he hinted it in Too Many Cooks) as a
playwright who, without any conscious effort at being "literary," at
being a "critic of life," makes real literature out of the acted play
because he chooses his subject from every-day life and writes about
it with his eye always on the object. In The First Year he writes
about the early married life of a young middle-class couple in any
small town, their quarrels, their domestic difficulties in trying to
give a grand dinner party in a tiny flat, their efforts to "get on,"
their discontents, their underlying affection, good humor, decency.
It is Main Street with a difference--the difference being Craven's
own sympathetic love for these folk instead of scorn of them. We
personally believe that so far as it goes it is a sounder, truer picture of American small town life than Main Street. And it is enormously amusing and affectionate without any resort to sentimentality.
The style is as American as that of a George M. Cohan play, or as
Turn to the Right, but, unlike the Cohan plays, it cuts below the
surface and gives us real human beings. There's health in our
popular theater when it can produce such a work.

                              --Walter Prichard Eaton in Shadow-
                                land, Vol. 4, No. 4 (June 1921),
                                page 64.

FIVE STAR FINAL (Louis Weitzenkorn; Cort Theatre, December 30,
    1930)

    This is Louis Weitzenkorn's much-discussed newspaper play.
It's a rapid-moving and kaleidoscopic affair in 21 short scenes, melodramatic, crude, inexpert, and full of white-hot indignation. Unlike
The Front Page and Gentlemen of the Press, it shows nothing of the
glamor of newspaper life, only its nastiness; and the chief figure
gets out of it in disgust instead of remaining a slave to its fascina-
tion.

    Mr. Weitzenkorn bases his play on an old scandal which a
tabloid editor unearths as a feature for his paper. When he hears
from the woman whose family will suffer from this revelation it is
too late to do anything about it. It's his business to boost circulation, and scandalous human-interest stories are the best means of
doing the trick. The story is printed, the victim and her husband
kill themselves, the woman's daughter and her fiancé suffer intense
agony, and come near losing each other; but the public is delighted.

    Five Star Final could be dismissed as a sentimental melodrama
if it weren't for a certain quality behind its sprawling plot and
sketchy characterization, a quality of mind or soul that you feel
urged Mr. Weitzenkorn to write the play he did. He had something

to get off his chest, because he felt deeply about it, and he didn't
take the trouble to disguise his wrath. I like this, if only because
so many writers seem to think it bad form to lose their temper.
Maybe it is, but all the same it's refreshing to see a temper lost once
in a while in a good cause. Five Star Final really cuts loose; it calls
names, and it defies in fine fashion the swinish public that gets its
daily kick out of private scandal.

But all the same it's not a very good play, because it doesn't
seem inevitable. Not that people don't do such things, only they
don't do them that way. To begin with, no tabloid would find
enough dirt in a 20-year-old murder case of this sort to base a circulation campaign on. The whole story wouldn't be worth more than
a couple of sticks at most. Next, the victim would certainly not kill
herself before she had made a better fight, and her husband wouldn't
have killed himself the moment he discovers her body. Next--well
there are a lot of weak spots like that: incidents put in in order
to bolster up a story at the expense of motivation. In this respect
Five-Star Final resembles most thesis plays, whose authors care more
for their ideas than they do about any mere adherence to the facts.

But even as a thesis this play has one weakness, which grows,
as a matter of fact, out of that fine scorn that I said I liked. I like
the scorn, but not the play. Mr. Weitzenkorn is always drawing
conclusions for us, which deprives us of the pleasure of doing it
for ourselves. If he had presented his facts dispassionately, I feel
I might (figuratively speaking of course) have stood up in the aisle
after the last curtain, and shouted to the audience: "For God's
sake, can't we do something about this iniquity!" But Mr. Weitzenkorn had already done the shouting for me.

I'd like to see his next play. Maybe by the time he has got
it down on paper he will have forgotten his indignation and learned
that all we want is truth and the glamor of life as it is.
                                        --Barrett H. Clark in The Drama
                                        Magazine, Vol. 21, No. 6 (March
                                        1931), page 9.

                            *   *   *

The avidity for circulation which characterizes all contemporary
periodicals has been excitingly concentrated in Five Star Final on a
tabloid which goes about the business disreputably. The pace of the
piece has been quickened by the method of staging, which allows
two or three sets to be shown at once or flashed from one to the other according to the demands of the action. We thus jump from the
switchboard to the publisher to the contest editor to the circulation
manager to the paper's speakeasy, etc., in less time than you can
say "Arthur Brisbane." The sheet which stirs up the plot is The
New York Evening Gazette, which endeavors to add fifty thousand to
its circulation by unearthing a story of twenty years ago out of which

a woman who justifiably murdered her seducer emerged anonymously
into a respectable life and the legitimate motherhood of a daughter
whose marriage is scheduled to take place on the day of the first
installment of the Nancy Vorhees tragedy. The desperate parents
try every means within their limited power to stop publication of the
scandal, but the hypocritical publisher and his henchmen are ada-
mant, even sending a fake clergyman up to get a photograph of the
girl on her wedding eve. (And what, by the way, is a paper like
The New York Evening Gazette doing with a religious editor?) On
the following day, one of their camera men and a sob sister use
burglars' methods to enter their flat, only to find Nancy and her
husband stretched out as suicides. That is sufficient for the central action, which is grim and thrilling. I was even more interested
by the general excellence of the types which contributed to it, from
the stereotyped courtesy of the drawling switchboard operator to the
perfect costuming and genteel animosity of the climbing matron who
wanted her son's fiancée's picture in the Herald-Tribune and who
had made out a long wedding list which approached the Social Register as nearly as it was possible for her to get. Ziggy, the contest
editor who wanted to race four hundred taxicabs from the Bronx to
the City Hall, enchanted me with his side rackets and breezy, go-
getting chicaneries, and Arthur Byron, as the managing editor who
had bluffed himself into the belief that "ideals won't put a patch on
your pants" only to find that money won't put a patch on your soul,
was as excellent as usual, and I hope, after One, Two, Three and
Five Star Final, that his next rôle will not involve the use of a
single telephone. Every other character deserves equally honorable
mention, even the policeman who slept fourteen hours in Corcoran's
speakeasy, and even the Rev. Ipsopod, who although tiresome and
out of place, was probably meant to be the former and was more or
less necessary to the plot.

> --Baird Leonard in Life (January
> 23, 1931), page 18.

FOLLIES   see   ZIEGFELD FOLLIES

FOLLOW THRU (Lawrence Schwab and B.G. DeSylva; 46th Street
       Theatre, January 9, 1929)

       Golf stuff set to music.

> --O.O. McIntyre in Life (July 19,
> 1929), page 26.

THE FOOL (Channing Pollock; Times Square Theatre, October 23,
       1922)

When an adaptation of a famous novel has been made for the movies, it is sometimes translated back into story form to run serially in the newspapers. The Fool sounds like a similar treatment of the New Testament.

Channing Pollock, the author, has taken on the rather gigantic task of having his hero, a young minister-philanthropist, behave in certain modern situations as it is figured that Christ would have behaved. Here is a rather fine idea, and it was inevitable that several situations of considerable dramatic power should result.

Not content, however, to let the intrinsic force of these moments carry them through, Mr. Pollock has fitted them out with a complete stage make-up of false whiskers and grease-paint, giving the effect of the Passion Play adapted for stock in Woonsocket, R.I. and, as a crowning touch, the final curtain on the young idealist and the little cripple looking out at the stars, when she says: "Is that the star of Bethlehem?" and he says (without laughing, mind you) that line which is getting too old now even for burlesques: "I ... wonder."

There is unquestionably a need for a play such as Mr. Pollock has written, and perhaps the way he has written it will bring it closer to the hearts of a greater number of people than would have been reached by a more subtle or original treatment. Even as it is, there are moments when the audience quite obviously feels that the Christ-like behavior of the hero is--well, perhaps just a bit eccentric, as, for instance, when he quietly accepts the slap on the face from the bounder. In fact, it might be possible to write a play in which the hero followed Christ's recommendations with such faithfulness that he would become a rather ridiculous figure in the eyes of a modern audience of red-blooded, he-men Americans.

James Kirkwood has come out of the movies to play the rôle of the young minister and he does it with enough repression to make up for some of the lines he has to speak. The really likeable character in the play, however, is the dastard as played by Lowell Sherman. He is probably one of the most pernicious influences in our stage today, so attractive is he continually making vice.
                              --Robert C. Benchley in Life (November 9, 1922), page 18.

THE FRENCH DOLL (A.E. Thomas, adapted from the French of Armont and Gerbidon; Lyceum Theatre, February 20, 1922)

Irene Bordoni is Irene Bordoni. You can't get around that, even if you can get around the play.
                              --Robert C. Benchley in Life
                              (March 16, 1922), page 19.

82

The Front Page

THE FRONT PAGE (Ben Hecht and Charles MacArthur; Times Square
Theatre, August 14, 1928)

Each season there comes one play with an advance reputation
which assures its success almost before it opens on Broadway. The
Front Page is the lucky one for 1928. This whirlwind of comedy
melodrama and rowdy dialogue can hardly help crashing along through
the season, chiefly because it is a darned good show.

It is another of the "Sock Chicago" series and was written by
two Chicago ex-reporters, Ben Hecht and Charles MacArthur, who
have remembered not only a lot of their Windy City playmates but an
incredible number of words they use. The action, which takes place
in the Press Room of the Criminal Courts Building while a condemned
murderer is being chivied about from gallows to gents' room, is
practically incessant after the first scene, and an uncannily selected
and directed cast makes the effect as near to perfect as such things
can get. Lee Tracy (formerly hoofing it in Broadway), the infallible
Osgood Perkins, Dorothy Stickney, Claude Cooper, Willard Robert-
son and a lot of bona fide reporters whose names we couldn't allocate
(we did recognize Joseph Spurin-Calleia as the waiter in Broadway
who jingled the change in his pocket), all helped to make The Front
Page the real and violent cross-section of life that it is.

We ought, perhaps, to warn prospective clients of The Front
Page that they are likely to hear a lot of talk that they have never
heard on the stage before, but it won't do them a bit of harm. Personally, we do not object to it, but we do feel that the authors have
made their reporters too consistently amusing. Some of the dullest
moments of our life have been spent in a newspaper office in New
York and we resent the implication that Chicago reporters are given
to cracking wiser than our local boys. If there had been as many
laughs covering the criminal courts in 1916 as there are in The Front
Page, we would still be working for the New York Tribune. (Voice
from the Managing Editor's office in the New York Tribune: "Oh,
no, you wouldn't!")

--Robert C. Benchley in Life (August 30, 1928), page 12.

FUNNY FACE (Book by Fred Thompson and Paul Gerard Smith, Music by George Gershwin, Lyrics by Ira Gershwin; Alvin Theatre,
November 22, 1927)

A combination of George Gershwin music, dancing and song by
that delicious pair, Fred and Adele Astaire, some superlative comedy
by Victor Moore and a lavish production by Aarons and Freedley,
all go to make this musical comedy at the Alvin one of the season's

joys. It offers nothing startlingly new. The book is certainly no
better than dozens of others and the lyrics have as little sense as
orthodox lyrics should have. But the whole event moves swiftly,
the chorus is well trained, and the above-mentioned principals have
a pleasant way of pervading the whole evening with good spirits and
an art which, of its kind, is not to be surpassed.

> --Grenville Vernon in The Common-
> weal, Vol. 7, No. 6 (December
> 14, 1927), page 817.

GARRICK GAIETIES (Music by Richard Rodgers, Lyrics by Lorenz
Hart; Garrick Theatre, June 8, 1925)

There are few things more surprising--pleasantly and other-
wise--than an art theatre on a spree. The business of taking one's
self seriously has, apparently, certain limits, and when those limits
are reached, something volcanic happens. In the case of the Neighborhood Playhouse, that volcanic thing has taken the name of the
Grand Street Follies and won the annual reputation of being about
the best summer show in town. But to have the elaborately sedate
Theatre Guild (junior section) break forth in similar fashion is a distinct shock. It demands some rapid adjustment. I went to the Garrick Gaieties last week all ready to be adjusted. And here is what
I found--

First and foremost--June Cochrane. A stellar imp of the first
magnitude--innocent of eye, delicately malicious of smile, crisp and
sprightly of toe, capturing not a little of the total charm of her pro-
totype in the Charlot review, Gertrude Lawrence. Miss Cochrane
henceforth has my allegiance as a real comedienne--one of that increasingly rare species on our quantity production stage.

Next--well, it's very difficult to set these junior players of
the Guild in a special order. Each clamors for first place. So,
without prejudice to the others, let's name at once a magnificent
young impersonator, Peggy Conway. In one scene Miss Conway takes
off Pauline Lord with a subtlety of caricature amounting almost to
genius. Whether she can do as well with artists whom she has had
less chance to observe is an interesting speculation.

This brings up the one great weakness of the Garrick Gaieties.
The show is nearly all satire on the senior activities of the Guild, a
sort of lampooning of the local dramatic faculty. If you have seen
the most important Guild productions, if you know the Guild directors
at least by name and reputation, then you get the full sting of the
evening. Otherwise, only a few numbers will explain themselves.
Of course the Gaieties were not intended at first for continuous performance. They were put on for one evening in something of the
spirit of a college show. This explains its tinge of local Rotary Club

atmosphere, but it does not alter facts. To appreciate the Gaieties, you have to know the Guild.

Edith Meiser, another Guild junior, also blossoms out into a capital entertainer. Anyone who has seen her in the minor parts allotted to her this last season would have suspected the qualities she now shows. It is refreshing to see them in full play. And then there is Eleanor Shaler and her dancing, satirical and otherwise, and Rose Rolanda, whose single appearance in the Mexican interlude lifts the show to real artistic eminence.

What of the men? Where, for example, is the Albert Carrol of the Garrick? Sterling Holloway, Philip Loeb and James Norris are probably the best, with House Jamieson running close on their heels. But none of them sparkles as one expects them to in this sort of enterprise. None of them approaches Carrol of the Grand Street organization nor Edgar Stehli of the Provincetown revival of Patience. The feminine talent is paramount at the Garrick--as distinctly as the male talent seems to have the upper hand along Broadway generally.

On the show as a whole, one can not shower blanket praise. In many places, it is distinctly disappointing. This applies not only to the intensely local interest of many of the numbers, but to the quality of the numbers themselves. The cheap and easy road of the double meaning joke has proved too alluring. Several times youthful sophistication is weakly substituted for real wit and sparkle. If this junior group thinks it is being naughty and daring, it is only being childish. Rich, clean satire is much harder to write and to get across the footlights. But it is infinitely more worth doing, and is certainly the one difference one would expect from a professedly clever group like the Guild juniors compared to the Broadway review factories.

The best general numbers by far are the Mexican interlude, reminiscent of Balieff's Russian Picnic, and the skit on the Scopes trial, in which monkeyland protests at the idea of having mere man as a descendant and Philip Loeb has a glorious revenge on Bryan. Of the song and dance specialty numbers, those in which June Cochrane and Eleanor Shaler officiate are the ones you remember. On the whole, it is unfortunate that the critics have been so generous with this review, because it ought to be much better. It is in no way the equal of last year's Grand Street Follies, nor of the Charlot review, on both of which it is visibly patterned. The brilliant work of a few individuals does not make up for the trite and obvious vulgarity which mars so much of it nor for the superlative quality of satire one expects and does not find. It is quite fair to hope for much better basic material next season. It is the job of the Guild--even the junior Guild--to give pointers to Broadway, not to be runners-up on the box-office magnates.

--Richard Dana Skinner in The
Commonweal, Vol. 2, No. 7 (June
24, 1925), page 190.

GARRICK GAIETIES OF 1926 (Music by Richard Rodgers, Lyrics by
    Lorenz Hart; Garrick Theatre, May 10, 1926)

The two summer shows which have already opened--The Gar-
rich Gaieties and The Great Temptations--represent the two poles of
revue-production (if we may use the word "pole" without infringing
on any New York Times copyright).

The Great Temptations at the Winter Garden is a frank appeal
to the roving and slightly bloodshot eye of the primate. The Garrick Gaieties is the last word in intimate and esoteric kidding. They
probably will not compete; so there would be no sense in comparing
them, yet each could learn something from the other.

The things that the Messrs. Shubert could learn from the
young folk at the Garrick are approximately legion. The Winter
Garden show has lifted its stuff from every conceivable source--the
Moulin Rouge in Paris, from which it gets its song hit "Valencia,"
costumes and all; the Fifth Avenue Club of New York, from whose
superior cabaret it has stolen the stupendous Koster and Bial's number, and the sweepings from back-room floors whence come the ideas
for its comedy sketches.

The Shuberts should know that right here in America young
men are writing original music and high-grade lyrics like those of
Messrs. Rodgers and Hart in the Gaieties, and original comedy
sketches like those of Benjamin Kaye, Newman Levy, Herbert Fields
and Edward Hope, all of which get laughs without recourse to the
offal container. After all, a sketch which gets laughs is better than
a sketch which doesn't, even though it may be clean. And Mr. Shubert's little gems don't get laughs.

The lesson for the enthusiasts at the Garrick is one which,
with a few more years of success, they will learn for themselves.
They could, however, hasten the process by observing carefully the
methods of Mr. Jack Benny, the interlocutor at the Winter Garden.

Mr. Benny is possessed of that most important attribute for
comedy--ease. He has an agreeable, but not too agreeable, manner.
His countenance expresses his emotions in some mysterious manner
without changing. He ambles on with a very good line of stuff, but
whether you like it or not seems a matter of indifference to him. It
is not that he is over-confident. Several of his remarks lie dis-
tressingly close to the footlights after delivery. Yet he takes it as
just a part of the day's work. He does his best, but no more, and
you may take it or leave it. It is something of the quality that Miss
Luella Gear has (by the way, isn't it about time for Miss Gear?) and
it bespeaks a cool and detached attitude of mind toward comedy which
immediately gives the comedian the upper hand in his fight with the
audience.

The youngsters at the Garrick are not cool, and are several thousand miles from being detached as yet. They try very hard, and are self-conscious about it. It is only their second year, and they are apprehensive lest you think that they are not so good as last year. As a matter of fact, they aren't, but that is nothing to worry about. They are still good enough to take it easy, and that means very good indeed.

It is interesting to note that the number which the Shuberts liked so well at the Fifth Avenue Club that they took it over, bag and baggage, as the saying goes, for the Winter Garden is one in which a chorus of large and buxom dames parade with spears in the manner of the old days at Koster and Bial's. This used to be considered pretty daring in the Nineteenth Century and nice people looked askance at these generously filled tights. In the present Winter Garden show, these old pioneers in display seem, in comparison with the other choruses, to be dressed in hoop-skirts and pantalettes. The number might almost be called "When Grandma Was a Girl" and played for sentiment to lend respectability to the show. The opening number of The Great Temptations is entitled, in a burst of transcendentalism, "Art Has No Frontiers." Mr. Shubert never spoke a truer word.

We are not a savage department at heart, and are in favor of every man's earning his living in the way which seems best to him, but somehow the prospect of a series of summer shows, each with a team of bare-torso dancers, the male member of which goes about lifting his partner up high in the air by one stiffened leg, arouses in our heart just the faintest hope that some day soon one of these ladies will slip when she leaps into the arms of her big boy and bruise herself rather badly. One or two good accidents and there might be less of this sort of thing going on.

> --Robert C. Benchley in Life
> (June 3, 1926), page 23.

THE GARRICK GAIETIES OF 1930 (various; Guild Theatre, June 4, 1930)

The Garrick Gaieties is herewith heartily recommended as a splendid evening's entertainment. Put forth by the young protegés of the Theatre Guild, it contains more humor, projected with a charmingly restrained enthusiasm, than any straight revue you are likely to see this summer. The twelve sketches are all good with two exceptions, and were apparently conceived on the sage principle that brevity is the soul of wit. They point the follies and foibles of our day in a lively spirit of burlesque, and they point so well that one of them, "They Always Come Back" has aroused the wrath of Mr. Grover Whalen, who is its protagonist to a pitch where he is rumored

to be planning to Take Steps.   The department store of which Mr.
Whalen has resumed management does business on the slogan that
"Anything Can Be Returned," and the underlying idea of the skit
is that Mayor Walker evidently felt that someone who had originally
come from it must go back.   He is shown directing the passenger
traffic by stop and go signals, and he sings a swell song about his
plight which elicits howls from the audience.   I feel obliged to print
one stanza of it:

I used to be commander of the coppers,
And my lightest word made criminals afraid;
But my radiance is wasted not now on shoppers,
And my genius I am squandering on trade.
This hand that handles corsets and pajamas
Is the hand that held the hand of Queen Marie,
But I'm back among the drapers just because the daily papers
Hadn't room enough for Jimmy and for me.

The women who lend their hypothetical prestige to commercial
enterprises were neatly burlesqued in a scene which showed four of
them trying to select the right bed and mattress in a blindfold test,
and the modern soda fountain, at which a wretched dyspeptic was
pleading for a bicarbonate of soda in the midst of clamors for chicken
livers and for kippered herring on marble cake, also awakened considerable audible laughter.   Several more of these skits were knock-
outs, but I must sacrifice their synopses in order to stress a feature
which I consider the main basis of the audience's evident pleasure in
this review.   Although none of these youngsters had a voice which
would cause Rethberg or Gigli to lose any sleep, it was possible,
even from the last row in the house, to hear every word they sang
and said.   Inasmuch as all the lyrics were good, this distinct enunci-
ation made a hit with me, because when a cavalier is pleading with
a young woman to try to be compassionate because there may even
be some cash in it, and when a tyro in a harem asks the favorite if
the incense takes away the sin sense, I like to know what is going
on.

                              --Baird Leonard in Life (February
                         21, 1930), page 16.

GENTLEMEN PREFER BLONDES (Anita Loos and John Emerson; Times
        Square Theatre, September 28, 1926)

        Reviewing Gentlemen Prefer Blondes at this late date is like
speculating on the chances of Abie's Irish Rose.   With every trans-
atlantic liner listing heavily under its load of gift-copies of Anita
Loos's book, with Chicago just recovering from its six-months' spend-
ing-debauch at the box-office of the play, and with every newspaper
in New York running serial press-stories on the local opening, all
that we have to do is to mention the name and add "Yes" to it.

No one ever claimed that it is a great comedy, any more than
Miss Loos claimed that it was a great book when she furtively allowed
it to be published. But it is highly effective entertainment. And
that, as the producer in The Butter and Egg Man said, "is a hot
piece of news" too.

In the rôle of Lorelei, the predatory ward of Mr. Eisman, June
Walker gives evidence of being an even better actress than we had
suspected, and we were never one to doubt Miss Walker's talents.
It may not be an expert play, but the part calls for an expert actress. It also calls for an actress who can hold her own in the
scenes with the unemotional Dorothy, who, as played by Edna Hibbard, is considerable competition. These two young ladies, with the
lines which have been given them, could be in no play at all (as,
indeed, they almost are), and furnish an elegant evening.

And when G.P. Huntley is added to the array, with lines
which only G.P. Huntley can say, our desire to be judicial melts
away and we unloosen our collar and settle back for a good, vulgar
paroxysm. Good playwriting or not, Chicago hit or not, Gentlemen
Prefer Blondes is funny.

                              --Robert C. Benchley in Life (Oc-
                              tober 21, 1926), page 23.

                          *   *   *

That most famous of best sellers, Gentlemen Prefer Blondes,
was at last presented to expectant audiences after a triumphant session in the provinces. Anita Loos and John Emerson had an easy
task of it: they simply took the book and put it on the stage, with
almost nothing left out and not much added. The book had made the
play a success before the latter was ever written; we have never
seen an audience more determined to laugh. Chuckles emanated
from every corner of the Times Square Theatre even while the first
curtain was rising on the de luxe cabin of an ocean liner--not a particularly amusing spectacle. We had laughed before when Lorelei remarked that it was wonderful to have your hand kissed but a diamond and sapphire bracelet lasts forever; we had become convulsed
when Dorothy said that you could no more injure her girl friend's
reputation than you could sink the Jewish fleet, and so we laughed
and became hysterical again. We were not alone by any means--
everyone was doing it. The last act flattens out considerably just
as the last part of the book does, but by then you should have got
your money's worth out of the blonde who was frail in everything
but finances. Some of the casting is simply fabulous: Georges Ro-
main and Adrian Rosley as Robert and Louis were priceless, and Mrs.
Jacques Martin as the sprightly Mrs. Spoffard was at her best.
Some of the others were not so good, but why go into post mortems?
We found ourselves being sorry for June Walker who plays Lorelei
Lee. True to her part, she fed lines to everybody in the cast with
such liberality that there was hardly a wisecrack left for herself.

Edna Hibbard as the cynical Dorothy came in for the best of them--
there was a ripple of laughter every time she spoke--but Miss Walker
played gamely on, conscious and consoled perhaps by the knowledge
that after all she was the blonde whom gentlemen prefer.

--Larry Barretto in The Bookman,
Vol. 64, No. 4 (December 1926),
pages 479-480.

GEORGE WHITE'S SCANDALS OF 1920 (Book by Andy Rice and
George White, Music by George Gershwin, Lyrics by Arthur
Jackson; Globe Theatre, June 7, 1920)

Politicians may be at a loss to lower the high cost of living
but theatrical producers--never. George White, who entered the
revue stakes a year ago, romps under the Broadway wire with a
new entry that not only is vastly entertaining but which satisfies
the longing for a reduction in the H.C.L. In brief, he proves that
silk hosiery is superfluous, particularly that of the fancy lace styles.
He displays several girls--and very comely girls they were--bare-
legged as usual. Then enter other groups with brushes and paint
pots, and decorate the exposed shins with imitations of lace stockings
now so much in vogue.

The effect was electrifying, and it deserved all the applause
that it gained. But old H.C.L. was not the only condition of life
here that was burlesqued. Old George W. Prohibition came in for
attention. So did a political convention. And piratical landlords
and Mexican revolution.

There was not a want of diversity, and Mr. White gives evidence of crowding hard upon Mr. Ziegfeld's preserves. He has an
unerring eye for dance novelties. He demonstrates excellent judgment in picking his peach crop. He knows that inspired burlesquers
such as George Bickel can coax unrestrained mirth from the most
blasé, and he capitalizes adroitly the spirit of the moment whether
it be jazz or jest.

His leading entertainer is Ann Pennington, of the sculptured
knees, the naive smile, the doll-like daintiness. Ann danced as
gracefully and tirelessly as ever. Bickel trotted out his amusing impersonation of Bryan and was hilariously funny as a get-rich-quick
landlord. Lester Allen displayed his acrobatic skill as a dancer.
His steps have an added quality of humor. Lou Holtz tried ever so
laboriously to be funny after the manner of Cantor and Jolson. La
Sylphe was as sinuous as ever in a couple of dances. Jack Rose,
Ethel Delmar, Lloyd Garrett and Frances Arms were others who contributed to the liveliness of the evening.

There were two picturesque ballets. The lyrics were sprightly.
The note of jazz was conspicuous in the music and the costumes were
uniformly beautiful in design and color.

Mr. White made a belated appearance, dancing agilely and amusingly. It would seem as if the cares of a producer were uppermost
with him now. Which is all very well. Last year he appeared often
in the various scenes and the show was not nearly as good.

                              --Louis R. Reid in The New York
                                Dramatic Mirror (June 12, 1920),
                                page 1201.

GEORGE WHITE'S SCANDALS OF 1921 (Book and Lyrics by George
    White and Bugs Baer, Music by George Gershwin; Liberty The-
    atre, July 11, 1921)

Is it "Youth must be served"? No, it's "Youth serves." The
youth in John Murray Anderson and the youth in George White. For
the joys in their revues are the youth. And the youth is doing the
serving to the public of the new things. Perhaps because the new
is ever youthful and the youth has the courage or the bravery or
the imagination.

The Scandals of 1921 is a success. A very considerable success. There's not the slightest doubt about it. But what interests
us most is that a boy should be able, in so few weeks, to assemble
a production so enormous and yet put into it beauty and fun. Just
which is the greater here is a matter of opinion. And a matter of
when you see the show. For as the weeks pass the fun must grow.
And so whether to credit Herbert Ward and Robert Law who are responsible for the beauty more than Bugs Baer, George White and
Arthur Jackson who are responsible for the fun is a colossal undertaking. And involves risks. Bugs Baer has some funny lines which
are what I have said of them before--Mark Twainish. And if occasionally some of them are rather--well, you know,--so were Mark
Twain's. They, like this entire production, set out to amuse and
entertain. And they achieve that. What more artistic? I know a
little of that job. I know that the man who hasn't written for audiences is always telling the man who has how rotten his stuff is. And
I know from some ghastly experiences that when an audience has
been made to laugh the job was a great one. "He plays for laughs,"
they say. "He works for laughs," I say. And so the explanation
of the Samson and Delilah ballet, the divorce court scene and the
patter throughout are laughs.

As to comics I didn't like Lester Allen when I first saw him a
year or two ago. He gave the impression of being so self satisfied.
That has passed. And now he lets us like him instead of liking him-

self. And in this show I like him well enough to predict a stardom
IF. He can do things. Of how many other comedians can it be
said? George Le Maire has nothing to do. I hope he will have more
anon. George Bickel, too, feeds Allen. Lou Holtz's work never
varies. His songs have the same quality. But he is always a hit.
Ann Pennington had nothing new. But again, like Holtz, she was a
hit. But again there's a tomorrow and Miss Pennington should learn
to fence, to skate, to throw a rope, and kindred things which she
could fit into a revue.

And Aunt Jemima! Who stopped the show. She weighs about
three hundred. And she is a personality which is so gorgeous--in
three hundred ways--that if you haven't heard her sing "Mammy" you
haven't lived. Extravagant praise? You'll see.

George Gershwin wrote the music. I am afraid that he has his
ears on the Metropolitan. I mean not that he took, but he forgot
he was writing for the Liberty Theatre.

> --S. Jay Kaufman in The New York
> Dramatic Mirror, July 16, 1921,
> page 85.

* * *

Although Mr. Hearst's name is not on the program of George
White's new Scandals as one of the authors, he must have cast at
least a paternal eye over the assembling of the book, for it is full
of little nuggets from his editorial page.

In fact, it is not the first time this season that we have detected his deft hand in the manipulation of a libretto to drag in a
reference to Admiral Sims or Governor Miller, but never before has
such glorious irrelevance been achieved in the name of Hearst propaganda as in the finale to the first act of Mr. White's Scandals. For,
in the midst of this extremely fluffy and inconsequential show, at
the close of a tuneful number about the charm of the South Sea Isles,
we are suddenly assailed by an elaborate song-formation, done with
deadly seriousness, the burden of which is that American shipping
should pass free through the Panama Canal.

First, in a green spot-light, comes the comedian George Bickel
in a Rough-rider suit representing Roosevelt, thereby starting the
thing off in the worst possible taste. Then Gen. Goethals, suddenly
grown as tall as George LeMaire, followed by girlies representing the
laborers who dug the canal, three statuesque blondes (Gold, Silver
and Copper from "the United States Mint, we gave without stint")
and a personification of Mr. Hearst's Mr. Opper's The Common People.

Then, to arouse the audience to a state of fury at the injustice of the thing, all the foreign nations are shown passing through

the canal on equal terms with the United States. The audience, however, is peculiarly apathetic, not quite remembering what the Panama tolls dispute is all about anyway and completely spoiling the spirit of Mr. Hearst's act by applauding John Bull as he is shown coming
through the locks. It is doubtful if any one of the cast (even including Mr. White himself) is really very much worked up over the
question of American shipping in Panama. Certainly a summer's-
night audience can take it or leave it alone.

Perhaps next season Mr. White will let Mr. Hearst have a scene
urging war with Japan or Mexico, or maybe later in the summer a
symbolic number showing the achievements of the Hylan Administra-
tion in New York City.

Aside from these few grim moments of political diversion, The
Scandals of 1921 is just one of those shows.

Some of Mr. Jackson's lyrics, especially those spoken by the
chorus at the beginning of the show, are excellent, and Mr. Bugs
Baer has interspersed some characteristic lines throughout the book,
but the comedy as a whole is difficult to reconcile with the theory
that the world is growing better, even slowly.

Mr. George White himself is the most pleasing feature and unfortunately he has given himself very little to do. Ann Pennington,
however, can't complain. Miss Pennington unquestionably has cute
legs, but, after all, she has only two of them and, as with circuses,
when you have seen one you have seen them all. Furthermore, she
seldom does anything new with them. But that is neither here nor
there, for there are crowds who think differently, and we have a
feeling that Miss Pennington is satisfied to please the larger number
and let this department look elsewhere for its excitement.

                              --Robert C. Benchley in Life
                              (July 28, 1921), page 18.

GEORGE WHITE'S SCANDALS OF 1923 (Lyrics by B.G. DeSylva, Ray
    Goetz and Ballard McDonald, Music by George Gershwin, Book
    by George White and William K. Wells; Globe Theatre, June 18,
    1923)

Returning to the scandalous school presided over by George
White, we find the usual lavish exhibition of young ladies, scantily
gorgeous costumes, fine lights, and many scenes. We find no more
wit than of yore, but we find three fellows who keep their humor
where no librettist can interfere with it--in their legs. They are
Lester Allen, a familiar of many Scandals, Johnny Dooley, usually a
supporter of Dillingham or Ziegfeld, and Tom Patricola, a newcomer
from variety.

It would seem a dangerous business to put three comic dancers
and no notable purveyors of fox-trot and glide into a revue, but
these three are so good and so individual that the result is something like a triumph. Allen is an exceptional comic gymnast who
works in very deft patterns. Dooley is the best of all those that
live by "funny falls." Patricola is the rarest of rarities, a dancer
whose legs are fat and funny and as swift and delicate in their comic
gestures as the arms of Ruth St. Denis making beauty. The music,
of course, and the various sketches make a nice, commonplace background of contrast to the beauty of the women and the talent of the
men.

                            --Kenneth Macgowan in Shadowland
                               (September 1923), page 52.

                            *   *   *

Each year there is a strange Messiah-complex manifested at
the end of the first act of Mr. George White's Scandals. He seems
to feel that it is his mission, as the producer of a summer revue, to
bring some Great Message or other to the world, to bring down his
first-act curtain on a scene which will send the audience out into
the lobby shaking their heads and saying to each other: "By George,
Moe, I am going to write to Congressman Minnick to-night about this
thing."

One year it was the Free Passage of American Ships through
the Panama Canal to which Mr. White devoted the services of his
shapely young ladies. It was a powerful and stirring sight to see
them, and brought home to many a roisterer in the audience who had
come out merely for a good time that there is something more than
just fun and frolic in being an American. We forget whether or not
the Newfoundland Fisheries case has ever been taken up in a serious way by Mr. White. At any rate, this year it is Prohibition, and
the New York World itself couldn't write a more bitter editorial than
that which is delivered by Mr. Johnny Dooley in the character of
Peter Stuyvesant on the gross injustice of depriving a free citizenry
of its right to beer and light Scotch.

Some day, when all the stirring issues of the day are settled,
Mr. White will produce an entertaining show, for each year he gets
better comedy, or rather, each year his comedy is less poor. We
miss W.C. Fields this season, but Johnny Dooley is always good for
a couple of violent laughs and Lester Allen will no doubt be greatly
relieved to know that we are getting around to thinking him funny
too. Either he is getting better or we are undergoing a softening
process in one of our brain lobes. We have a horrible suspicion
that the latter is the case.

Among the assets of this year's Scandals are (1) a Jewel Shop
number, (2) the London Palace Girls, who keep step much better
than we could ever possibly do, (3) Winnie Lightner, who, by dint

of very hard work, succeeds in putting over several songs which
are hardly worth the trouble, (4) Tom Patricola, a very good dancer
and comedian, (5) the curtain from the Folies-Bergère.

Things we could have easily dispensed with were (1) you won't
believe it, but there is a Hawaiian Hula-Hula number right out of
the files of 1921-22, diaphragms and everything, (2) the aforementioned Prohibition editorial, (3) a song called "Let's Be Lonesome
Together," all right as a song, but confusing in its setting of goldfish and canaries. If there is some symbolism in goldfish and canaries which we missed, we will print a retraction later.

                              --Robert C. Benchley in Life
                              (July 12, 1923), page 20.

GEORGE WHITE'S SCANDALS OF 1924 (Book by William K. Wells and
    George White, Lyrics by B.G. DeSylva, Music by George Gersh-
    win; Apollo Theatre, June 30, 1924)

It was bound to happen sooner or later that Mr. George White,
by the simple process of improving his Scandals each year, would
overtake and pass the comparatively static Ziegfeld Follies. This is
Mr. White's year. He has turned out a show which is better than
the Follies in almost every department. Its only point of inferiority
is that it isn't named the Ziegfeld Follies.

There was a time when Mr. White felt that he had to hand out
a little lesson in civics along with his fun-making and consequently
was accustomed to introduce strange pageants and satiric thrusts
aimed at such res publicae as the Panama Canal Tolls Repeal or the
Sundry Appropriations Bill. This year he has let the country go
to the dogs and has devoted himself almost entirely to entertainment,
at which he succeeds remarkably well.

True, there is one number which takes upon itself the task of
holding censorship up to ridicule and which succeeds, as most attempts of this sort do, in making censorship seem almost a virtue.
The best way in dealing with things like censorship is to let them
hold themselves up to ridicule, which they will do ably in about three
days if left alone. Somehow our revue authors lack something of the
subtlety necessary to the delicate task of gilding the lily.

But, on the whole, the Scandals are a great credit to Mr.
White. He has taken a tip from John Murray Anderson in the matter
of black and white as an effective combination for settings, and has
also observed the simple Charlot folk in their comedy sketches and
noted that one good idea as a basis for a comedy sketch is worth
more than one bad idea.

An especially smart trick is the elimination of the opening
chorus entirely, and the substitution of a little song, with an excellent lyric, sung by two young ladies named Williams (sisters, according to a lobby-rumor). The burden of the song is that you
(the audience) have come in so late that you have missed the opening chorus, and then they proceed to tell you some of the delectable
features which your tardiness has cost you. The only trouble is
that most of the audience will really believe that they have miseed
the opening, as most of the audience will have come in late

We are now willing to admit that Lester Allen is funny, this
marking the end of a six-year struggle on our part. One reason may
be that this year he has been given some funny material. A performer is practically helpless with bad material, and Mr. Allen has
served more than his fair amount of time at hard labor with heavy
jokes. We have never had any struggle to enjoy the work of Tom
Patricola, and it is easier in this show than ever before.

There is also a super-burlesque of a mammy song, done with
great feeling by Mr. Will Mahoney in partial black-face. This number, with its devastating kidding of the "goin' back" school of melo-
dic hoke, brings back the original function of the American revue
as founded by the Great Master Cohan in his two revues of dear
memory (reverent bowing and genuflection). If there were any justice in the world at all, our revues would devote themselves almost
entirely to kidding the truck of the previous legitimate season, instead of laying themselves open to kidding by taking themselves so
seriously. Perhaps, after Mr. Cohan stops being cross, he will
come back and do a Cohan revue burlesquing the Follies, the Music
Box, the Scandals and the rest.

An interesting psychological point (if any psychological point
may be called interesting) is brought out in the technique of singing
the burlesque mammy song. Mr. Mahoney, by copying Mr. Jolson's
hysterical frenzy, with the gradual crescendo of emotional fervor and
volume of orchestral accompaniment toward the culmination of the appeal to be taken back to the dear old Mammy, impels exactly as much
applause with his burlesque as Mr. Jolson does with his earnest effort. There is something about that crescendo which brings an audience to its feet even though it knows that the thing is being spoofed.
Proving that it makes no difference at all what you say or sing, so
long as you gradually increase the volume of sound and emotion toward the end. This is a trick known to all successful public speak-
ers, especially to Mayor James Curley of Boston, who could make a
hallful of hundred-per-cent. white Nordic Protestants applaud wildly
at a papist speech, simply by building up to his climax in the manner
of Mr. Jolson singing a mammy song. There is nothing else for you
to do but applaud when the thing is finished in that manner.

We might try ending A PAGE LIKE THAT!
                                        --Robert C. Benchley in Life (July
                                        31, 1924), page 18.

GEORGE WHITE'S SCANDALS OF 1926 (Sketches by George White and
  William K. Wells, Lyrics by B.G. DeSylva and Lew Brown, Music by Ray Henderson; Apollo Theatre, June 14, 1926)

    Now, Mr. George White's Scandals is Broadway de luxe. It
makes no attempt at satire (except possibly in the opening chorus);
its appeal is strictly localized; it is flip and shallow and, in one
sketch, the winner of the Pulitzer Bad Taste Prize. And yet it is
a real show. Whatever it sets out to do, it succeeds in doing. And
its aims are by no means unworthy.

    It is lavish to the point of hysteria and, in its Harper's Ba-
zar way, beautiful. It has served comedy sketches with good tag-
lines, thereby setting up a revue record, and, with that "very,
very charming and very, very gifted" entertainer, Mr. Harry Richman, to talk and sing, and Willie Howard at his best to be comical,
and Tom Patricola to do everything that he does, the comedy of the
show is in expert hands. Perhaps in that word "expert" lies the
answer to the superiority of Mr. White's show over its downtown de-
tractor.

    But, of course, the chief feature of a George White show would
have to be the dancing, and here is dancing, as you might say, ga-
lore. Ann Pennington, Buster West, Frances Williams--who also
sings--and, according to the program, the Fairbanks Twins, although
we must have been looking the other way when they came on.

    Mr. White must have spent a lot of money on his show, but he
ought to make a lot of money also; so that end of it works out all
right. As far as the public goes, it can have no kick at all.

    Granted that applause during an intricate dance step is grati-
fying to the dancer and designates the applauder as a connoisseur,
it does, nevertheless, make it impossible to hear the following steps,
which may be very nice, too. Applause at any time, except at the
end of an act, is a pretty silly procedure. You like something, so
you make it difficult to hear.

    We don't want to have to speak about this again.
                              --Robert C. Benchley in Life (July
                                 8, 1926), page 21.

GEORGE WHITE'S SCANDALS OF 1928 (Book by William K. Wells and
  George White, Music and Lyrics by DeSylva, Brown and Henderson; Apollo Theatre, July 2, 1928)

    The new season may not open technically until some time in

August, but to theater-goers who have fidgeted through the shoe-
string ventures of May and June Mr. George White's Scandals early
in July mark the gala take-off. Just to see a show in which the curtain works correctly is excitement enough.

And Mr. White's curtains all work to perfection, and very pretty curtains they are, too. Several other things were probably fixed
before the second night; so there wouldn't be much use in listing
them here. If Mr. White was sitting out front with a pad and pencil
he caught them. And we regret to say that Mr. White must have
been sitting out front, as he didn't appear in the show at all, not
even in a spot which seemed to have been built for him--"The Origin of the Tap-Dance."

And while we are on the subject of building up spots and entrances, no young lady ever had an entrance built up for her more
elaborately than Miss Pennington's, when the entire orchestra, with
megaphones, arose and sang a song about "Pennie" to bring her on.
And, speaking entirely from our own personal taste, what followed
was something less than a sensation. The older we grow as a reviewer of revues, the less inclined we are to go on giving Miss
Pennington's knees a good notice. Pretty knees are all right, but
the world moves and we have been spoiled by dancers who spend
their vacations working up something new for their next show. If
we sound like a cross old bear in saying this it is because we have
wanted to say it for several seasons and have, through our repression, grown slightly peevish about it. The whole thing probably
boils down to the fact that the beast in us has never been aroused
during one of Miss Pennington's numbers.

Most of Mr. White's principals, however, we could stand seeing
year after year, even if they never changed their stuff (and we certainly have been put to the test). We have been following Harry
Richman around ever since he began singing "There was an old man
about ninety" at the old "Wigwam," and if we were going to tire of
him, we should have done so long ago. We would follow Miss Frances
Williams around just as long if it weren't for what people would say.
Miss Williams and Mr. Richman have several of their regulation numbers together and succeed in making a great deal out of not much.
Their duet, "What D'ya Say?" is the one this year to be done in
front of the rose-bower. It is to their credit that they do not yield
to the temptation to appear during the second chorus framed in the
little oval above the bower. But there is the oval, just crying out
for two heads to appear through it. It would be pretty terrible if
this notice gave them the idea.

And, while we are on the song-hits, it seemed that the usually worthy De Sylva-Brown-Henderson trio have not quite come up
to their standard this year, although probably in two months we shall
be unable to believe that we didn't see the virtues of such established
successes as "On the Crest of a Wave" and "Pickin' Cotton." Our

chief objection to the score is its synthetic quality, at least three
numbers containing passages to which words of earlier song hits
could be sung in unison.   (If you must know, "On the Crest of a
Wave" brings back the verse of "Tea for Two" in its opening bars,
"Origin of the Tap-Dance" even more of "Miss Annabelle Lee," and
"What D'ya Say?" in effect at least, is a sister ship to "Give Us a
Little Kiss.")   Needless to say, all of the songs go over big.

The sketches, practically all of which end with the customary
revolver blackout, are funnier than usual, although a couple of them
have been done before in other shows--the one on "Credits" being
practically identical with one done in the Garrick Gaieties, and
"Chicago," a combination of one from Americana and Mr. White's own
The Feud of last year.

The sketches which are original, however, are very original,
such as the burlesque on Strange Interlude, in which the characters
act what they are really thinking as they read their lines, and the
"Vocafilm" act between Harry Richman and Willie Howard.

As most of the sketches contain the Phoenician personality of
Mr. Willie Howard they would be funny anyway.   It seems to us that
Mr. Howard grows more and more comic as the years go by, or else
we grow easier and easier to amuse.   And Tom Patricola's tremendous
vitality and varied talents constitute another feature of which we
never weary.   Mr. Patricola has that same friendly personal quality
which is Will Rogers' great asset on the stage, making it possible
for him to please you even when he is doing nothing particularly
pleasing in itself.

For those to whom excursions into the more animal forms of
comedy are distasteful, we issue the warning that there are several
sketches, as there usually are in the Scandals, which will offend, but
if Mr. White was out front counting the laughs on the opening night
he will already have omitted one or two of them as not worth the
risk.

If we seem to have been a bit carping toward a show which is,
almost from beginning to end, a good show, it is because we have
had more space at our command for this one and because we have
set out, during the coming season, to spot as definitely as possible
any features which have been lifted from the past.   This habit among
revue and musical comedy writers of appropriating things they have
heard in other shows is becoming so taken for granted and so almost
universal that it constitutes one of the main defects of our native
output and, wholly aside from the professional ethics of the thing,
it makes for duller evenings among those of us who have to see
every show every year.

But, even with those reprises which we have listed, the Scandals are never dull, and they fill a long-felt want in the summer

schedule. Mr. White has done it again and is in line for congratu-
lations.

Although it is not in our field, we should also like to compli-
ment whoever is responsible for changing the type-face in the pro-
grams. It makes it a pleasure to look up names, especially when
they are such names as have been here assembled.
                              --Robert C. Benchley in Life
                              (July 19, 1928), page 16.

GEORGE WHITE'S SCANDALS OF 1929 (Book by William K. Wells and
    George White, Music and Lyrics by Cliff Reid, George White
    and Irving Caesar; Apollo Theatre, September 23, 1929)

The tenth birthday of George White's Scandals finds the mixture much the same as ever. A lavish scenic display, music of a
fair order for this type of review, a generous dosage of off-color
material and a few numbers of merit. The best you can say is that
the Scandals do not sail under false colors and are quite frankly
vulgar. They are a product of one extreme of the time, just as A
Hundred Years Old and Many Waters and Sweet Adeline reflect the
reaction setting in at the other extreme.
                              --Richard Dana Skinner in The
                              Commonweal, Vol. 10, No. 24
                              (October 16, 1929), page 617.

GETTING GERTIE'S GARTER (William Collison and Avery Hopwood;
    Republic Theatre, August 1, 1921)

Those theatre-goers who, on looking over the list of plays,
come to Getting Gertie's Garter, and say: "Let's go; that sounds
funny," will unquestionably like it. The name is all the advice that
is necessary, and it is excellent advice, too.

For those who would buy tickets for anything with such a
name, the play can not be too highly recommended. They may be
just a little disappointed in that it is not quite so naughty as it
sounds, but it is good for at least a couple of dozen nudges and
countless giggles on the part of the ladies in the audience. And to
the eternal credit of the male sex let it be said that the laughter is
preponderatingly feminine, mostly in a hysterical tone from large
ladies with pink ribbons showing through their shirt-waists. Sigmund Freud could spend an interesting afternoon at a matinee of
Getting Gertie's Garter taking notes on the ladies who giggle.

As a farce, it has its moments, but they are moments which almost every farce has had for the past fifteen years. Doors are slammed, heads are poked out from barrels, people say "What the hell?" and "My Gawd!" and whisky is drunk for comedy effect by a butler who blows out the last mouthful with a loud noise. It is all perfectly splendid, and a great credit to Messrs. Hopwood and Collison. Oh yes, and there is, of course, the reference to B.V.D.'s, which makes a tremendous hit.

Hazel Dawn is in the cast. As we remember it, she played a violin in The Pink Lady. She should have kept up her music instead of going in for this sort of drama. You meet such nice people if you are a violinist.

And, in an entirely serious vein, let us warn people suffering from hay-fever not to attend Getting Gertie's Garter during the sneezing season. The second act is laid in a barn, and bales of hay send out clouds of vicious dust which can not help but throw sufferers sitting in the first ten rows into violent relapses. People who do not have hay-fever will think that this is a funny paragraph. Those who do, will understand.

> --Robert C. Benchley in Life (August 18, 1921), page 18.

GIRL CRAZY (Book by Guy Bolton and John McGowan, Music by George Gershwin, Lyrics by Ira Gershwin; Alvin Theatre, October 14, 1930)

George and Ira Gershwin have contributed lavishly their respective talents for music and lyrics to this latest production of Aarons and Freedley. Donald Oenslager has done good work with the settings and George Hale has invented some new dancing routines which take full and brisk advantage of Gershwin's inimitable score. Also, it may be remarked that Willie Howard emerges every now and then at his best as a versatile comedian. But the show as a whole suffers from the usual generous sprinkling of vulgarity--especially in contrast with that recent refreshing gust, Fine and Dandy.

Ginger Rogers as the heroine of this dude ranch story is "cute" and little else. One Ethel Merman tries a few variants on the Libby Holman technique--but they are not an improvement. In the end, we come back to George Gershwin and the dancing inspired by his music as the only thoroughly worthwhile part of the entertainment. There is a sustained and almost ecstatic vitality in his score of which only he seems capable. He is the summation of the jazz age, with all its self-conscious blueness, and its strident display of physical energy, covering up something quite mysterious which may ger-

minate unexpectedly--something which seems to include the search
of disillusioned youth for some new illusions by which it may hope
to live. I do not believe that the jazz spirit in itself is constructive.
But it may be furnishing materials upon which new forces can work.
It is fast reducing us to a pulp.

> --Richard Dana Skinner in The
> Commonweal, Vol. 12, No. 26
> (October 29, 1930), page 673.

*   *   *

This is the second musical show I've seen this season. When
I call Girl Crazy a formula piece I mean that it is competently written, produced and acted, but quite without a certain something that
ought to have come out of any combination that included Guy Bolton,
John McGowan, George and Ira Gershwin, and Donald Oenslager, not
to mention a good cast and chorus. Every single element that ought
to be there seemed present, but they didn't total up right. Perhaps
the best way to express what I mean is to say that George Gershwin's music sounded like a clever imitation of George Gershwin's
music. But after all, maybe the trouble was that this show was laid
in the Southwest and had a lot of cowboys, and I had seen Green
Grow the Lilacs across the street at the Guild Theatre only a few
weeks before. And that "give me idees," as almost any of Mr.
Riggs' characters might say. I know nothing about musical shows
and I'm probably all off anyway, but I throw out the suggestion that
Mr. Riggs should set himself to the writing of a real American musical comedy, devoid of "routine" with its professional funny man and
its so pseudo music and its more than so pseudo dances; let a real
American composer (like young Lamar Stringfield) arrange the songs,
and the Guild, or Jed Harris, or Hopkins, or Chester Erskin do the
directing.

Is this sort of thing impossible?

> --Barrett H. Clark in The Drama
> Magazine, Vol. 21, No. 7 (April
> 1931), page 10.

THE GLASS SLIPPER (Ferenc Molnar; Guild Theatre, October 19,
1925)

There are only two plays laid in Budapest this week,* but you
have to expect slack periods when you are dealing with countries
as far away as Hungary. Sometimes, too, the shipments aren't
packed carefully and they reach here with several dozen scripts in
bad condition. So don't blame the producers.

---

*The other play was Antonia.

One of this week's tiny batch, Molnar's The Glass Slipper, is
a work of real beauty. Occasionally it shifts into second speed, it
is true, but for the most part it is a fine and tender telling of the
old story of Cinderella, a Cinderella whose Prince is a middle-aged
boarder who eats with his knife and is a prince only in the wide,
adoring eyes of the little slavey.

Much of its poignancy may come from the heart-breaking intensity of June Walker as the romance-ridden little heroine. Having
emerged only as recently as Processional from the domestic-farce
group, Miss Walker shows an amazing sensitiveness to the pathos of
Irma and, in several instances, makes a personal contribution to the
part which Molnar could hardly have looked for from any actress.
To stand alone on the stage and apostrophize knives and forks while
setting a table is an assignment so difficult that Miss Walker's success in it is a tribute to her alone and no one else. It is a beautiful performance of a beautiful part.

> --Robert C. Benchley in Life (No-
> vember 12, 1925), page 20.

* * *

Ferenc Molnar has done an extraordinary thing. He has created one character of amazing beauty and poignancy, and tried to
hide the fact by a curtain of cheap twaddle. There are incidental
passages in The Glass Slipper as vulgar, as trite and as cynically
affected as anything yet imported from the Hungarian stage. (Can
one possibly be more explicit?) Yet in his treatment of the two main
characters--the little boarding house drudge with the soul of an elfin
poet, and the middle-aged carpenter whom her fancy transmutes into
a hero--Mr. Molnar has spoken with a tenderness, an understanding
and a delicate and veiled symbolism that not only quicken the heart
but cleanse the crust of the spirit.

For the most part, these are sordid and hardened people with
whom Molnar deals, and he pays them the unnecessary tribute of
too much pseudo-clever treatment, at times ironical, nearly always
satirical, and again simply gross. He is like an orchestral leader
with an over-fondness for his drums and brasses. What should be
restrained background becomes blatant foreground--or, if you prefer, what should be an insistent, perverse but subdued accompaniment, ends by nearly drowning out the melody. Molnar, the cheap
showman, has tried to efface Molnar, the tender poet. The result
is a play one cannot recommend, in which is embedded a theme and
a portrait of such beauty as to demand rare praise.

The Theatre Guild has assigned to Miss June Walker the part
of little Irma Szabo, the orphan drudge in a Budapest boarding house
reeking with degradation. Those who saw Miss Walker in the Guild's
production of Processional last year will not be surprised to learn
that she has created from the lines of Molnar a portrait of astonish-

ing honesty, elusiveness and tender beauty--the child turned woman, whose soul rebels so heroically against the miserable realities of her life that she creates a poetic reality of her own, an imaginative life in which she moves and breathes and has her being--a girl who saves her pennies to take a gallery seat weekly at the theatre to revel in the creations of that dramatist "with the common first name of Shakespeare and the beautiful family name of Repertory"--who loves the blue light of the moon--whose fierce passion for beauty and goodness sublimates the least detail of her drab and sordid life.

Not an easy part to play before prosaic audiences--not easy lines to save from ridicule--not a truth easy to translate in gesture, in voice, in futile pathetic movement, in a sudden awakening of mature instinct and fierce rebellion--not easy--but June Walker has done it. She has refused to let her soaring melody be dimmed by the kettledrums--she has made it the triumphant song of a little pilgrim, crude in expression, sublime in instinct.

And Lee Baker as the middle-aged carpenter--a failure, a weakling, but also with an ever-increasing rebellion in his soul-- has created the full complement of Miss Walker's Irma. Far beneath his wavering outer mass, beneath his surface brutality, lies a spirit like her own, slow to be aroused, slow to summon its own strength, but full of the rumor of beauty and a stronger will. When Irma falters, Lajos finds himself. These two incongruous spirits meet at last, freeing each other of their ignoble chains. This is the theme and these are the characters that should have made The Glass Slipper a great play. Mr. Molnar has sinned greatly against his own art in engulfing them with maudlin trash.

--Richard Dana Skinner in The
Commonweal, Vol. 2, No. 26 (No-
vember 4, 1925), page 650.

THE GOOSE HANGS HIGH (Lewis Beach; Bijou Theatre, January 29, 1924)

The Goose Hangs High is a defense of the much deplored younger generation. Lewis Beach, the author, maintains that the youngsters of the present time are not unlike the youngsters of other times--more thoughtless, perhaps, more assertive, but when the need comes they rise to responsibility as their parents did in their youthtime. And they respond to it with gusto and initiative and generosity; they "shoot the works," "go the whole hog"--or whatever the current phrase for the good gambler and good sport may be. Furthermore, they are not merely sympathetic; they do things.

For two acts The Goose Hangs High is vigorous and effective comedy. The careless selfishness of the children is portrayed with

sympathetic understanding, the scene in which they return from college for the Christmas holiday has a touch of Barrie in it. The
third act is disappointing. We are shown at the second curtain how
the children react to their father's failure and the sacrifices it imposes on them. After that there is nothing more to tell.

Norman Trevor, departing from his usual rôle of suave,
polished, mundane middle age, gives a sincere impersonation of
Bernard Ingals, the father; Katherine Grey, as his wife, is tender
and not too sweet. Miriam Doyle is the most convincing flapper of
the season, and Eric Dressler is a manly and forceful juvenile. Mrs.
Thomas Whiffen plays the grandmother with her usual skill and grace.
                              --David Carb in The Bookman,
                                   Vol. 59, No. 2 (April 1924),
                                   page 203.

GRAND HOTEL (W.A. Drake, from German of Vicki Baum; National
     Theatre, November 13, 1930)

     I see very little in Grand Hotel, by Vicki Baum, adapted from
the German (and very ably adapted) by William A. Drake. This
show is a tremendous success, and in these parlous times I'm pleased
to record as much of any play. I'm glad for the author's sake, and
Mr. Drake's, and all the actors', and for everyone else connected
with it. It is so successful that my little adverse notice couldn't
possibly damage anyone's financial interests. But if by some incon-
ceivable combination of circumstances these lines would result in disaster to the enterprise I'd still be forced to say that Grand Hotel
left me cold.

     What is claimed for it? Speed, pace, the feeling of multi-
tudinousness; many scenes revealing the vertiginous peripeties of
life. Here are birth and death, ambition, love, disillusion--all
cleverly embodied in a group of people gathered by chance at a
Berlin hotel. Here is the unscrupulous financier, there the accom-
modating stenographer, here, too, are a loving couple, and there
again a group of business men at each other's throats; life, life,
ebbing and flowing.

     There is movement, assuredly (as in any movie), there are a
few surface details, it is true, that remind you of life; there is suspense (better handled in the movies); there are many characters
(but there were more in The Ten Commandments)--and what else?

     No accent that rang true; no fusion of diverse elements; no
real understanding of character; only hustle and a somewhat kaleidoscopic view of life; in a word, there was life as viewed by an alert
hotel detective through the keyhole. What Grand Hotel lacked was a
playwright who saw and understood.

The German author has translated the superficialities of certain aspects of modern life in the terms of a medieval morality play. Everyman up to date, The Adding Machine, From Morn to Midnight, Processional, all attempted the same sort of thing, and accomplished it better, while Daniel Rubin, in Women Go on Forever, surpassed them all.

> --Barrett H. Clark in The Drama
> Magazine, Vol. 21, No. 4 (January 1931), page 12.

THE GREAT GOD BROWN (Eugene O'Neill; Greenwich Village Theatre, January 23, 1926)

The thing that really worries us is that the entire last half of Eugene O'Neill's The Great God Brown was an unintelligible jumble to us. We did recognize that here was something containing great beauty in its writing, something with individual scenes of dramatic power and, so far as we have been able to collect data in thirty-six years of sheltered living, great truth. We could wish that we had got even more from it.

But, in the first place, we were oppressed by the feeling that the use of masks to indicate changes and conflicts of character was not the step forward in dramatic art that it is supposed to be. We seem to remember equally subtle changes and conflicts of character having been expressed in the old-fashioned theatre simply by good acting. And, progress or no progress, masks do muffle the voice and faintly suggest children at Halloween, a fact which does not make for illusion. And if you have not illusion in the theatre, what have you? Simply William Harrigan with a mask on.

It was when Mr. Harrigan, by having to juggle two masks-- his own and Robert Keith's--thereby expressing the slightly bewildering fact that he was both Billy Brown and Dion Anthony (a fact which was not suspected by Dion's wife until Billy one time forgot to change into Dion's clothes, certainly an inconsistent mixture of mind and matter as a basis for the proceedings), that the thing got quite out of hand as far as we were concerned, and we were just a little bit irked, possibly at our own obtuseness. Leona Hogarth, as Dion's wife, was the only one that we understood all the way through to the end, although Anne Shoemaker, as Cybel the kept woman, was at times refreshingly clear. If Samuel Shipman, however, had written a scene in which a prostitute teaches the Lord's Prayer to a dying man, we wise boys would be tittering yet.

We should like to read The Great God Brown. It must be O'Neill's finest reading play. Fifty per cent. of its failure as drama we will mark off against our own faulty perceptions. The other fifty

per cent. we insist belongs to that theory of dramatic writing which
ignores the fact that, things being as they are, a play <u>must</u> be
acted on a stage, by human beings, and for human beings who come
into the theatre with no equipment save their eyes and ears and
minds, such as they are, quite virgin to the author's secret intentions.

> --Robert C. Benchley in <u>Life</u>
> (February 11, 1926), page 20.

* * *

A season which had developed heaves and almost blind staggers suddenly exhibited such a burst of speed and strength during
the past month as to draw it up to the goal post, if not a winner,
at least able to make a respectable showing with the more successful
theatrical years which have gone before. The reason for this aus-
picious event that in some cases nailed S.R.O. signs outside theatres was a covey of plays that flocked into town almost within the
week of one another. But before these are glorified two very important and very sad experiments must be mentioned, <u>The Great
God Brown</u> and <u>Goat Song</u>. In the former Eugene O'Neill has come a
cropper while riding on a brave quest. It is probable that the increasingly strong limelight that has been turned on him these last
few years and the larger audiences attracted to his plays have made
him conscious, aware fo the innermost parts of his being, that he is
indeed a playwright, and as such has or ought to have a message.
Messages have been the curse of the theatre before this, but always a new figure arises to deliver them. One can imagine O'Neill
drawing pad and pencil to him and saying, "This must be significant;
important in fact, and concealed in its lines must lie the story of all
mankind." Having delivered this tall order to his subconscious he
sets to work and the result is <u>The Great God Brown</u>, a queer, jum-
bled, inchoate thing, a sort of <u>Everyman</u> whose characters indulge
in a deal of talk about why the elements of failure are found in success and vice versa, and a deal more about Mother Earth whose children we are and who receives us at the end when our petty strug-
gles are over. The theme contained beneath this welter of words is
interesting enough: That man's nature is dual--that he goes through
life playing a part before a curious or indifferent world, and never
exposing his real self. To carry out the illusion the cast were
equipped with masks which they flicked on and off their faces with
great facility. When this ceased to be a novelty it became merely
confusing, and along toward the end of the play when the actors began exchanging masks the doubt in the mind of this spectator was
truly piteous.

> --Larry Barretto in <u>The Bookman</u>,
> Vol. 63, No. 2 (April 1926), page
> 213.

THE GREEKS HAD A WORD FOR IT (Zoë Akins; Sam H. Harris The-
     atre, September 25, 1930)

     Zoë Akins is a playwright who has often been on the verge of
doing something really fine. She's not afraid to try new ways of
saying the same old thing--as in The Furies--and even when she follows beaten paths, as in Déclassée, she manages to achieve neatness
and a kind of glitter that's agreeable. But up to now I've not seen
her in the role of serious writer, I mean as a playwright particularly
worth watching. Either I was wrong all the while, or Miss Akins
has at last reached maturity as a writer. But whatever the reason,
she is today a person whose work cannot be dismissed. Her new
comedy, which looks like a success, is not a happy accident. I have
read another late play of hers, The Morning Glory, a study in character that's far and away the best thing of its kind she has ever
written.

     The Greeks Had a Word for It, is a hard-surfaced bright little
comedy about three New York gold-diggers who go on the assumption
that the cleverest girl gets the man with the most money. The scenes
with the girls alone are the best, while the plot proper, showing how
one of them tries to make a career for herself under the guidance of
a famous popular pianist, smacks somewhat of the more obvious type
of Belasco show. But even such true and tried incidents as the
planted necklace cannot ruin the inherent qualities of authenticity
that underlie the quieter scenes.

     I've forgotten to tell you what the Greek word is: it's Hetairai,
meaning "free woman." The Hetairai (if I haven't forgotten how to
make the feminine plural) were members of that class in ancient
Athens that stood somewhere between the courtesans and the respectable matrons.

                              --Barrett H. Clark in The Drama
                                Magazine, Vol. 21, No. 2 (Novem-
                                ber 1930), page 16.

THE GREEN GODDESS (William Archer; Booth Theatre, January 18,
     1921)

     William Archer lays down his critical axe, looks sneeringly at
his highbrow pencil, regards with interest the huge bank deposits
of popular melodramatists, and proceeds to write a play. "I shall try
to do a thrilling, spectacular melodrama," he might have been heard
muttering to himself, "with plenty of intrigue, a touch of satire at
British conventions and a picturesque villain."

     And he succeeds admirably.

The Green Goddess is a thriller which maintains suspense, excites and generally entertains.

The action concerns the fate which is in store for English folk who have suddenly dropped in an aeroplane among a barbaric and fanatical people of India. The Raja's three brothers are being put to death for a political crime at a distant English post, and the Raja, in accordance with the traditions of his people, seeks revenge. There is conspiracy and a thrilling rescue, which is not without its casualties.

George Arliss gives a vivid and sustained performance of the sinister Raja. Ivan Simpson is excellent as a reptile servant. Olive Wyndham gives color and charm to the heroine's role. Cyril Keightley and Herbert Waring are capital as the other distressed but courageous English.

The play has been magnificently staged.
> --Louis R. Reid in The New York
> Dramatic Mirror, January 22,
> 1921, page 188.

* * *

William Archer's The Green Goddess left us puzzled. How could such a melodrama--suave and adroit tho it be--have been written by Mr. Archer? For Mr. Archer has long held a distinguished position in the English theater. He contributed mightily toward introducing Ibsen to the English speaking theater. He wrote a standard text book on dramatic construction, Play-Making. He has long been a critical power in London.

Small wonder, then, that New York awaited his first drama with unusual interest. Yet The Green Goddess left it cold, for it proved to be merely an orthodox melodrama. True, Mr. Archer had given it an unusual finish and a fine dexterity of handling, well brought out in Winthrop Ames' production, but The Green Goddess fell short--by many miles.

Naturally, after the coming of The Green Goddess, you will learn again that a critic is a man who can not write a play and, of course, if he cannot write a drama, he can not, by all the processes of reasoning, appreciate a good one when he sees it. To which we need only repeat that famous response that it is not necessary to know how to lay an egg in order to tell whether or not it is good.

All of which is a bit beside the point. Mr. Archer's The Green Goddess is what it is because its creator plainly believes more in technique than in life, more in dramaturgic skill than in humanity. He has taken three people--two British officers and a woman--and dropped them from a wrecked aeroplane over the desolate Himalayas

into the lonely realm of Rookh.   The woman is the wife of one of the
Englishmen and beloved by the other.

But the rajah of Rookh--a cynical Oriental educated at Cam-
bridge--is malignity incarnate.   He coolly kills the British husband
as the man sends a wireless call for help.   Of course, the rajah
makes improper overtures to the English lady in return for her
lover's life and, naturally, a British force arrives in aeroplanes in
the nick of time.   Everything moves on melodramatic schedule.

Mr. Archer has related all this with an eye to the theater.
The piece holds one's interest but it is wholly and completely mechanical.   Mr. Archer has lost his perspective upon life in his love of
dramatic mechanics.

Mr. Ames has given The Green Goddess an excellent presentation.   The various settings are fine instances of scenic investitures
in the proper dramatic mood.   And the acting is excellent.   George
Arliss gives one of his typically silken and sinister performances as
the rajah, while the hit of the melodrama is scored by Ivan Simpson
as his scoundrelly refugee valet.
                              --Shadowland, Vol. 4, No. 2
                              (April 1921), page 58.

THE GREEN HAT (Michael Arlen; Broadhurst Theatre, September 15,
   1925)

Unless, like this department, you were unable to finish reading The Green Hat owing to frothing at the mouth, you will remember the gloriously expensive death which closed the career of that
most constant of all nymphs, Iris Fen'ick, Iris of the what-shall-I-
say, Iris of the this-and-that, Iris of the mad Marches, of the mad
Varicks, out of Ouida by the doorman at the Embassy Club.   You
will remember that she ran her costly, aristocratic, high-powered
Hispano-Suiza, which in its day had got thirty miles to the gallon of
Narcisse Noir, into a large and British tree on the elegant estate of
Major-General Sir Maurice Harpenden, Bart.   Probably more upstairs
work was left undone when The Green Hat came out than at any
time since the big Second-Maids' strike in 1913.

In order that the play might end in the same manner as the
book, it was necessary to simulate the sound of a dying Hispano-
Suiza off-stage.   This was done by placing a Little Colonel washing-
machine motor in the wings (left) and letting it run for forty seconds,
followed by a glass-crash and a pastille of red fire.   The illusion was
not startling.

This incident, in its essence, is typical of The Green Hat, just

as it is typical of the rest of the public prose of Michael Arlen. Ex-
tensively billed as "Hispano-Suiza" sophistication, it has the sound,
even to an untrained ear, of the homely hum of the Little Colonel
motor. "Phony" is a word which grates harshly when set against
the patrician cadences of Mr. Arlen. "Brummagem" would be more
in keeping. But we will let it go at "phony."

The Green Hat, however, deserves to be as popular as it unquestionably is, if for no other reason than that it gives Miss Katharine Cornell an open field. She is magnificent. We can think of
no more difficult assignment for a young actress than to play a scene
in competition with Miss Cornell, and yet it is done with thrilling success by Margalo Gillmore in a smaller and much less grateful rôle.
These two young ladies wear the paste jewelry of The Green Hat
with such distinction as to make it seem almost real--a record feat.
And, given some of the most luxuriant verbiage a man has ever been
called upon to deliver, Leslie Howard makes the tragic Napier even
more than bearable, probably because at heart he is an excellent
comedian. May we not please some afternoon have a special matinee
of The Green Hat in which this sensible cast are allowed to broaden
their performances one-eighth of an inch, making the whole thing
the most delightful burlesque of the season?
                              --Robert C. Benchley in Life
                                (October 8, 1925), page 20.

                        *   *   *

Katharine Cornell has returned to New York at last, bringing
Michael Arlen's The Green Hat with her. Of her exceedingly fine
acting--so fine that for the first time, I lost the delight of seeing
Miss Cornell in the greater satisfaction of seeing the new and vivid
character she had created--I shall say more presently. For the moment, let us assume that the play's the thing, and see what sort of
a drama Mr. Arlen has fashioned.

It is all the easier for me to consider the play by itself, as I
have never read the book--and quite possibly never shall read it.
I entered the Broadhurst theatre with no preconceived visions and
found--a rather loosely and at times very poorly constructed play
wound about a theme which might have been poignantly beautiful,
but which missed both beauty and song by that vast space which
separates the right from the left hand slope of a mountain crest.

Here you have Iris March, conscious of a neurotic and erratic
inheritance, thwarted in the only real love of her life by prejudice
and parental interference, married to "Boy" Fenwick because he
loves her so intensely, only to discover that he was physically un-
fit to marry and to have him commit suicide on their bridal night.
To save Fenwick's reputation before the world, and particularly before her weak-willed brother, to whom "Boy" had been an idol and
inspiration, Iris makes it known that he killed himself because of

shock at discovering her own past. Here you have the start of a
theme of quixotic self-sacrifice emerging from a character otherwise
self-indulgent and essentially selfish; for Iris subsequently gives
herself, though not her love, to many men for the mere sake of
being loved.

In the course of her notorious career, Iris guards but two
treasures--this secret of Fenwick's death, and her love for Napier
Harpenden. The latter, she gratifies three days before his marriage
to Venice Pollen; the former, she betrays on the same occasion by
telling it to Napier himself. From then on, her life is perpetual
retribution, beginning with the still-birth of her child, and ending
with her disillusionment in Napier himself, when, in a well meant
effort to justify her before the world, he tells his father and a group
of friends the truth about Fenwick. Iris had planned, with the sad-
eyed consent of poor Venice, to leave England forever with Napier.
But when she finds that he is not great enough to keep the secret
which she herself had not kept, she sends him back to Venice, by
telling him the lie that Venice is about to have a child. She then
drives her car headlong into a tree, the quicker to end her own in-
tolerable existence.

What a drama this might have been, if Iris had raised her love
for Napier many degrees higher by never seeking to make him her
own; or, if that temptation had proved beyond the power of her
will, had she kept "Boy's" secret to the end of her days. Either
act would have brought Iris to a certain moral importance; would
have given her a faint claim to be numbered among the great romantic heroines of the drama. But to the end, her self-love exceeds
any power of will or self-sacrifice she can summon. She is a pro-
foundly unhappy woman, forever seeking and never finding inner
strength; nearly approaching heroism, only to find it smothered by
her own impotence.

Mr. Arlen, then, has painted in his play the portrait of a
tragic failure, important only as all self-created tragedies are important, and in no wise kindled with the spark of greatness. I
should say that by the self same token by which Iris informs us that
she is not really bad, that she "only misbelieves," she also confesses that she cannot be really fine or noble. It is seldom that the
lukewarm sinner becomes the heroic saint. Where the will is dormant,
it generally leaves the valleys as well as the heights unexplored.
Stripped of all glamor, the Iris of Mr. Arlen's play is a weakling,
with magnificent impulses far beyond her power of achievement. For
this reason, she is simply--unimportant.

Not so, however, with the living impersonation of Iris as sub-
limated by Miss Cornell. This great artist of our stage has written
into the play a beauty, a richness and an importance with which Mr.
Arlen certainly never endowed it. Mr. Arlen's lines say one thing
(rather cheaply, too); Miss Cornell's presence, her movements, her

gestures, even her silences, convey another. She makes you believe, for the moment, in the importance of Iris Fenwick in spite of
all that your reason can say to the contrary. In a sense, this is an
imperfection in her art. She has, it is true, thinned out her own
womanliness to a remarkable degree, but not to the degree indicated
by the playwright. She has pitched the moral importance of Iris far
too high, too near the pinnacle to which her own personal ideals
would leap. But if this is an imperfection, it errs at least on the
creative side. She gives all that Mr. Arlen had to give (which is
very little) and much more beside. If the play is ever presented
with another actress, you will, I am sure, hear people discussing
two distinct characters, the Iris of Mr. Arlen, and the Iris that
shared also the imaginative power and the humane sympathy of Katharine Cornell.

                    --Richard Dana Skinner in The
                      Commonweal, Vol. 2, No. 21
                      (September 30, 1925), page 508.

THE GREEN PASTURES (Marc Connelly; Mansfield Theatre, February
     26, 1930)

        No play of recent years has loosed such a torrent of emotional
praise from at least one section of the critical press as The Green
Pastures by Marc Connelly. The vocabulary of several of our leading critics seemed to crack under the strain of trying, for the first
time in months, to express a genuine stir of feeling and intellect.
Only here and there--as in the conspicuous case of John Mason
Brown of the Post--was the small voice of discrimination raised to
point out the ways wherein Mr. Connelly had failed to achieve a
masterpiece of classic proportions.

        This, I submit, is an unusual state of affairs. Our press
critics are not easily reduced to an emotional pulp, nor easily prodded
to a sincerity of praise which, by their own confession, beggars
words. Yet the play which has done this, and more, is simply a
representation of the Negro's idea of heaven and of the world in the
days when "God walked the earth in the likeness of a man." In
view of some objections I shall have to make to the method and to
certain underlying ideas of the play, it is only fair to let the author
state his purpose in his own patently sincere words. The play is
an attempt, writes Mr. Connelly, "to present certain aspects of a
living religion in the terms of its believers. The religion is that of
thousands of Negroes in the deep South. With terrific spiritual hunger and the greatest humility these untutored black Christians--many
of whom cannot even read the book which is the treasure house of
their faith--have adapted the contents of the Bible to the consistencies
of their everyday lives."

Further, they "accept the Old Testament as a chronicle of
wonders which happened to people like themselves in vague but actual places, and of rules of conduct, true acceptance of which will
lead them to a tangible, three-dimensional heaven. In this heaven,
if one has been born in a district where fish frys are popular, the
angels do have magnificent fish frys through an eternity somewhat
resembling a series of earthly holidays. The Lord Jehovah will be
the promised Comforter, a just but compassionate Patriarch, the Summation of all the virtues His follower has observed in the human
beings about him. The Lord may look like the reverend Mr. Du
Bois, as our Sunday school teacher speculates in the play, or He
may resemble another believer's own grandfather. In any event, His
face will have an earthly familiarity to one who has come for his re-
ward."

Now the most conspicuous failure of The Green Pastures lies in
not achieving this very simple theme which Mr. Connelly outlines
with such clarity and sympathy--a theme, certainly, to which no one
familiar with the mediaeval morality and miracle plays could take exception. The veil between the finite and the infinite will always be
such that man will seek to represent the unknown, whether in art
or in the recesses of his mind, as somehow like the known. Even
the most abstract philosophers and the most advanced scientists cling
to the need of objective illustration of their ideas. The upheaval
in science today is largely due to the difficulty of creating mechanical models of the atom. Philosophers living in space and time have
had the utmost concern in trying to find words to describe concepts
of God in terms that imply neither space nor time. Anthropomorphism
is purely a matter of degree and not--as those who gently patronize
the illiterate Negro imply--a distinct cleavage in viewpoint between
the primitive and the educated. We can afford, then, to treat the
mental images of the Negro with sympathy, understanding and tenderness. We may discard all thought of irreverence in the gentle familiarity these images imply with things divine. But what we can not
accept, either emotionally or intellectually, is a mixture of images,
a scrambling of pictures we may easily ascribe to the Negro mind of
the deep South with pictures obviously concocted, on behalf of the
Negro, by a sophisticated mind of New York. This is a sin against
real simplicity--and it is this which mars what might have been the
great beauty of Mr. Connelly's work.

The pattern of the play starts with a Sunday school lesson on
the book of Genesis for a group of Negro children. One of them
asks what God looks like. The preacher replies that no one knows
exactly, but that he himself has always imagined God must look like
the Reverend Mr. Du Bois, a famous Negro preacher of his own
youth. Soon after this, the scene shifts to heaven--during one of
those celestial fish frys Mr. Connelly mentions in his explanation.
It is, of course, a Negro heaven, in which the Lord moves about in
the dignified semblance of old Mr. Du Bois in a frock coat. From
then on, we follow the scenes of creation, of the fall of man, of the

Deluge and the Ark, of the exile in Egypt and of the winning of the
promised land--all in terms of supposedly Negro images in which the
modern and the ancient are mixed with a forced naiveté. Some of
the scenes are simple and moving, the more so because of the dignity
and directness with which they are acted by the Negroes who compose the cast, and because of the rich accompaniment of Negro spirituals. But the general mood--and here is something which must be
felt even more than sensed through reason--is one of unconscious
patronizing, as if the author were constantly asking the audience
the question "Isn't this childlike simplicity utterly charming and
captivating?"

Moreover, there are many scenes in which the images, as I
have suggested, are distinctly false. I can only compare them to
the rich man's idea of "roughing it"--to that deliberate effort at
simple living which consists in traveling back to nature in a Pullman
car, in hiring an expert chef as camp cook, and in calling a steam-
heated log cabin a "shack." In other words, many of the scenes
have a spurious simplicity forced upon them, a feeling which is not
simple at all but, under surface appearances, highly complex and
mentally exacting. Other scenes again have a distinctly satirical
twist; and throughout the play there is a lack of that solemn grandeur
which, in my limited experience, even the most uneducated Negro
mind attributes to things divine. It is characteristic of the truly
simple mind to exaggerate greatness, to run to excess in hero worship. It is the boy brought up in the slums who imagines every
rich man's house to be a marble and gold palace. It may be, as
Mr. Connelly indicates, that the Negro imagines the business office
of the Lord to be a tiny room with a couple of stiff-backed chairs
and a roll-top desk; but I doubt it. The majesty and panoply of
the throne are much more in keeping with the dreams of the naive
and the humble. It is precisely the sophisticate who suspects behind
the trappings of royalty the banal domestic life of the king. The
simple or the childlike mind conceives the king at breakfast in ermine and wearing his crown. I cannot imagine, then, that the Negro, even of the deep South, thinks of Jehovah in commonplace surrounding, any more than the Jewish people themselves expected the
King of Kings to be born in a manger. It is the person of Christ--
with Whom this play does not deal--Whom the mind of the child
clothes in the familiar simplicity of humble friendship.

None of these defects of authorship and idea can, however,
rob the play of the deep sincerity of its acting by the Negro cast.
It is the powerful and sturdy directness of their work, I am sure,
which has done the most to stir an emotional response. They reflect
the substance of a faith in their every action, and this alone, in a
day of doubt and unbelief, comes almost with the impact of a revelation. At various incongruous moments in the play, one feels very
much as if their inner integrity were being violated and exploited.
Certainly Marc Connelly has not produced this effect intentionally.
But faith, no matter how humble, can never be truly and honestly

conveyed except by those who share it, if not in its pictorial images
at least in its flaming essence, if not in its particular idiom then
certainly in its universal language. The Green Pastures impresses
one, rightly or wrongly, as being written by a playwright who undoubtedly has a deep respect for but does not share the essential
qualities of the faith of the Negro people.

> --Richard Dana Skinner in The
> Commonweal, Vol. 11, No. 20
> (March 19, 1930), pages 561-562.

GREENWICH VILLAGE FOLLIES OF 1920 (Book and Lyrics by John
    Murray Anderson, Thomas J. Gray and Arthur Swanstrom,
    Music by A. Baldwin Sloane; Greenwich Village Theatre, August
    30, 1920)

The new Greenwich Village Follies, true to its traditions, opens
in Greenwich Village. But it will not be confined there long. It
will march triumphantly to a larger field in the vicinity of Mr. Ziegfeld whose domains it threatens seriously in pictorial appeal, artistic
effects and dancing features.

John Murray Anderson continues the strikingly novel stage-
craft--novel for girl-and-music shows--which he displayed in What's
in a Name, two of the numbers, a Russian executed amidst the barbaric costumes of the fourteenth century with a bizarre Greenwich
cafe as a background and a Persian danced with Oriental abandon
and color being splendid examples of his skill.

But there are many, many other features, most of which are
worth while. Stunning costumes, youthful and agile dancers, comedians of subtlety and clownish broadness, settings of rare charm
and originality--all these contribute to the appeal of the revue in
Sheridan Square.

Among the performers there are noted the droll and ingenious
Savoy and Brennan, comedians who are always reliable and always
funny. There is Ivan Bankoff dancing with unusual fervor and
athletic grace, assisted by the accomplished Mlle. Phebe. Collins
and Hart contributed their comic business with an invisible wire.
Myers and Hanford extracted music from a saw and amused after the
manner of Arkansas travelers. Sylvia Clark sang and jested with
her usual good humor. Frank Crumit as a master of ceremonies
found a niche for his quiet methods. Venita Gould was another capable singer and impersonator and a highly personable young woman
named Margaret Severn won a substantial success in a series of
dances in masks, the latter the work of W.T. Benda.

> --Louis R. Reid in The New York
> Dramatic Mirror (September 4,
> 1920), page 415.

GREENWICH VILLAGE FOLLIES OF 1921 (Lyrics by Arthur Swanstron
and John Murray Anderson, Music by Carey Morgan; Shubert
Theatre, August 31, 1921)

This notice of the Greenwich Village Follies is fortunately a
month late, and is therefore able to include mention of a recently
added number which, together with Irene Franklin, constitutes the
only bearable comedy in the bill. The act is so good that the management was evidently ashamed to put it on the program; so we can
designate it only as "Mulligan and Mulligan from the West," which is
the title of the song that the team makes several futile attempts to
sing throughout the performance, finally ending up with a remarkable dance, the name of which is: "King Charles Brothers Chasing
Bubbles."

It is incredible that John Murray Anderson can dream and put
into reality the beautiful settings that one sees at the Greenwich
Village Follies, and yet allow such unsanitary comedy conditions to
exist on the same stage. The best way to enjoy the performance
would be to sit in the last row in the gallery (or just near enough
to see the detail of the Benda masks in Oliver Herford's "Blue Law's
Ninth Wife") and read a book during the more repellent comedy
scenes.

                              --Robert C. Benchley in Life (Oc-
                              tober 13, 1921), page 18.

THE GREENWICH VILLAGE FOLLIES OF 1924 (Lyrics by Cole Porter,
Irving Caesar and John Murray Anderson, Music by Cole Porter;
Shubert Theatre, September 16, 1924)

It is common talk that critics see so many plays that they become fed-up and disagreeable and are incapable of judging anything
at all fairly. This is not true as a generalization (as the girl said to
the sailor), but in the matter of revues we must admit that we have
reached the saturation point and are no longer able to view their magnificence with the clear eye of the layman. After seeing three revues on three successive evenings we felt that one more yard of gold
brocade, one more ounce of glittering jet, or even one more young
lady built to represent one of the sixteen steps in the process of
making an overcoat, and we would set fire to the theatre.

It was The Greenwich Village Follies which fed us up to the
eyes. At 11:30, when the first act was over, we could not remember having spent a duller evening since we were a little boy and
heard Dwight Elmendorf lecture on the Holy Land. For hours the
thing had gone on. Bolt after bolt of white goods had been un-
rolled; ton after ton of the heaviest comedy ever mined in these

parts had been dumped out of the cars, and bar after bar of synthetic music had lulled us into a stupor from which we had to be
awakened by an usher. And, as we fumbled our way to the sidewalk with just ten minutes in which to catch the 11:40, we noticed
that no one else had his hat and coat on. "Why is this?" we asked.
"Have you all no homes?" There was general laughter among the
wiseacres, who explained that only the first act was over. This left
just one thing for us to do, and we did it. We sat down on the
curb and cried as if our little heart would break.

One feature of The Greenwich Village Follies, and one alone,
reconciled us to going back for the second act. Moran and Mack,
black-face artists from vaudeville, had aroused us at 10:45 during
the first act, with an unforgetable bit of comedy. And they were
worth going back for. They would be worth going back into a burning building for. And this in the face of our fear that, if we did
go back, the management would bring on that coloratura again. We
can pay Messrs. Moran and Mack no greater tribute than to say that
we braved a coloratura soprano for a second glimpse of them.
                              --Robert C. Benchley in Life (Oc-
                              tober 9, 1924), page 18.

GREENWICH VILLAGE FOLLIES OF 1925 (Lyrics and Music by Harold
    Levey and Owen Murphy; 46th Street Theatre, December 24,
    1925)

We are getting pretty sick of saying about our native revues
that they are gorgeous spectacles but that they lack comedy. Probably the producers are even more sick of its being said. Their
reply might well be, "Show us some comedy and we'll use it." And
yet we doubt very much that the management of the Greenwich Village Follies know good comedy when they see it, for they have placed
"The Spy," one of the best revue sketches we have ever seen, comparatively early on the bill and have given the author no credit. As
played by Tom Howard, this was the high spot of the revue season
for us. The rest of the show, even with our beloved Florence Moore
working her hardest, is as devoid of laughs as (Notice to printer:
Insert good simile here).

It is gay to look at, yes. But as is usually the case with Mr.
Short's elaborate concoctions, the stage crew on opening night was
in a panic and during the more quiet periods of the show it sounded
as if they were building on the entire back wall of the Chanin Theatre. They ought to be through with the riveting by now; so perhaps things are better.
                              --Robert C. Benchley in Life (Jan-
                              uary 28, 1926), page 18.

THE GREENWICH VILLAGE FOLLIES OF 1928 (Sketches by Harold
   Atteridge, Music by Ray Perkins and Maurie Rubens, Lyrics
   by Max and Nathaniel Lief; Winter Garden Theatre, April 9,
   1928)

   The Greenwich Village Follies can hardly be classed among the
"new" summer shows, as it has been running a month and a half,
but it was new to us, which, after all, is the only standard one has
in this world, isn't it? While we wouldn't say that it is a knock-out
among revues, it also seemed rather pleasant to these world-weary
eyes. From vaudeville again has been drawn a headliner in the person of Dr. Rockwell, known for many years to patrons of the two-a-
day as the diagnostician of the banana-stalk and general therapeutic
expert. If you haven't seen him before (or even if you have), it
wouldn't do any harm to go and hear what he has to say. He has
some charming ideas about anatomy.

   And while we are on the subject of anatomy, The Greenwich
Village Follies is one of those summer Winter Garden shows.
                              --Robert C. Benchley in Life
                              (May 24, 1928), page 20.

THE GUARDSMAN (Ferenc Molnar; Garrick Theatre, October 13,
   1924)

   Ever since the days, early in our theatre-going career, when
we used to run out to Versailles to invitation performances of whatever the new Molière thing happened to be, we have been asked by
playwrights to believe that a man could don a thin disguise and, by
holding a cloak about his jaw and turning his head to the right, de-
ceive his wife and entire household into thinking him "a mysterious
Stranger" or "a certain Doctor Bogo from Tasmania."

   And, in all this time, we have never once believed it. Even
Shakespeare could never make us believe it, although now that he
is gone it might be better form to say nothing about his failure in
this respect. Nil nisi bonum, you know. De mortuis, that is.

   And then along comes Alfred Lunt in The Guardsman and convinces us that it might be possible. He dresses up as a Russian
soldier and makes love to his own wife with such skill that she would
have been just silly to suspect him. It turns out, however, that she
did suspect him from the first and just allowed him to run on. So
the only character on the stage that we have ever believed could
fool his wife like that, didn't. And now we don't know what to
think.

As a play, The Guardsman is not particularly important, except in so far as it is smooth and facile and entertaining. After all, that is pretty important when you have to sit through it.

But Mr. Lunt's performance is important, especially for Mr. Lunt. It marks him as a young actor who can be trusted. There was a time when he made faces a bit too much for our particular fancy, but in Outward Bound we knew that he was headed for Class A, Group One, and here he is. Lynn Fontanne, although not quite so richly supplied with opportunities as she has been in the past, makes the rather generic rôle of the suspected wife something quite different. To see the two of them together is to experience that peace of mind which comes only when you realize that the lines of a play are entrusted to experts and that you needn't worry from then on.

> --Robert C. Benchley in Life (October 30, 1924), page 18.

THE HAIRY APE (Eugene O'Neill; Provincetown Theatre, March 9, 1922)

The Hairy Ape, Eugene O'Neill's latest play to be produced in New York, may well be considered the most powerful thing he has done. The little stage at the Provincetown Theatre fairly bursts its seams with the brute force of the message and the almost terrifying strength of its expression. (And, incidentally, in that tiny space are produced scenic effects which make those of up-town theatres appear like something you might do in the barn.)

The downward course of the giant stoker, who seems throughout the play to be the baffled embodiment of Rodin's "Le Penseur," from the stoke-hole of his ship to the cage of the hairy ape, is made all the more impressive by the vivid performance of Louis Wolheim.

The combination of the strength of O'Neill's conception and the force which Wolheim brings to its execution constitutes an experience in the theatre which is moving in so far as the congested conditions in the Provincetown Theatre will permit one to be moved. For all these conditions, however, it would be well to see The Hairy Ape before it moves up-town (as it unquestionably must), for Jones and Throckmorton have achieved a focus with their effects on this miniature stage which may be lost or diffused in a larger and more commercial theatre.

> --Robert C. Benchley in Life (March 30, 1922), page 18.

HAMLET (William Shakespeare; Sam H. Harris Theatre, November 16,
    1922)

        Having avoided seeing as many preceding Hamlets as I possibly
could, I am in no position to offer any very valuable comment on the
Hamlet of John Barrymore.   All that I can say is that while watching
him I understood Hamlet for the first time, and for the first time
felt any personal contact with a character from Shakespeare on the
stage.   Consequently it was the first time that I have not been bored
stiff at a Shakespearian production.   I doubt if this is very high
praise under the circumstances, but it is from the heart.
                                    --Robert C. Benchley in Life (De-
                                        cember 14, 1922), page 18.

HAY FEVER (Noel Coward; Maxine Elliott Theatre, October 5, 1925)

        Noel Coward, an Englishman and Mr. (Michael) Arlen's chief
rival for the favors of publicity and invitations to theatrical supper
parties, is the author of Hay Fever, which will probably not last as
long as his now celebrated Vortex.   It is a comedy of bad manners
written about a retired actress and her family, which consists of a
novelist husband, an insolent son, and a bumptious daughter.   Again
there is no meat, but only a delightful amount of pastry.   Laura
Hope Crews as the middle aged actress panting to return to the
boards and taking out her thirst on her family by "acting" persistent-
ly, carries off a very delicate task with all the intelligence for which
she is known.   She provides a superb composite portrait of all the
middle aged actresses in the world temporarily out of work.   Frieda
Inescort is charming as the normal, healthy young daughter who
never had a chance in such a preposterous household, and Harry
Davenport is entirely authentic as the absent-minded novelist who is
always poking into the characters of other people.   We wonder at
the vast amount Mr. Coward knows of that manifestation popularly
known as "the artistic temperament."
                                    —Louis Bromfield in The Bookman,
                                        Vol. 62, No. 4 (December 1925),
                                        pages 477-478.

THE HERO (Gilbert Emery; Longacre Theatre, March 14, 1921)

        Sam H. Harris has to his credit the production of a play which
is almost great.

        The author is not Gilbert Emery as programmed, but Pottle, a
well known novelist I am told.

The theme is relentless. And what a theme! What a courageous theme! The hero was a hero at the front but he is the "heavy"
at home. That's all there's to the story. He steals, he seduces, he
is lazy. At home. His brother's wife almost becomes his victim. A
Belgian girl adopted by the wife is already his. The hero talks in
church and the brother is the custodian of the money. Which the
hero eventually steals. But as he is going away there's a fire. A
kindergarten. The brother's child is there. The hero saves its
life. But gives his own. The wife tells the brother that the hero
was on the way to the bank to deposit the money.

As a story it may seem trivial. But when you see it as you
must if you would see a fine piece of work you will begin asking
yourself why it interests you. One has the feeling, or at any rate
I did, that one wants to leave it. It's bitter. And yet it holds one
completely. I suppose that the hero being no hero does it. Or it
may be that we wonder just how far the hero will go. Or it may be
the old mother which is a gorgeous character and gorgeously acted
by Blanche Frederici.

Mr. Harris gave it a splendid cast. Grant Mitchell was NOT
the hero. He was the brother. And therein is the point. It isn't
the better part. Robert Ames was the hero. And both men were
corking. I have not seen Grant Mitchell do anything so well as he
did this insurance agent brother. The touches were many and they
were in character. Robert Ames, who is with Miss Larrimore in
Nice People, has more opportunities here. I predicted a career for
him. He is always sure but he doesn't make his audience feel it.
There's a difference.

Kathlene McDonell reminds me of Clara Joel. Why doesn't someone make them forget themselves? Sam Forrest is one of the best of
directors and I am surprised that he allowed Miss McDonell to indulge in the well known McDonell peculiarities. What a really fine
actress she might be!

But Gilbert Emery Pottle is the hero of The Hero.
                              --S. Jay Kaufman in The New York
                                Dramatic Mirror, March 19, 1921,
                                page 488.

                         *   *   *

Another significant native play, produced in the spring at a
special matinee, thanks, one fancies, to the ambition of Grant Mitchell,
the actor, who proposes to play it in regularly next season, is The
Hero, by Emery Pottle. The drama dares to tell a truth it has been
dangerous to blurt out of late--namely, that a physical hero in war
may be a moral scoundrel in peace. The drama punctures a certain
balloon which has been inflated with hysteria rather than hydrogen.
                              --Walter Prichard Eaton in Shadow-
                                land, Vol. 4, No. 4 (June 1921),
                                page 64.

HOLIDAY (Philip Barry; Plymouth Theatre, November 26, 1928)

Salutations to Philip Barry for the one well-nigh perfect play
of this unhappy season! If ever there was a justification for the
belief that a thoroughly honest play can also be highly diverting and
enormously successful from the box-office viewpoint, Mr. Barry's
latest and best play stands forth as that justification. There is not
an off-color line from beginning to end. Yet the comedy is clean,
swift and high-spirited. The design is as simple as a landscape, yet
the substance of human emotion is there in full measure. The play
is firm, true and often poignant without once bordering on sentimentality. And it happens also to be the most outstanding and even
sensational success of the season.

The story, as I have suggested, is simple enough. A young
lawyer, Johnny Case, who is on the verge of success, meets Julia
Seton at Lake Placid. Julia is the oldest of Edward Seton's three
children and very much wedded to her father's views on how the
family and the world in general should be run. Her father--other-
wise dubbed "Big Business" by his second daughter, Linda--is one
of those conservative crustaceans thoroughly accustomed to having
his own way in everything. He is somewhat horrified to discover
that Johnny Case has no social background, but is slightly mollified
by the fact that Johnny has just arranged a successful merger of
public utility interests and shows evidences of making a name for
himself. Serious trouble begins just after Mr. Seton has agreed to
announce the engagement of Julia and Johnny at a large New Year's
party. It then turns out that Johnny has some ideas of his own
about relative values in life. Having made a little money of his own
and being something of a vagabond at heart, he is rather inclined
to take some of his leisure while young. He is fully prepared to stop
business for a little while and to resume it only after he and Julia
have had a period of leisure and travel. This comes as a bombshell
of the first magnitude in the Seton household--to all, that is, except
the forthright and rebellious Linda and her younger brother Ned.
The conclusion is, if you wish, obvious. The engagement is broken,
and Linda, who has understood the vagabond in Johnny all along,
finds her way clear at last, after making doubly sure that Julia no
longer cares for him at all.

Now, in many ways, we have here only a repetition of the
familiar Cinderella theme. You could tell the story in a way to make
it seem almost ridiculous. But Barry does not handle his material
that way. In the first place, the Cinderella characteristics in Linda
are well concealed by her abrupt, almost boyish mannerisms, her
quick wit and apt tongue. She is the dominating figure throughout
the play. Then, too, we find a perfection of characterization which
convinces us that we are dealing with individuals and not with age-
old types. There is authenticity in every detail, and many side
touches give the picture depth and inner meaning. For example,

there is the brother, Ned--well on his way to becoming a drunkard
for the simple reason that the whole atmosphere of the stuffy household has got on his nerves. He needs spiritual fresh air and plenty
of it. There are Linda's best friends, Nick and Susan Potter, who,
in their unassuming way, have made a real art out of life and extract
plenty of amusement and meaning from it by using their sufficient
means intelligently. They do not make accumulation of money or
power an end in itself. There is also the constant battle of the two
sisters, carried on in an undertone and rarely flashing into heat,
but forever keeping before us the sterility of wealth as a thing in
itself.

    I am well aware that in describing these things, I may make
them appear as mere platitudes and moralizations. The point is that
Barry, with consummate art, has concealed their obviousness, given
them fresh verbal expression, and surrounded them with a sensitive
breeze of comedy that takes all the curse off of them. He never
strains an emotional point to sentimentality. He never permits fierce
denunciation. He lets the audience do its own thinking for the most
part, and creates a complete illusion of real human experience. Perhaps the finest touches of all are in his handling of dialogue between
the conflicting family groups. Linda and her friends know the worth
of nonsense. They never lose the spirit of play--and in that alone
lies the secret of the "moral of the play" never becoming tiresome.
No American playwright can create such delicious nonsense as Barry
at his best, and in this play he has given us the cream of those
qualities which made certain parts of White Wings and In a Garden
enchanting. He has avoided the main fault of those earlier plays,
however, by not getting carried away by nonsense and fantasy. He
has set about to write a real play and has introduced whimsicality
only where it serves a dramatic purpose.

    Of course a play of this character gains enormously from in-
telligent production, and be it said now and with emphasis that
Arthur Hopkins has lavished on Holiday an almost perfect cast, and
settings by Robert Edmond Jones that fairly burst with authentic
atmosphere. Jones has often demonstrated his power of imaginative
design. He is surpassingly fine as an impressionist. But, like every
true artist, he also has the ability to turn realist in a heightened degree. When the curtain goes up, the Jones settings speak for themselves. They tell you what kind of house this is and what kind of
family lives in it. And that is worth pages of "exposition."

    Hope Williams makes of Linda Seton an almost unique character
in dramatic literature. I am unable to say whether this is the result
of perfect "type" casting, or of superb acting. So far as the audience goes, this makes little difference. Linda stands forth as clear
as a cameo--a strong, clear-thinking, direct-acting, whimsical and
lovable girl without a trace of self-consciousness, and with a breadth
of understanding which can flow only from a strong though concealed
maternal quality. In the thankless part of Julia Seton, Dorothy Tree

manages to retain just as much sympathy as the exigencies of the
situation permit. Her father, as played by Walter Walker, is anything but a caricature of "big business." He is a perfectly credible
older man who has become ossified. Monroe Owsley gives a very
sympathetic interpretation of Ned, and Donald Ogden Stewart contributes so much of reckless drollery to Nick Potter that he becomes
for a moment in the second act a full play in himself.

   To some people Holiday may seem a trifle thin and lacking in
the flame of drama. But to my mind its very restraint is what gives
it its universality. By keeping true to character it permits the audience to fill in the gaps, as to how they would act in a similar position. In brief, Holiday is a masterpiece.

--Richard Dana Skinner in The
Commonweal, Vol. 9, No. 14
(February 6, 1929), page 405.

*   *   *

   Last year we had occasion to complain that too many of our
personal friends were taking to writing plays. Even when they are
good, it is a little embarrassing for us. Mr. Philip Barry is perhaps
the most thoughtless of all our writing acquaintances, for, not only
has he followed Paris Bound with Holiday, but he has gone out of
his way to write a part in it for Donald Ogden Stewart, who is
practically the illegitimate son of this department. He did have the
decency to write him a very good part, and Mr. Stewart has had
consideration enough for our feelings not to fall down on the stage
or forget his lines, but the whole thing has been quite a nervous
strain for us and we rather resent having been subjected to it.

   Furthermore, this business of authors going on the stage has
got to stop. We old actors who have given the best years of our
life to the theatre are in no mood to see our places taken by a lot
of literary whipper-snappers who are in the thing for a lark. It
was bad enough when Heywood Broun donned one sock and half a
buskin and did a monologue in Herman Mankiewicz's Follies of 1924,
but during the past season there has been a positive influx of
scriveners into the green-room, headed by Russell Crouse and his
understudy, Ward Morehouse, in Mr. Morehouse's Gentlemen of the
Press. Backstage is practically alive with writers, and one never
knows whether they are there to interview the star or to act. It
is all very confusing.

   As for Mr. Stewart's performance in Holiday, we are fortunately able to commend it without laying ourself open to the charge of
log-rolling. If he could see his way clear to remembering that he
bet $25 on Yale we could give him a better notice. As it is, he will
have to content himself with the vociferous approval of non-partisan
audiences each night.

Supporting Mr. Stewart in Holiday are Hope Williams (the star),
Ben Smith, Dorothy Tree, Walter Walker, Monroe Owsley (superb as
the bitter brother) and Mrs. Donald Ogden Stewart in a vivid bit as
Delia, the maid. If Mr. Barry's play keeps on pleasing people at
the pace it has been doing (and with the best dialogue in town there
is no reason why it shouldn't) it will run long enough for the Stewart
baby, second in a long line of dramatic artists, to join the cast and
make the Stewart family 100% Equity.

--Robert C. Benchley in Life
(January 4, 1929), page 21.

HUMORESQUE (Fannie Hurst; Vanderbilt Theatre, February 27,
1923)

One of the best indications of Laurette Taylor's acting ability
is the manner in which she emerges unscathed from bad plays. Aside
from its first act, Humoresque is pretty nearly all paste. The only
trick that Miss Hurst has omitted to wring tears and thrills from her
audience is the one where the old couple are forced to leave their
home for the poorhouse. There is the playing of the Marseillaise
off-stage for no reason at all, the speech about its being Humanity's
war, the idiot boy sobbing and laughing about the house, and, supreme in ruthlessness, the actual parting between mother and son
on the eve of his sailing for France, which Miss Taylor aids and
abets by moaning and groaning in an unbelievably cruel manner.
Added to Miss Hurst's utilization of the blind soldier in Back Pay,
this scene places her among the first ten in the Bad Taste tourna-
ment.

And yet, out of all this mass of imitation jewelry, Miss Taylor
shines forth as genuine. Not a genuine Jewess, perhaps, for there
is always the sparkling Irish eye of the ever-young Peg to belie the
assumed dialect and the wig. But certainly a genuine actress, crying out for a genuine play.

--Robert C. Benchley in Life
(March 22, 1923), page 18.

ICEBOUND (Owen Davis; Sam H. Harris Theatre, February 10,
1923)

It isn't until you have left the theater that you realize that
Icebound isn't really much of an opus. While you are there, the
acting fools you.

Owen Davis has written something which, while it is far su-

perior to the scented soap he used to manufacture especially for the
William A. Brady hotels, is still just a fairly ordinary tale of New
England village life. Especially does his last act lose itself in the
bureau drawer with the pile of other and similar last acts, even to
the scene in which the heroine goes upstairs and comes down again
bearing a nice, new, empty black satchel, with which she says she
is going to catch the 5:45, at which point the hero suddenly realizes
that he loves her, yes, that he has loved her all along. Some time
ago we offered a handsome prize to any heroine who, once having
gone up to get her black satchel, would choose a time to sneak out
when she would <u>not</u> be intercepted at the foot of the stairs by the
hero, and who would really catch the 5:45. Our bankers still have
the prize in their vaults.

Mr. Davis has, however, filled his rice-pudding with a large
number of good lines which make it taste like something entirely
fresh. (We do not refer to the deliberate comedy lines, most of
which can be heard coming two blocks away.) But above all, Mr.
Harris and his director, Mr. Forrest, have assembled a cast each
member of which contributes a few moments of really exceptional
acting.

This department tries to avoid mentioning lists of actors who
"also did well," believing that it doesn't make very sparkling reading
for anyone except the actors mentioned. If you happen not to have
seen a play, or aren't familiar with many stage names except those
of Ethel, John and Lionel Barrymore, it isn't going to be worth your
while to wait long on a page to find out that George Spelvin was
excellent as the District Attorney or that Hilda Gerble furnished a
vivid few minutes as the runaway nun.

In the case of Icebound, however, we must record the fact
that we consider the following bits of acting as good in their way as
anything the Russian boys and girls could compress into moments of
equal length. (1) Robert Ames recalling the lace on the French girl's
dress, (2) Phyllis Povah's reading of the letter, (3) Willard Robert-
son's wordless exit in the last act and (4) Edna May Oliver's practically wordless entrance in the first act. This does not exhaust the
list of worthy bits, or of names deserving mention, but it <u>is</u> making
a pretty dull paragraph; so the best thing to do is to advise you to
see Icebound and take note of the acting.
                                        --Robert C. Benchley in <u>Life</u>
                                        (March 1, 1923), page 18.

* * *

Icebound won this year's Pulitzer Prize for the best American
drama, etc., etc. Much objection from certain critics followed! In
my opinion Icebound is one of the finest plays ever written by an
American. Mr. Heywood Broun prefers <u>You and I</u>. He does not believe in Icebound's people. Now, Mr. Broun, does it ever occur to

you that possibly you know the inhabitants of Westchester better
than you do those of northern New England? Not long ago I attended
a family reunion: clans assembled from the northern countries. "Do
you remember Nelly?" asked one. "She was the spit-and-image of
Hannah in Icebound." So it went, one after another we found them
all, those members of the Jordan household. Look far enough and
you'll find a black sheep Ben in practically every New England family. Owen Davis has taken the worst side of the Yankee temperament and softened it here and there, in Ben, in Judge Bradford, in
Doctor Curtis and in Jane, with broad humanity. The story is an
old one. The money is left to Cinderella and Cinderella reforms the
Prodigal Son, then marries him. It was, however, the development
of all these characters around that central theme that interested Mr.
Davis. This he has done superbly, with economy of incident, faithfulness of dialogue and quick moving emotional development. Henry
Jordan speaks and it is the very soul of the small-minded Yankee
speaking:

> There hasn't been a Jordan, before Ben, who's disgraced
> the name in more'n a hundred years; he stands indicted be-
> fore the Grand Jury for some of his drunken devilment. If
> he hadn't run away, like the criminal he is, he'd be in the
> State's Prison now, down to Thomaston. Don't talk Ben to
> me, after the way he broke mother's heart, and hurt my
> credit!

And again, Ben, the prodigal speaks:

> BEN. Look out there! (He points out of the window at
> the drifted snow.) It's like that half of the year, froze up,
> everything, most of all the people. Just a family by itself,
> maybe. Just a few folks, good an' bad, month after month,
> with nothin' to think about but just the mean little things,
> that really don't amount to nothin', but get to be bigger than
> all the world outside.
> JANE (sewing). Somebody must do the farming, Ben.
> BEN. Somebody like the Jordans, that's been doin' it
> generation after generation. Well, look at us. I heard a
> feller, in a Y.M.C.A. hut, tellin' how nature brought animals
> into the world, able to face what they had to face--
> JANE. Yes, Ben?
> BEN. That's what nature's done for us Jordans--brought
> us into the world half froze before we was born. Brought
> us into the world mean, and hard, so's we could live the
> hard, mean life we have to live.

There are two speeches in Icebound that I don't believe. Perhaps you do. I remember that they cried out at me as I saw the
play and they do the same now that I read it. Each one is laugh pro-
voking; but the laughter is not, I think, legitimate. They are both
in the last act where laughs, I suppose, are precious. The Jordans
are grouped in the parlor, discussing that frigid room:

ELLA.   I don't know as it was ever what I called a cheerful room.

HENRY (Severely) A parlor's where a person's supposed
to sit and think of God, and you couldn't expect it to be
cheerful!

Now, do you honestly think, Mr. Davis, that Henry Jordan
would have made that speech? Mind you, the stage direction reads,
not ironically but severely. Then, again, Orin, the ten year old
comments: "Say, Mum! What do you s'pose Uncle Henry thinks he
means when he says things?" Perhaps Orin is simply Mr. Davis,
puzzled by his own character of Henry. Surely, that speech isn't
Orin! However, here is a fine play, finely and truly wrought.

--John Farrar in The Bookman,
Vol. 58, No. 1 (September 1923),
pages 59-60.

JANE CLEGG (St. John G. Ervine; Garrick Theatre, February 23,
1920)

Cheered by the very substantial success of John Ferguson,
the Theatre Guild now sets out to make an equally good go at another
play by the same author. It requires no great foresight, however,
to predict that such will not be the case. To begin with, the author has made things immeasurably harder by writing a play that is
dull most of the time. Then, too, Margaret Wycherly, who enacts
the title role, is not by any means up to the requirements of the part.
Judging from the first performance, "Henry Clegg" would have been
a more fitting title for the play, for it was Dudley Digges who carried off the largest share of whatever honors there were.

The story is slight for a whole evening's entertainment. It
contains drama, to be sure, but much of it is lost in the intermin-
able scenes which are merely conversation. Jane Clegg is the wife
of a pretty low sort of man. She has discovered that he is keeping
a mistress, and he has promised to reform, but he has neglected to
do so. His one idea is to get from Jane some of the money which
an uncle has left her, but which she absolutely refuses to let him
have. Eventually he steals from his employer so that he and his
mistress can flee to Canada and begin life again. Of course his
theft is discovered and Jane pays up for him. But it is something
of a surprise to him when she bids him godspeed on his journey to
the new world, and raises no objection to his deserting her.

Miss Wycherly plays Jane with such repression that she is very
nearly inaudible through most of the play. At no time does she dom-
inate the scene, even when the situation is all in her favor. One is
left constantly in doubt as to what she is really thinking of the things

that transpire about her.   In sharp contrast, is the work of Dudley
Digges as the husband.   His every move reveals some mental impulse, some essential mood.   Henry Travers as an irate "bookie" also
gives a capital performance.   Helen Westley will undoubtedly improve
when she is more familiar with her lines.   Taking the production by
and large, no amount of improvement on anybody's part will succeed
in making Jane Clegg either good drama or good entertainment, and
the lion's share of the blame must rest with the author.

> --John J. Martin in The New York
> Dramatic Mirror (February 28,
> 1920), page 363.

* * *

It isn't so awfully difficult to be "direct" in a play.   As a rule,
however, the public likes side issues, plenty of irrelevant characters
and "comic relief."   In sombre problems playwrights try assiduously
to "lighten things up" with a few quaint types who have little to do
with the case.   They seem to imagine that they can hammer in their
points much more vigorously if they steer away from them from time
to time.

But St. John G. Ervine, in Jane Clegg at the Garrick Theatre,
doesn't worry his head about side lights.   Nor does he prolong the
agony.   The play at the Garrick comes to an early finish, with no
dreary interruptions and no irrelevancies.

It is a vital, intense and singularly attractive little drama of
domestic unhappiness, and it has no mission at all.   The Heroine
suffered long and wretchedly from the infidelities of her husband,
but there was no attempt to hyper-heroineize her.   On the contrary.
In spite of her misery, I thought she was a somewhat disagreeable
person, hard as nails, and filled with a sense of her own superiority.   Hubby was the "absolute rotter" with no doubt at all, but the
mere idea of spending one's life with such a perfect specimen of self-
satisfied femininity as Jane Clegg is quite horrible to contemplate.

Mr. Ervine held no brief for Mrs. Clegg.   All he did was to
show us how sorely tried she was, how utterly right she was, and
how logically her ideas worked.   The playwright even made the
"absolute rotter" admit that Jane was a very fine woman, but too
fine for him.   He gave over his previous affections to a woman who
was more "like himself," and Jane quite understood it.   Jane was intelligent enough for that.

And, by-the-by, I love the name of Jane.   It is so curt.   It
is so significant.   It has no epigrammatic twist to it.   It is so sensible.   It is almost tailor-made.   When you say "Jane!" you feel that
you haven't wasted time and haven't catered to any frivolity.   It is
an ideal name for a neat heroine.   Of course, one could make it
"Jennie," but only the weak-minded would do that.   Jane will stand
by itself--always.

Miss Margaret Wycherly made Jane even more superior than
she need have been. Her Jane would have driven any well-regulated
chap to musical comedy or burlesque. But Miss Wycherly gave an
extremely interesting performance and made the little play interroga-
tively entertaining--that is to say, distinctly discussable. Dudley
Digges was quite admirable, and so were Henry Travers and Erskine
Sanford.

The Theatre Guild deserves congratulation. Jane Clegg is
one of the best features of the season. And, by-the-by, why has
the Theatre Guild dropped its "Inc."? I did enjoy the "Inc." It
sounded so incongruously commercial.

> --Alan Dale in New York American
> (February 29, 1920), page CE-
> 11.

THE JAZZ SINGER (Samson Raphaelson; Fulton Theatre, September
    14, 1925)

George Jessel as a Jewish boy with a Big Problem, settled not
without reference to sentimentality.

> --Robert C. Benchley in Life (De-
> cember 3, 1925), page 56.

JOURNEY'S END (R.C. Sheriff; Henry Miller Theatre, March 22,
    1929)

Mr. Gilbert Miller left the New York theatre and America flat
several months ago with a huzza of hate for our lack of appreciation
of a good play. I wish one of these pouting producers would actually stay away some time just to restore my wavering faith in press
agents. But Mr. Miller, like the rest, returned with a play and a
good one and as any sub-normal critic could have told him in the
first place New York ate it up. And now he thinks America is just
perfectly grand!

The play is Journey's End with an all-English company of nine,
and all men. Those who liked What Price Glory?--and I didn't--
spangled with its guttery oaths and salty sonovas will find an entirely different picture of war. It is a stirring pastel revealing with
deft strokes the tenuous thread of humility as well as the ineffable
sublimity and beauty that death may attain.

The entire play takes place in the crepuscular gloom of a blood-
soaked dug-out with intermittent gaseous blobs of light from No Man's

Land as a background. With that same deadly monotony that has
squeezed out their lives to the bitter rind, they hear the crepitant
hiss of powder and the dolorous zoom of shrapnel. Zoom, hiss!
Zoom, hiss! Zoom!

Here stalwart soldiers, with an eager hunger for life but not
afraid to die, await what the Eddie Guests call The Great Adventure.
It is ironic. It is harsh. But its embittered rapture is the most
astonishing dramatic highlight New York has ever beheld. One could
not help but sigh while watching the unfoldment that it was not an
American play by an American author for we would need no longer
keep an eye peeled for The Great American Drama.

As an illustration of its devastating simplicity there was a time
in the mud-smeared cavern with its rotting effluvia, its slime-sluicing
filth, its cooties, and unbearable strain when a visionless and dull-
witted second-lieutenant, apropos of nothing at all, yawned: "I
heard a bird singing this morning!" And even a crisp mustached,
steely-jawed Old Big Business across the aisle beat me to a handker-
chief for an out-loud snivel.

The central figures are Leon Quartermaine as Lieutenant Osborne, an ex-schoolmaster caught in the philosophy of his noble
heredity--a gentleman; Colin Keith-Johnston as the still decent but
alcohol soaked Captain Stanhope, and Derek Williams as Second Lieutenant Raleigh, a young shavetail suckled in the creed of English honor. This young second lieutenant worships the kindly
and gentlemanly ex-schoolmaster with that rare ardor that seems only
possible when the world is young.

Life melts in his mouth like butter. He is as clean as a fresh
north wind. The zero hour nears. The lad wants to "go west" like
a man with whoever is assigned to go with him, but he is so young
and life is glamorous. They talk--he and the ex-schoolmaster--of
white and black pigs, of anything! Finally, he inquires timidly who
is to creep with him across that scorched and barren hell to almost
certain death. "I am going with you!" replied the schoolmaster.

And there never has been, nor do I believe ever will be, a
more arresting moment on the stage with the curtain falling slowly on
that youth's shining and eager expression and the choked back happiness of his "Oh, I see!"

The play offers nothing so absurd as a plot. Out of the drab
dross of trench triviata the author, R.C. Sherriff, has plaited a
golden strand of philosophic loveliness. My new pearl-gray hat,
fresh from Gelot's in Place Vendome, soars high in the air. His
taste is superb. So is his play.

--O.O. McIntyre in _Life_ (April 19,
1929), page 28.

* * *

Rendered practically incapable of criticism by my excitement at
any play which has in it some khaki and the sound of a machine-gun
reproduced from the wings, I find myself what is flatteringly called
speechless at Journey's End, by R.C. Sheriff, which has arrived at
Henry Miller's Theatre from London. For Journey's End is not only
about the war but is a singularly beautiful play.

The war it reveals is a gentleman's war in contradistinction to
the profane scrap of What Price Glory. It is war seen from the dug-
out of British officers, most of them public-school men. There's
hardly a "damn" in the play, not a woman, and only a faint hint of
an offstage love story. This sounds dull, but curiously enough its
spectacle of nerves and self-control, and drunkenness and magnificence, all phrased in the quiet language which becomes public-school
men, tears one apart more thoroughly, if anything, than did the
Homeric roar of What Price Glory.

The most acid thing I can think to say about Journey's End
is that at times one feels it might with justice have been called
Tom Brown in the Trenches, by An Old Boy. For American con-
sumption, perhaps such things as young Lieutenant Raleigh's enthusiasm on learning that Lieutenant Osborne played football for England
should be muted. There are, however, worse things a play could
be like than Tom Brown. Mr. Sherriff could make one remark in
favor of his characters' admiration of pluck, and tenacity of manners,
and general understatement of any difficulty they are called upon to
meet. He could say, "But that's the way we are at our best," and
I should be inclined to believe him. An astounding race, and Journey's End deserves a place in its permanent annals.

There is so little story that it is difficult to summarize it.
Captain Stanhope is a youngster who's been on the front line for
over three years and fallen into habits of drunkenness which seem
horrible to his brother officers and to himself, though to eyes grown
accustomed to post-Volstead standards their manifestations appear
rather mild. The brother of the girl he was in love with before he
came to war is assigned to his company, to his humiliation. The boy
and Stanhope's best friend are detailed by orders from Stanhope's
superior to go on what promises to be a fatal mission. Stanhope's
friend is killed, but the boy returns, only to be killed the next day.
Stanhope's death is indicated at the final curtain. It is as plotless
and unreasonable as a casualty list, and as moving.

The casting and direction seemed to me just about perfect.
Colin Keith-Johnson, as Stanhope, and Leon Quartermaine, as Osborne, merit particular praise.

                              —Charles Brackett in The New
                              Yorker (March 30, 1929), page
                              27.

JUNE MOON (Ring Lardner and George S. Kaufman; Broadhurst Theatre, October 9, 1929)

   If I can buy a seat, I am going back next week to see Ring
Lardner's and George Kaufman's June Moon again and make a serious
report on it. On the first night, I began laughing shortly after the
curtain went up on the prologue and never quite recovered. By the
end of the second act, I had got lockjaw, my abdominal muscles were
twisted into hard, aching knots, and I was bleeding profusely from
the nose. I hadn't caught a breath for ten minutes.

   Then, Harry Rosenthal picked up a sponge and washed a window. A simple gesture in itself. But when it happened, I tore open
my shirt and fell, writhing and shrieking, into the aisle. Happily,
the aisle was piled high with the bodies of first-nighters and friends
who had died laughing.

   At the end of the play, the ushers (who were carefully selected
for their posts from the city's deaf and dumb asylums) cleaned us up
and sent us to hospitals, where we were given copies of Chic Sales'
The Specialist to sober up on.

        See June Moon when you are low.
                              --Robert C. Benchley in Life (No-
                              vember 1, 1929), page 22.

JUNO AND THE PAYCOCK (Sean O'Casey; Mayfair Theatre, March
   15, 1926)

   Not having been in town to hear all the preliminary smooch
about Juno and the Paycock, we were not so disappointed in it as
many seemed to be. It smacked a little of the days when three curtains out of five arose on Rollo Peters huddled in front of a peat-
fire muttering "Da," and there were long stretches in it when the
pace would have permitted travelers to get out and pick daisies by
the track and still keep up, but, on the whole, it was a pretty impressive performance with a grand idea behind it. The talk is rather
Irish, but as the scene is laid in Ireland, there doesn't seem to be
anything else possible. And Augustin Duncan and Claude Cooper
are, in the latter's words, a "darlin" pair.
                              --Robert C. Benchley in Life
                              (April 8, 1926), page 27.

                         * * *

   A young Irishman, Sean O'Casey by name, stirred up a deal
of excitement for himself and some trouble by writing a play called

Juno and the Paycock. It had a stormy career in Dublin, but subsequently London took it to its heart, where it is still cherished.
That accolade bestowed, it was inevitable that we should see it here,
and so three producers combined--such being the fashion lately--to
give it to us. The name of this piece is pretty; the theme isn't.
It tells about the horrors of life in Ireland during the Republican
movement, but whether the English or the Irish are responsible for
these is not clear. At any rate the play concerns the household of
one Jack Boyle and the sordid clutter in which they all live. What
with Irish whisky, break-downs, and ballads, one thing leads to
another until presently the family fortune vanishes, a daughter is
betrayed, and a couple of young men are shot by somebody. Only
a Russian or an Irishman could so pile on the horrors and keep a
straight face. These tragic deaths gave each mother concerned the
opportunity to advance firmly to the footlights and deliver herself
of a speech beginning. "What were me pains in bringin' him into
the world compared with me pains in takin' him out of it?" The rest
of the cast, at attention and Eyes Right, listened respectfully to this
funeral oration. It would have been funny if it had not been boring.
A considerable cast headed by Augustin Duncan gallumphed through
the piece with a variety of accents that would have startled the playwright could he have heard them. We have been fooled before by
plays that try to prove something, but we go right ahead in our innocence being caught.

> --Larry Barretto in The Bookman,
> Vol. 63, No. 3 (May 1926), pages
> 343-344.

KID BOOTS (Book by William Anthony McGuire and Otto Harbach,
     Music by Harry Tierney, Lyrics by Joseph McCarthy; Earl Car-
     roll Theatre, December 31, 1923)

     Eddie Cantor alone would make Kid Boots worth while, for, as
he toyed with a mallet preparatory to mashing the fingers of an unfortunate young golfer, we elected him one of the leading legitimate
actors of the day. And any time he wants to make us cry, he can
do so without half trying.

> --Robert C. Benchley in Life (Janu-
> ary 24, 1924), page 18.

THE KINGDOM OF GOD (G. Martinez Sierra, translated by Helen and
     Harley Granville Barker; Ethel Barrymore Theatre, December 20,
     1928)

     Miss Ethel Barrymore recently complained in a magazine article

that the critics gave her credit for only beauty and personality and
seldom for skill. She should thank her stars that her beauty and
personality were on tap in the first two acts of The Kingdom of God
and that she could save her skill for the third. The third act is
splendid, thanks to this skill, but the first two are pretty terrible.

In the first act, Miss Barrymore is seen as Sister Gracia at
the age of nineteen, in the second at the age of twenty-nine and in
the third at seventy. By the time she is seventy there has been a
noticeable improvement in her vocal methods due to advancing age,
and that high, breathless monotone which, at nineteen, made it a
little difficult to understand just what she was saying, has given way
to a rich, full voice which snaps out the words in thrilling fashion.

Miss Barrymore and her much-imitated voice have given rise
to a school of acting which might be called the Episcopalian Method.
In this, each line is chanted like a response, with no differentiation
in tone between lines, and sometimes goes on like that for hours.
Now Miss Barrymore does this usually when she thinks the rôle needs
it and can shift at will, as she does in the third act of The Kingdom of God, but it would be too bad if a standard were set whereby
young actresses chanted exclusively and one were never again to
hear a human voice in natural conversation on the stage. Little as
Miss Barrymore esteems her own beauty and personality, they would
come in very handy for anyone who wanted to follow in her steps.

> --Robert C. Benchley in Life (Janu-
> ary 18, 1929), page 23.

LADY, BE GOOD! (Book by Guy Bolton and Fred Thompson, Music
by George Gershwin, Lyrics by Ira Gershwin; Liberty Theatre,
December 1, 1924)

Gershwin's best score, with the Astaires and Walter Catlett to
make it even better.

> --Robert C. Benchley in Life (Janu-
> ary 29, 1925), page 19.

THE LAST MILE (John Wexley; Sam H. Harris Theatre, February 13,
1930)

I would like to see a sign over the door of the Sam Harris theatre, where The Last Mile is playing, which reads "For Men Only!"
... having sat speechless through one performance, including intermissions, and listened to the chatter of the womenfolk around me,
I decided to go again a few nights later for the thrill of re-seeing

the play and also to make sure if other women reacted the same way
... they did ... while I sat enthralled by the terrible intensity and
realism of this gruesome drama, such remarks as these filtered into
my ears ... "For Goodness Sakes! What did you ever pick out such
a thing as this for!" "My Dear! This is simply terrible! Let's go
some place and dance!" "Why, in Heaven's name, did the critics
rave about this melodrama!" etc., etc., etc. ... here is a play which
reenacts faithfully what actually happened up at Auburn just a few
months ago; here is the rawest, truest slice of life which has been
put on the stage in years, and yet it seemed to make no more impression on the dear girls, at least the ones within my earshot, than
a strawberry festival! ... if it had been a mystery play, with revolver shots in the dark and sliding panels, they would have shrieked
and tore their marcelled hair but this thing, for some strange reason,
left them cold ... "Why?" I mumbled in my beard, as I wandered up
Broadway in a cold daze ... is it because they don't realize they are
seeing something real, something terrible? Is it because they don't
know such things actually happen? Is it because they lack imagination? Is it because they are dumb, or is it just because they are
women? ... maybe that's it ... probably the men in an audience witnessing a play which pictured a woman in the throes of childbirth
wouldn't be expected to get as much kick out of it as the ladies but
no, that can't be it, because I've never seen the inside of a prison
and yet, The Last Mile moved me more than any play I've seen in a
long time ... will some kind lady who has seen the play put me out
of my misery?

                              --"Knickerbocker Jr." in Life
                              (March 7, 1930), page 16.

THE LAST OF MRS. CHEYNEY (Frederick Lonsdale; Fulton Theatre,
     November 9, 1925)

     There can be no risk at all in recommending The Last of Mrs.
Cheyney to almost any one. Mr. Lonsdale's comedy is smart (not
quite so smart as we had been led to expect, but smart enough), and
the combination of Ina Claire, Roland Young and A.E. Matthews
makes for just about as delightful conversation as any cast-picker
could dream of. When a play is as generally satisfactory as this,
and the players are as deft, we are left with nothing much to say
about it except to state the facts. What we need to fill this page
with sparkling comment is more bad plays.
                              --Robert C. Benchley in Life (No-
                              vember 26, 1925), page 22.

LAUGH, CLOWN, LAUGH! (David Belasco and Tom Cushing, from the
     Italian of Fausto Martini; Belasco Theatre, November 28, 1923)

Laugh, Clown, Laugh! and Sancho Panza are two plays which, while they have distinct faults, contain much that is beautiful and some really great acting. The second act of Laugh, Clown, Laugh! has a holding power that recalls the great scenes of Galsworthy's Justice. The clown story is always fresh, and here it has new treatment. If the last act is anticlimactic it, at least, affords Lionel Barrymore a chance to display fine character portrayal and unusual restraint. Ian Keith's performance immediately challenges comparison with that of Mr. Barrymore, and he holds his own well. While neither so fine a part nor a performance, it is possessed of fire and grace.

> --John Farrar in The Bookman,
> Vol. 58, No. 6 (February 1924),
> pages 653-654.

LET US BE GAY (Rachel Crothers; Little Theatre, February 19, 1929)

The moderately good plays which we were complaining of include Flight, Let Us Be Gay--well Flight and Let Us Be Gay. The latter is a little better than moderately good, but nothing to go home and fling yourself on the couch over. Miss Francine Larrimore comes back to us in it, and if we could always be quite sure of what she was saying, we would be glad to see her, for she has a dynamic quality which helps lift things along whether you follow them or not. And Charlotte Granville is now running neck and neck with Alison Skipworth as our favorite dowager.

> --Robert C. Benchley in Life
> (March 22, 1929), page 20.

* * *

Let Us Be Gay is Miss Rachel Crothers in an amusing vein of light comedy. A marriage dissolves before our eyes in Act I and the victims meet some years later, when the wife is called upon to vamp the husband away from a young woman whose relatives would reserve her for better things. The confrontation of the sundered couple obviously offers opportunity for the Comic Spirit and, helped by Miss Francine Larrimore and Miss Charlotte Granville, the author secures her efforts. I recommend this effort to those who think that "sophisticated" comedy is purely a (sic) English invention, that Gerrard double-two-double-one is a smarter effect than Rhinelander two-two-one-one.

> --Ernest Boyd in The Bookman,
> Vol. 69, No. 2 (April 1929),
> page 180.

LILIOM (Ferenc Molnar, translated by Benjamin F. Glazer; Garrick
Theatre, April 20, 1921)

There is something radically wrong with Liliom. But until the
printed text of the play is available, it is impossible to say with any
degree of certainty whether it is Molnar's fault as author, or [Frank]
Reicher's as director, that after five scenes of ironic realism the play
suddenly shifts to fantastic farce. At any rate, such is the case,
and one leaves the theatre wondering, frankly or surreptitiously, as
is one's wont, what it was all about.

At least one thing is perfectly clear, however, and that is that
Eva Le Gallienne gives a beautiful performance. One wishes her dic-
tion were a little less cultured, but that is a small matter in comparison with her deep sincerity and her fine restraint. These qualities
in her no doubt make Joseph Schildkraut's playing of the title role
seem more markedly inadequate. He swaggers and clucks and hitches
up his trousers and resorts to most of the theatrical devices that one
goes to Theatre Guild productions to avoid. Dudley Digges plays
"The Sparrow" with all the grim comedy the character contains and
Evelyn Chard does the child well.

One or two of Lee Simonson's settings are particularly good,
especially the railroad embankment, but the heavenly courtroom is
woefully insipid. It is a fitting spot for the play to choose to go to
pieces in.

--John J. Martin in The New York
Dramatic Mirror, April 30, 1921,
page 733.

LITTLE NELLIE KELLY (George M. Cohan; Liberty Theatre, November 13, 1922)

Little Nellie Kelly, being a George M. Cohan production, moves
at a rate which doesn't give you time to think whether it is good or
not. As a matter of fact, it is mostly good, especially the singing
and dancing of Elizabeth Hines and Charles King and the others in
a light-footed cast.

--Robert C. Benchley in Life (November 30, 1922), page 18.

LOYALTIES (John Galsworthy; Gaiety Theatre, September 27, 1922)

In the face of a really good play this department finds itself dumb. There are so many ways of saying that a play is rotten, but only three or four ways of praising it. "Holds the attention till the final curtain," "a splendid performance," "delightfully gay," "intensely interesting," or any of the things we said above about Miss Barrymore.

Galsworthy's Loyalties is a good example of a play we hate to write about because we enjoyed it so much. In the first place, we were so interested that we forgot to pay attention to our job (i.e., jotting down nasty remarks on the margin of our program alongside the Rogers Peet advertisement, which we are unable to decipher the next morning owing to having written one on top of another in the dark).

In the second place, we don't know any words for "interesting" except "interesting," and that, above all things, is what Loyalties is. Another snappy phrase that we could use would be "well-acted." If we had been drinking, we might loosen up to the extent of adding "well-written." And there you are! Loyalties is interesting, well-acted and well-written--and a whole lot more. Its plot, by the way, concerns the cross-cutting of pet loyalties of its characters, the loyalty of one Jew to his race, of the English soldier to the army, of the lawyer to his profession, of the determined "gentleman" to his fellow "gentlemen," all leaving the audience where it was at the beginning, but conscious of having seen a real play.

> --Robert C. Benchley in Life (October 19, 1922), page 18.

MACHINAL (Sophie Treadwell; Plymouth Theatre, September 7, 1928)

Just to show that our aesthetic sense has not been dulled by all these years of sordid living, we are happy to announce that two of the biggest kicks we got during the past week were from lighting effects. One was at the final curtain of Machinal, which comes on an empty stage gradually brought from darkness into refulgent dawn (it would have been Mr. Arthur Hopkins who first found the drama of an empty stage), and the other was in the musical comedy, Good Boy, when a brilliant white light was thrown on a ballet maneuvering on moving floor panels. We hope that you won't think that we have gone pansy in our excitement over these things.

We were pretty well prepared to be moved at the final curtain of Machinal, for the whole drama had been stirring in its simple and episodic forward march. Miss Treadwell has not exactly improved on her models in this modernistic monotone and her characters are, by now, fairly recognizable as having played their sad roles before in several tragedies of modern wives with dull husbands. But she has eliminated most of the trying features of the earlier expressionism

and her play is a good, bed-rock combination of the best features
of them all. It also had a dash of realism in the presence of circumstances highly prized last year by the newspapers during the
Snyder-Gray trial, although the characters are in no way related to
those unfortunate people. Oddly enough, it is only in the trial
scene that the play sags. We have been seeing stage-trials now for
quite a time and some of them much better than this.

The work of Miss Zita Johann seemed to us to add immeasurably
to the effectiveness of the play and her scene in the bedroom of
her lover (also well played by Clark Gable) was as delicate and lovely an idyl of illicit love as we remember seeing for a long, long time.
                        --Robert C. Benchley in _Life_ (Sep-
                            tember 28, 1928), page 17.

                        *   *   *

I wish I could agree with several of my intelligent friends who
told me that in Sophie Treadwell's _Machinal_ I should find something
of a masterpiece. This Arthur Hopkins offering is an episodic play
about a melancholy girl who marries her elderly employer for his
money and in desperation kills him. We see the "Young Woman"
(very properly anonymous) during successive stages of her career
from stenographer to murderess, and so far as I'm concerned I can
only say that she and her fate left me absolutely cold. As the play
opened she was unaccountably disagreeable, inefficient and dull.
She is suffering from some complaint--unhappiness will describe if
not explain and justify it. To solve her problem, as she thinks, she
marries a good-hearted if fatuous Babbitt. This fellow is supposed
to be unsympathetic, but I vow and declare I felt sorry for him,
and in the scene where his wife refused to carry out the most ele-
mentary item in her contract as a bought wife, I would have cheered
if he had carried her bodily to the window and chucked her out.

In her quest for happiness she finds one short hour of bliss
in the arms of a casual young man, and this scene was wholly charming and convincing. The succeeding scenes carried us along into a
court scene that failed to thrill, and then into another that dupli-
cated the setting and situation of _The Valiant_, but omitted everything
that makes that little play so powerful and moving.

Machinal is an unimaginative string of episodes mechanically arranged for the purpose of showing a supposedly pitiful woman in the
throes of circumstances. But in order to make these episodes live
the dramatist should have created at once a creditable and living
woman. But she asks us to take for granted that the Young Woman
is not only unfortunate, but deserving of sympathy--a special and
heightened kind of sympathy. Life shows us many such people, but
until their existence is put before us with motives and reasons, we
cannot properly understand or passionately care. Here the Young
Woman is just out of luck--literally that. At most she is presented

as a stupid, sullen, dishonest, uncontrolled female. And I say,
What of it? If I feel this way about Miss Treadwell's heroine, it
isn't my fault: the character is not realized.

That Mr. Hopkins has mounted and directed the play with skill
and understanding, serves only to show what is not in it.
                              --Barrett H. Clark in The Drama,
                                 Vol. 19, No. 2 (November 1928),
                                 page 45.

MAMMA'S AFFAIR (Rachel Barton Butler; Little Theatre, January
    19, 1920)

Mamma's Affair, which won the Harvard prize play contest in-
stituted by Oliver Morosco, is an intriguing little comedy. It is as
thin as a wafer but quite as toothsome. And it reflects unusual
promise on the part of its author.

Miss Butler has not worried herself over the intricacies of
plot. She has been more busily engaged. She has endeavored to
create vital and interesting characters who pass in and out of situations that bear a close fidelity to life. The dialogue, more humorous
than witty, also reflects the casual chatter of life as it is lived by a
group of luxurious hypochrondriacs. A small cast contributes a good
performance.

It is the freshness of the author's viewpoint that is most engaging. The conventional and the hackneyed in technique are passed
by with just a fleeting nod. Nothing is overdone. No obvious efforts at a laugh intrude upon the consciousness. No fixed mechanism regulating the activities of the characters seems visible and the
result is an impression of wholesome spontaneity.

Ida St. Leon is very charming as the distressed daughter of a
professional invalid who exercises herself so much over her mother's
imaginary condition that she suffers a real nervous collapse herself.
The scene is a resort hotel in the Berkshires and when the country
doctor--a most alert and enterprising fellow--is called in he grasps
the situation immediately. He isolates the girl from her mother and
the anaemic sentimentalist to whom she is betrothed.

And the girl promptly falls in love with him. He is slow in
responding, for he has some amiable theories about professional ethics. But he does prescribe for himself eventually--a heart stimulant
that is customarily called love.

Robert Edeson gave an excellent performance of the doctor--
frank, personable and authoritative, while Effie Shannon as the hypo-

chondriac was capital in her assumed nervous tension. Katherine
Kaelred played her companion with spirit and George LeGuere and
Amelia Bingham contributed worthy aid.

--Louis R. Reid in The New York
Dramatic Mirror (January 29,
1920), page 132.

MARY ROSE (James M. Barrie: Empire Theatre, December 22, 1920)

Sir James Barrie's newest dramatic contribution, Mary Rose,
has aroused all sorts of critical discussion, pro and con. We quite
agree with the learned authorities who pronounce this eerie and uncompromising fantasy to be some planes below the Barrie of Peter
Pan and A Kiss for Cinderella or even Dear Brutus.

It depends upon your Pollyanna needs as to just what message
you get out of Mary Rose. That is, you will either think Barrie is
driving home the gentle philosophy that time heals all wounds and
happiness always breaks thru or you will suspect that he is actually
touching upon the bitter forgetfulness of humanity.

Far be it from us to attempt to outline the whimsy. Barrie
does not intend it to be taken literally. It is simply the story of a
young wife who disappears upon a strange isle of the outer Hebrides
--a place of ill repute among the country folk--only to return to her
family twenty-five years later, unchanged and as young and fresh as
upon the tragic day of a quarter of a century before. But she finds
her parents old and life weary and her husband strange and grey,
indeed, they have all suffered--and forgotten.

There are touching moments of pathos in Mary Rose. We found
it distinctly interesting, but we hesitate to recommend it impersonally.
It will depend upon you whether it leaves you puzzled or moved.
But we think you will agree with us in resenting the way Barrie re-
fers to a visitor from the other world as a "ghostie." The critics
banged away unmercifully--and unjustly--at Ruth Charterton as the
ever-young Mary Rose. We liked her playing of the part and also
admired Tom Nesbitt, who played both the husband and the son of
the fantasy.

--Shadowland, Vol. 4, No. 1
(March 1921), page 63.

* * *

After all, why argue about Barrie's Mary Rose? Why try to
find out what he meant when he wrote it? Must everything in the
world mean something?

There are many who will go and hear this story of the young
mother who disappeared from "The Island That Likes to Be Visited"
and returned in thirty years as young as on that mysterious day,
and who will shake their heads, saying, "This is symbolic of the return of the dead," or, "Barrie meant by this that Time heals all
wounds." And a great many more will say, "I can be as eerie as
anyone, but this is too much to ask. It doesn't even make sense."

And then there are those sentimental, childish, slightly queer
people who will sit through the three acts and never notice that the
meaning is hazy, or the situations strained, or that Ruth Chatterton
is not the best possible-actress to play the part. Most of the time
they won't be able to see the stage at all because of a slight blurring
of their vision. All they will know is that they themselves died only
a short time before in the Empire Theatre and that they are very,
very happy in their new life and have no desire whatever to communi-
cate with their friends.

To this third class I must admit that I belong, but all three
classes are right. There is no argument about it. It all depends
on how firmly your feet are on the ground.
                          --Robert C. Benchley in Life (Janu-
                             ary 27, 1921), page 136.

MARY STUART (John Drinkwater; Ritz Theatre, March 21, 1921)

John Drinkwater's newest drama, Mary Stuart, left the critics
in puzzled disagreement. Some of them went so far as to call it
more vivid and imaginative than the poet-dramatist's Abraham Lincoln, while the other half of the critical contingent pronounced it
disappointing.

From our own point of view, we believe it to be interesting,
but falling short in a curious, cramped way. One or two other com-
mentors have made this same point and the analysis of one writer
comes close to the mark. In Abraham Lincoln, Drinkwater, at heart
the poet rather than the practical man of the theater, wrote a gently
realistic chronicle play within a poetic and symbolic framework. The
play succeeded, the public disregarding the poetry and symbolism
in its applause for the reincarnated Lincoln. This disregard of intentions seems to have caused Drinkwater himself to follow the public.
In Mary Stuart he seems involved and labored in his efforts to trans-
form a character from the poetic symbolism of his mind's eye to a
queen, conventionalized and modernized for the public taste and cast
amid pageantry and passion. Not that Mary Stuart lacks elements of
distinction. It has color, many fine speeches and the touch of an
understanding imagination.

Mary Stuart is written in odd form. It runs in a single, continuous scene for about an hour and a half, introduced by a modern
prolog. In this opening interlude Drinkwater seeks to show how the
life of Mary Stuart is applicable to a problem of today, specifically
the question of a husband who finds his wife in love with another
man, altho she vows her love for him also. Can a woman love more
than one man at a time? asks Drinkwater and, curiously, he seeks
to prove his answer in the life of the unhappy Mary who did not find
one real love. For this daughter of the house of Stuart greatly
loved, tho chance brought her only trash. As Mary herself says,
thru the words of Drinkwater:

"I'm hungry--do you understand? All this--my body, and my
imagination. Hungry for peace--for the man who can establish my
heart.... There are tides in me as fierce as any that have troubled
women. And they are restless, always, always. Do you think I
desire that? Do you think that I have no other longings--to govern
with a clear brain, to learn my people, to prove myself against these
foreign jealousies, to see strong children about me, to play with an
easy, festival mind, to walk the evenings at peace? Do you think I
chose this hungry grief of passion--deal in it like a poet?"

The action of Mary Stuart moves thru a single night, the
evening of the unlucky Rizzio's death. In it appear three of the men
to whom the passionate queen gave of her love: the sulking and de-
praved Darnley, her husband; the fawning, whining, perfumed Rizzio;
and the bullying swashbuckler, Bothwell. Obviously, this is but a
mere fragment in the life of the complex queen, living her drear
and lonely existence in dour Scotch Holyrood. But, as we have
noted, Drinkwater draws his picture with intelligence and imagination. It will interest you.

The acting, too, is compelling. No player of the season, save
Jacob Ben-Ami, received the critical acclamation accorded Clare Eames
as Mary Stuart. One would have thought a new genius had flashed
across the theatrical horizon. We see Miss Eames as possessing an
imperfect equipment, a flintlike personality, a manifest intelligence
and occasional flashes of something more than mere force. One of
these lies in the scorn and fire that mark Mary's vehement denunciation of the pitiful Darnley. But about Miss Eames' Mary there is
less of the beauty and passion that must have belonged to the heart-
lonely queen, than of the subtle, politic and high-bred princess. She
is shrewdly prim rather than beguiling, keen and cold rather than
the hot-blooded Mary who knew the warmth and intrigue of France.

The remainder of the cast is satisfying. There are Frank
Reicher's excellent performance as the perfumed and cowardly Rizzio,
and Leslie Palmer's skilful portrayal of Queen Elizabeth's ambassador,
for instance. The other characterizations are quite as good.

--Shadowland, Vol. 4, No. 4 (June
1921), page 51.

MARY THE THIRD (Rachel Crothers; 39th Street Theatre, February
    5, 1923)

    A delightful comedy of manners, Victorian and contemporary
jazz mores, with a funked ending. The disillusionment of children
apropos of the idyllic lives of their parents is real and poignant; but
the way out suggested by Miss Crothers balks, in my view, as quite
dubious.
                              --Pierre Loving in The Drama, Vol.
                              13, No. 7 (April 1923), page
                              250.

MERTON OF THE MOVIES (George S. Kaufman and Marc Connelly,
    from the story by Harry Leon Wilson; Cort Theatre, November
    13, 1922)

    Then comes Glenn Hunter in Merton of the Movies. Harry Leon
Wilson's book has been dramatized by George S. Kaufman and Marc
Connelly and has been tampered with but very little in the process.
At times it seems as if it had been merely poured out of the cup into
the saucer. Which, after all, is probably the safest method to adopt
in dramatizing a good book like Merton of the Movies. In the last
act, however, it stands on its own as a play, and sends you home
with the glow of having had a real good cry.

    For however much comedy there may be hung on Merton, the
fact remains that as Glenn Hunter plays it, it is one of the most
poignantly sad plays in town. The rôle of the movie-crazed youth
who thinks that he is a heroic figure while all the time he is being
used as a comic, is one which Mr. Hunter fills with such appealing
wistfulness and quiet pathos that, instead of laughing as you did in
the book, you find your heart gradually but surely being torn from
its moorings until it seems as if you could hardly bear it any longer.
And even though, at the final curtain, Merton has become reconciled
to being a leading low comedian, it is pretty certain that anyone
passing his room that night would hear an unmanly snuffling going
on as he faced in the dark the spirits of his shattered ideals. And
somehow you don't like to think about it. It is impossible to judge
just how much of a show Merton of the Movies would be without
Glenn Hunter. With him it is a great deal more than a mere comedy.
                              --Robert C. Benchley in Life (No-
                              vember 30, 1922), page 18.

MICHAEL AND MARY (A.A. Milne; Charles Hopkins Theatre, Decem-
    ber 10, 1929)

Just as the Theatre Guild has become producer extraordinary
for Bernard Shaw in this country, it is beginning to appear that
Charles Hopkins has acquired a similar commission from A.A. Milne.
Both The Ivory Door and The Perfect Alibi were produced at Mr.
Hopkins's own tiny theatre (and both, be it remarked, with distinct
success) and now we have a third Milne play, written this time especially for Mr. Hopkins. Michael and Mary has some startlingly good
scenes and many poignant and sensitive moments, interspersed with
a good deal that borders on the trite in dramatic situation and a
good deal that comes dangerously close to the saccharine philosophy
that "love is all that matters"--meaning, of course, that the play
stirs your sympathies deeply for deeds and decisions which are essentially wrong.

The play furnishes two distinct comments upon a serious decision made and acted upon by Michael and Mary. They are thrown together by chance. Mary has been deserted by her husband, and
has no idea where he has gone. She cannot (in England) obtain a
divorce on grounds of desertion. And so it comes to pass that a
tender and honorable friendship between Michael and Mary grows into a deep love which they can solve (according to their own ideas of
courage) only by going through a marriage ceremony in the full
knowledge that their act constitutes deliberate bigamy. They feel
that, because it involves danger and risk, it is a far more courageous
thing to do than to enjoy illicit companionship. The third possible
choice they never consider. They "marry." Michael makes notable
progress as a writer. They have a son. Thirteen years pass before "deed"--as the Hindus would express it--begins to show its
power of everlasting life, its curious quality of permanence in the
affairs of men: the past, in a very direct though complicated sense,
always molding and directing the present. The nearly forgotten husband returns.

He is, of course (and this is where the play turns trite for a
period) a blackmailer and a crook, also a man with a weak heart.
He and Michael quarrel. Michael pushes him violently and suddenly
finds him dead. Then what to do? The truth means a scandal--
unhappiness for their son, David. Falsehood means piling one lie
on another. They finally decide, for their son's sake, to string together the chain of lies. In a novel and extraordinary scene,
Michael, before calling in the police, rehearses every detail of what
he will say--the story of the pretended ex-soldier who comes to beg
money, becomes insolent when refused and falls dead when pushed.
The police come in. At every instant it seems as if Michael's story
would break down through some neglected detail. One of the police
sergeants with a turn for writing romantic fiction is certain that the
dead man is Mary's former husband--but adds such fantastic em-
broidery to his theory that the whole suggestion is laughed at.
Michael's story holds water. Michael and Mary are safe again--for
the moment.

But in their apparent safety they find--being thoroughly sensitive natures--the very reverse of the danger which had once lent an aspect of courage to their great decision. It eats into their souls-- until that day, another decade later, when their son announces his secret marriage to a very lovable girl. No longer able to bear the hypocrisy of their concealment, they tell the children the truth, only to find sympathy and approval. The retributive power of "deed" is at last apparently dead forever. But not quite. Just as the last chapter seems to close, the police sergeant of an earlier act, who has always kept in close touch with Michael (admiring him as a "fellow-author") drops in to have a nip of whisky and to tell of a strange discovery. It seems that the soldier imposter found dead in Michael's rooms years before was a notorious criminal--yes, connected with an important gang just brought to justice. The police are trying to piece together his life as part of the evidence. There is indication of an early marriage. Soon they will know to whom. As the play ends, Michael and Mary are once more faced with danger--with a public disclosure of all that seemed buried in their lives, with danger, too, for their son and his new wife. "Deed" thus still lives on, demanding its inevitable toll of consequences.

It is important to give this brief outline of plot in order to indicate the double comment which Milne makes. He takes you inside the minds of Michael and Mary. He shows you the devious processes by which they find a mental justification for what they want to do. He shows you all the sensitive fineness of their affection, and why they choose the way they do out of their supposed impasse. In the ultimate approval of their son and his wife, Milne seems to indicate his own approval. And yet, with a touch that is almost Greek, he shows the nemesis. The living lie will out--no matter how great the first provocation, nor how pitiful the extenuating circumstances.

The Greek influence is, I believe, important in estimating this play--that doctrine of retribution upon which Greek tragedy is built, and which was to find its only solution in the deeper understanding of Christianity--the possibility of the forgiveness of the guilt of sin without, however, escape from the temporal punishment which might be its due. Michael and Mary is essentially a Greek tragedy, ending in that (to the Greeks) insoluble conflict between mistaken deed and its retribution. Because of the very tenderness and humanity with which it is written, it is a play of misleading values--exaggerated in its premises and never more than half true in its conclusions. More things than human love must count if life is to reveal its richest mysteries and its magic truth.

In the casting of the play, Mr. Hopkins has done an almost perfect job. Michael in the hands of Henry Hull becomes an intense and vivid part. Edith Barrett as Mary gives an amazing portrait of a woman to whom all lengths of devotion--even mistaken devotion-- are possible. The minor parts are taken with a rare perfection of

ensemble--well worthy of the delicate shadings which only Milne and
Barrie can give to characters.

> --Richard Dana Skinner in The
> Commonweal, Vol. 11, No. 9
> (January 1, 1930), page 257.

MINICK (George S. Kaufman and Edna Ferber; Booth Theatre, September 24, 1924)

Not having read Edna Ferber's short story, "Old Man Minick,"
we went to the play which she and George S. Kaufman have fashioned
from it with no preconceived ideas of what it should or should not be.
Consequently, we were delighted with almost every minute of it.

For a play of that kind (and we are definitely committed to
plays of that kind) it couldn't be much better. Its pathos is there
by implication, for you to take or leave (the second-act curtain ex-
cepted). Its comedy is the solid comedy of observation. Only once,
during the chaotic women's committee-meeting, does it seem to border
on exaggeration, and this is merely because the audience laughs so
boisterously. If read in the 'script, we doubt that there is a line
in the scene which is not true. The direction of Mr. Ames is well
nigh perfect, and Woodman Thompson's setting, showing the vistas
of a Chicago apartment, if done by Mr. Belasco, would have left the
newspaper reviewers weak with excitement.

O.P. Heggie, as Minick, the old gentleman who escapes from
filial confinement to the open spaces of an old men's home, is at
times rather obviously an Old Man character part, but it would be
idle to deny that there are thousands of old men who are just like
him. Phyllis Povah is so good as the daughter-in-law that it hurts.
In fact, taking the play, the entire cast, and the production as a
whole, we have no qualms in grouping Minick next to What Price
Glory? in importance at this point in the season.

> --Robert C. Benchley in Life (Oc-
> tober 16, 1924), page 18.

THE MIRACLE (Max Reinhardt and Karl Vollmöeller; Century Theatre,
January 16, 1924)

All that we can say about The Miracle is that we have never
witnessed anything one-half so magnificent in the theatre before, and
never expect to again.

> --Robert C. Benchley in Life (Jan-
> uary 31, 1924), page 18.

*   *   *

The fact first. In The Miracle, the combined talents of Max
Reinhardt, Norman Bel Geddes and Morris Gest have brought to the
American theatre the most vividly impressive and thunderously beautiful spiritual spectacle, not that it has ever known--for it is too
easy to say that--but, more, that it has ever dreamt of. These
three men, the foremost active producing genius in the world, a
young American scenic artist of rare talent, and a man who is the
leading showman of his country, have realized, within the walls of
what until yesterday was merely a millionaires' red and gilt dream of
some transcendental bawdy-house, a super-theatre and in that super-
theatre, imagined with a soaring fancy, and made true with a remarkable panurgy, have lodged further what is beyond question the
greatest production, in taste, in beauty, in effectiveness and in
wealth of rich and perfect detail, that has thus far been chronicled
in the history of American theatrical art. All the elements that go
into the life blood of drama are here assembled into a series of
aesthetic and emotional climaxes that are humbling in their force and
loveliness. The shout of speech, the sweep of pantomime, the sob
and march of orchestral music, the ebb and flow of song, the peal
of cloister chimes, the brass clash of giant cymbals, the play of a
thousand lights, the shuffle and rush of mobs, the rising of scene
upon scene amid churning rapids of color, these directed by a master hand are what constitute this superb psychical pageant brewed
from an ancient and familiar legend and called now The Miracle.

The theatre that we have known becomes lilliputian before such
a phenomenon. The church itself becomes puny. No sermon has
been sounded from any pulpit one-thousandth so eloquent as that
which comes to life, in this playhouse transformed into a vast cathe-
dral, under the necromancy that is Reinhardt. For here are hope
and pity, charity and compassion, humanity and radiance wrought
into an immensely dramatic fabric hung dazzlingly for even a child
to see. It is all as simple as the complex fashioned by genius is
ever simple. There is in it the innocence of a fairy tale, and the
understanding of all the philosophers who ever were. There is the
sentiment that is eternally implicit in gentle faith, and the stern-
ness that one finds always in the heart of beauty. It is, in its pantomime, as silent and yet as articulate as a tune that haunts one in
the far confines of the brain. For such a melody, as we all know,
can be heard distinctly by the ear of the mind, for all its being a
prisoner in the cells of silence. The only trouble with a thing like
The Miracle is that it induces in the beholder an eczema of adjectives
and other parts of speech. It converts the critic into a mere honk-
honk, or circus press-agent. It makes him glow, like a reformed
chillblain. It deprives him of a certain measure of cool sense, as
does beautiful music; but what the need of cool sense on such occasions? So complete is the spell of illusion which Reinhardt works
that critical penetration is considerably blunted. Where, in other
circumstances, one might conceivably be dumfounded at seeing in the

aisles a procession of nuns that appeared to include Al Woods and
Archie Selwyn, it here matters not in the least. Belated seat-
searchers, aye, even Dr. John Roach Straton himself, fail for a moment to diminish the pervading air of sanctity and piety. The spectacle is too long; it might be cut down to two hours with much profit. But as it stands it is still a triumphant contribution to the theatre. Never before has this legend that Karl Vollmöeller has retold,
that Engelbert Humperdinck has veined with melody, that Geddes
has framed, that Reinhardt has worked his wonder on and that Morris Gest has brought to life for the American theatre taken on such
grandeur. Many a Sister Beatrice and Sister Megildis, in literature
and in drama, has found her place taken in an old gray nunnery by
the Mother of God since first the legend grew, but never until now
has the legend itself found its place taken in the temple of Thespis
by such artists as these. They have served the legend as only
real artists of the theatre could hope to.

The vagrant nun of the American girl, Rosamond Pinchot, is
a youthful, vital and dramatically picturesque figure. The Madonna
of Lady Diana Manners is well-composed and of tender suggestion
compact. The lesser rôles are handled without flaw.

> --George Jean Nathan in The Amer-
> ican Mercury (Vol. 1, No. 3),
> March 1924, pages 369-370.

MISS LULU BETT (Zona Gale; Belmont Theatre, December 27, 1920)

The recent realistic trend of our literature produced, along
with Main Street, Moon-Calf, Poor White and kindred others, an interesting and unusual tale of small-town life, Miss Lulu Bett, written
by a middle Westerner, Zona Gale.

Like the other stories of its type, Miss Lulu Bett concerned itself with the little things that go to make up the average middle class
life of our land. Specifically, it depicts the soul revolution and re-
generation of a near-spinster of thirty-four, smothered in the smug,
platitudinous and selfish family that surrounds her. The vital problems range between the mounting price of canned salmon and whether daughter shall or shall not be permitted to go to the library in
the evening. But Miss Gale succeeded in probing the souls of these
folks to their depths. Her story became almost an epic of family
life, as vital and as tragic in its minor key as Balzac or Meredith.

We thank the Gods of the Theater that Brock Pemberton, in
producing the play, permitted Miss Gale to do her own dramatization.
The result is an exceedingly human play with superbly real dialogue
and an utterly un-theatrical viewpoint upon actualities.

Did the critics praise Miss Lulu Bett? Most of them did not.
They noted its "microscopic dissection" with pain and actually de-
clared it to be undramatic! So Miss Lulu Bett has been forced to
struggle for its existence.

Yet if the theater has seen anything more real than the family
group on the front porch in Miss Lulu Bett we want to know it.
Here is reflected all the tragedies and the futile maladjustments of
life. Aside from the discernment it reveals in its painting of the
various family members, it cuts neatly into several vital things. The
unbending attitude of age to youth, for instance. Again, the supreme and unconquerable tragedy of old age.

Miss Lulu Bett is superbly played. Out of the fine ensemble
stands Louise Closser Hale's faultless performance of the grandmother,
a cameo of character acting. By deft strokes she enmeshes and
epitomizes all the humorous cynicism and feeble retrospect of old
age. Carroll McComas' Lulu Bett is straightforward and sincere.
All the others are admirably done.

The fate of Miss Lulu Bett remains to be seen. Be that as it
may, we look upon it as the best native play since Eugene O'Neill's
Beyond the Horizon.

> --Shadowland, Vol. 4, No. 3 (May
> 1921), page 57.

* * *

If St. John Ervine had done the dramatization of Miss Lulu
Bett which is now being produced at the Belmont, and if it had been
just a little duller, it would have been hailed as another Jane Clegg.
And even as it stands, the work of Miss Zona Gale, the author of the
novel, one has to be very careful not to wax chauvinistic and say
that it has the makings of another Jane Clegg.

Perhaps it is not quite so good a play as its parent was a book.
If it had been, it would have been the best play in New York. But,
aside from a little slowness of action (and since when has slowness
of action militated against the amiable reception of our advanced
drama?) and perhaps several pages too many of 'script, it comes
very near being a great play. It is great because of its pitiless fidelity to every-day people and every-day life, and because of this
very fidelity it sometimes seems dull. But the glory of it is that
Miss Gale has made it seem dull because she knows better, and it
takes an artist to be dull on purpose.

In one particular Miss Lulu Bett has an advantage over most
dramatized novels. The author herself has brought her character
to life. And Mr. Brock Pemberton, the producer, has lived up to
his reputation as a judge of casts made in his first production,
Enter Madame. It is hard to see how Miss Lulu Bett could have been

much better cast. Carroll McComas, as Lulu, accomplishes a miracle and makes herself extremely plain for a greater part of the play,
and even her blossoming is accomplished gradually and much as a
married spinster of thirty-four might blossom on determining to
strike out for herself in the world. She plays her early scenes a
little too much in the mood of Russian peasant tragedy, but certainly
no Russian peasant was ever much more tragic than Lulu Bett. Lois
Shore makes Monona Deacon the most disagreeable child ever seen on
any stage, which is no small triumph. Louise Closser Hale takes the
part of the grandmother and makes it the outstanding comedy feature
of the play. It would have been difficult, however, for anyone to
spoil such a part, and it might, perhaps, have been done less as a
"character" and more as a real old lady. William Holden and Catherine Doucet could not possibly offend the sensibilities of the most
ardent hater of the Dwight Herbert and Ina Deacon of the book.
The entire cast, in fact, is superbly undistinguished, which is just
exactly as it should be to speak the superbly undistinguished lines
of Miss Lulu Bett.

> --Robert C. Benchley in Life
> (January 13, 1921), pages 64-
> 65.

MRS. PARTRIDGE PRESENTS (Mary Kennedy and Ruth Hawthorne; Belmont Theatre, January 5, 1925)

It is perhaps unfair to follow the hilarious endorsement of Jolson and Is Zat So? with such gentlemanly applause as is called for
by the very nature of Mrs. Partridge Presents----. This is a play
by Mary Kennedy and Ruth Hawthorne (Miss Kennedy, like Mr. Glea-
son, is on the stage), and is a most amusing and delicate reversal
of the old problem of juvenile freedom. Blanche Bates is the mother
who is so anxious for her children to lead their own lives that she
tries to lead their lives for them, and Sylvia Field and Edward Emery, Jr., are the young people who would rather not have careers
if it is all the same to Mother. What is known as a "bit" is developed
into an "act in one" by the skill of Ruth Gordon, who wanders on
and off the stage with no particular reason and certainly no rhyme,
carrying the works on her smartly dressed shoulders.

> --Robert C. Benchley in Life
> (January 29, 1925), page 18.

THE MOON-FLOWER (Zoë Akins, adapted from the Hungarian of Lajos Biro; Astor Theatre, February 25, 1924)

Within a single week two dramas were produced with much the

same theme and leading characters. The Moon-Flower at the Astor
is "by Zöe Akins after the Hungarian of Lazos Biro"; Fata Morgana
at the Garrick is "by Ernst Vajda, translated by James L.A. Burrell." Because of these program announcements Miss Akins must be
held responsible for the former, and Mr. Burrell escapes responsibility for the latter. It should be the other way round. Anyone
would be delighted to accept responsibility for Fata Morgana--and
few for The Moon-Flower.

Both plays might have been called One Night of Love. They
are both concerned with a midnight-to-noon affair between a boy,
to whom it means everything, and a mondaine to whom it is but one
incident among many. Miss Akins has decorated her work with "fine
writing," which is neither fine nor beautiful nor literary--just high-
falutin and unreal. And Sidney Blackmer mumbles the fancy lines
with expressionless dullness. Elsie Ferguson in a red wig is lovely
and alluring; in the moments when she has the chance to be human
she is vibrant. But those moments are rare.

There seem to be no virtuous women in the Akins theatre--not
even as colorless contrasts to the flaming ladies. That is unfortunate,
because it is fairly generally believed that some women at some time
in their lives were virtuous.

> --David Carb in The Bookman,
> Vol. 59, No. 3 (May 1924), page
> 331.

MUSIC BOX REVUE (Music and Lyrics by Irving Berlin; Music Box
     Theatre, September 22, 1921)

There is no use in beating about the bush in the matter of
Irving Berlin's Music Box Revue. It looks, from the eminence of
this judge's box, to be just about the best revue that has yet been
staged in these parts (always excepting, of course, the two immortal
Cohan revues). From beginning to end, the numbers are consistently amusing, tuneful, or pictorially pleasing, according to what the
blueprints have called for. And they are short. Perhaps that is
the secret. You never have a chance to get tired.

And when you consider that the cast includes William Collier,
Sam Bernard, Florence Moore, Wilda Bennett, Hugh Cameron, and
Joseph Santley (Mr. Santley showing himself to be not only a graceful dancer but a graceful comedian as well), with Irving Berlin himself coming on at the end in a wistful and harmonious resumé of his
liabilities, there really is no reason at all why The Music Box Revue
shouldn't be the best revue in town.

A word, too, must be said for Hassard Short, who staged the

production, and who, in spite of a passion for freight-elevator effects and now and then a colored post-card touch, has made the whole revue a beautiful thing to watch. This trick-elevator craving which Mr. Short has is something that will have to be watched or, progressing at its present rate, it may reach gigantic proportions in a few seasons. In last year's Equity show Mr. Short had his Shakespearean heroes brought wabblingly into view, one by one, on a private elevator. In the Music Box, Mr. Santley and Miss Bennett are lifted bodily while eating at a table, and the whole chorus is later given a ride. Next year, maybe the entire stage will go up, followed perhaps by the first ten rows of orchestra chairs. Mr. Short must be made to stop before this happens.

--Robert C. Benchley in Life (October 23, 1921), page 18.

MUSIC BOX REVUE OF 1922 (Lyrics and Music by Irving Berlin; Music Box Theatre, October 23, 1922)

The success of last season's Music Box Revue was a bad thing for this season's Music Box. In the first place, it set an almost hopelessly high standard, and, in the second place, it gave Mr. Berlin too much money to spend on doodads, tinsel, diamonds, and freight elevators in staging his present production. There has been such a dazzling display of wealth in mounting the revue that the imagination at first cowers appalled before it, which makes the reaction of resentment only stronger when one finally realizes that, under cover of this cloth of gold, a really very ordinary show has been slipped across.

And even the scenic effects themselves, for all the money that has been poured over them, lack a certain soundness which John Murray Anderson gets with much less expense or Cleveland Bronner with a few strips of cheesecloth. Hassard Short, who has had the prodigal job of shopping with Mr. Berlin's money, has a way of obtaining a perfectly gorgeous effect and then, for fear that it may not be beautiful enough, giving a hysterical extra fling and shooting up a lavender jet curtain over the whole affair or sending the chorus wabbling up on solid gold dumbwaiters.

The use of mechanical or electrical features, to which Mr. Short is passionately devoted, may sound very well when he talks it over with Mr. Berlin in the Spring, but one must always count on at least two of the electric sunbonnets refusing to function when the time for the performance comes, or one of the gadgets shooting up too early, and an abortive effect of this sort, which was intended to be smashing, is much worse than no effect at all. One of the most trying sights on the stage today is that of the lovely members of the Music Box cast attempting, one by one, to descend in a non-

chalant and graceful manner a precipitous flight of stairs which ought
really to be climbed down backwards with a rope around the waist.
There is always the human element in things of this sort which Mr.
Short, with his transcendent imagination and unlimited funds, seems
always to disregard.

The revue itself, once you get your eyesight back, is all
right, but, in the opinion of this department, not to be compared
with last year's. Bobby Clark has come up from the burlesque
wheel and, as predicted in these columns a year or so ago, is very
funny. There is one act, a burlesque melodrama in which none of
the properties work, which makes up for a lot of waiting, and, of
course, there are reliable features, such as the leisurely Rath
Brothers and Mr. Berlin's music, which always turn out well.

The rest of the show is made up of a generally pleasing series
of pictures, with singing by John Steel (just a little flat now and
then, but who cares in a great big show like that?), Grace LaRue,
Charlotte Greenwood and the Fairbanks Twins. It is a little ab-
normality of ours that the Fairbanks Twins, even when dancing,
leave us at a temperature of about 45° F.; so when they sing we
are in no mood to take a joke.

From which summary, you may gather that we had a rather dismal time at the Music Box Revue. Oddly enough, we didn't. It was
only when we began to think it over that we realized how little it
takes to keep us awake.

--Robert C. Benchley in Life (November 16, 1922), page 18.

THE NERVOUS WRECK (Owen Davis, based on a story by E.J. Rath;
    Sam H. Harris Theatre, October 9, 1923)

After all, whatever a play may be about, wherever it may rank
in the artistic or technical scale, the one thing we demand of it
really is that it be theatrically effective. Two plays this month, for
me, at least, answer this demand completely. To any person who is
not the type that belittles Charlie Chaplin, I recommend Owen Davis's
farce, The Nervous Wreck. It is shrewd, rollicking, and finished.
To those who like "strong drama" well played, with a tone of reality,
Tarnish is the best play of the new season.

I am more convinced than ever that Owen Davis is one of the
finest craftsmen of our theatre. It is not so much the actual lines
of The Nervous Wreck that convince one of this--they, many of
them, are old timber, given a new tint by excellent playing; but Mr.
Davis has a sense of public psychology, an ability to write a scene
that clicks, which is the summum bonum of the playwright. The

Nervous Wreck is all about a young man who thinks he is sick and isn't, and in the course of his recovery becomes bandit, waiter, and lover. The incidents which attend his progress through the western country are not important; but they are exceedingly funny. A brilliant piece of satirical writing jumps out in the last act, where Davis burlesques the psychological detective and his word-association tests. Although its tone is burlesque it seems to me penetrating enough to be called satire. Otto Kruger, having weathered a rather heavy season last year, emerges as a brilliant farceur. He is as funny as, if not funnier than, Harold Lloyd--and June Walker is entertaining and good to look upon. Her part is by far the most difficult which Mr. Davis has created--yet with the most improbable material in a highly improbable play, she creates an illusion of reality. While the character she portrays is possibly the biggest liar to be seen on any New York stage, she manages to keep the sympathy of the audience.

> --John Farrar in The Bookman,
> Vol. 58, No. 4 (December 1923),
> pages 439-440.

THE NEW MOON (Book by Oscar Hammerstein II, Frank Mandel and Laurence Schwab, Music by Sigmund Romberg; Imperial Theatre, September 19, 1928)

All of these shows* are good enough entertainment, Billie being the best of the three. They lack, however, the distinction of The New Moon, with which Messrs. Schwab and Mandel duplicate the success of Good News, surely one of the greatest musical comedy hits of late, and offer an operetta comparable to The Desert Song, but better, I think. As I sagaciously insinuated in this place some months ago, musical shows are more competently and understandingly produced, as a rule, than the average play. The New Moon, for example, was tried out last season and taken off because nobody could be found to take the part now so beautifully played by Miss Evelyn Herbert. Meanwhile, changes were made in the libretto and score. The result is a melodious and delightful evening, picturesque settings, fine choruses, such as "Stouthearted Men," and songs like "One Kiss" and "Lover Come Back to Me," and not a note of syncopation in the lot.

> --Ernest Boyd in The Bookman,
> Vol. 68, No. 4 (December 1928),
> page 456.

*   *   *

Last week I indulged in an explosion. It was all about the

---

*Cross My Heart, Just a Minute and Billie.

crass stupidity of managers who failed to see the opportunity at their
doorstep in the way of finely romantic plays. Half an hour after
this explosion, I dropped in at the Imperial Theatre and saw The
New Moon. And now I wish to record that Laurence Schwab and
Frank Mandel have done precisely what I hoped someone would do.
They have taken a romantic story from old French New Orleans of
1788, and turned it into one of the most utterly engaging light operas of many seasons.

The managers themselves wrote the book with Oscar Hammerstein 2nd, had Sigmund Romberg write the music, and Donald Oenslager design the settings. There are, to be frank, a few dull moments. The book is a trifle too long, and a few of the chorus evo-
lutions could be eliminated to the advantage of the story. But those
are details. The interesting point is that the story is strong enough,
dramatically, to make one resent the chorus--the exact reverse of
most musical plays. The entire performance has that thing which is
the birthright of all good theatre--glamour. You find it in the delightful costumes. You find it in the lilting and romantic music.
You find it in the fresh enthusiasm of the players. You find it in
the absence of current smut and in the exuberant fun of the comedy.

Robert Halliday and Evelyn Herbert for the romance, Marie
Callahan and Gus Shy for the comedy, and William O'Neal for the robust action--there you have an excellent combination to start with,
and for good measure you can add Esther Howard for more comedy
and Rosita and Ramon for glamourous dancing. No one in the cast
really merits superlatives. Neither does the music by itself, nor the
book, nor the staging. But the combination of all the elements is
so well balanced, the spirit of the production is so pleasantly obvious, and the overtone so constant, that you would have to search
far to find the best magic of the theatre better expressed. The
New Moon is not exactly a work of art, but it is most emphatically a
work of theatrical distinction.

--Richard Dana Skinner in The
Commonweal, Vol. 8, No. 24
(October 17, 1928), page 605.

NO, NO, NANETTE! (Book by Otto Harbach and Frank Mandel,
Lyrics by Irving Caesar and Otto Harbach, Music by Vincent
Youmans; Globe Theatre, September 16, 1925)

We had a preconceived notion that No, No, Nanette! was a
pretty dull show, probably because it had been running so long before it came to New York. We knew the music from hearing unpleasant people whistling it, and were willing to let it go at that. In
fact, we took considerable pride in not going to see it. Imagine our
surprise, then, on dropping in at the Globe one afternoon, under the

impression that we were going into the Astor to see The Big Parade,
to discover that No, No, Nanette! is really very amusing, and that
Charles Winninger and Wellington Cross, with that ease and facile
kidding which comes to comedians after a long run, are a highly
comic pair. We were probably the last white man to see No, No,
Nanette! for the first time.

There is always something disappointing, however, about hearing music played in its original arrangement after it has become popular about town. It never sounds so good. This, we have figured
out, is because in the show it has to be sung by stars, which means
that all rhythm has to be sacrificed to the singer's desire to hold on
the ripe notes. A dance orchestra playing "Tea for Two" gets fifty
per cent. more real stuff into it than a theatre orchestra following
the singers, if for no other reason than that the dance orchestra is
concerned with the tune alone and its swing. Also, the audience
gets less out of a tune in the theatre, because in the theatre the eye
is attracted by the motions of the singers and the lights and scenery, whereas in a setting by itself the music has no competition.
The best way to hear a good popular piece of music is to have it
played by a good pianist in the dark. A good pianist is hard to get
in the dark, however.

> --Robert C. Benchley in Life
> (February 4, 1926), page 20.

OH, KAY! (Book by Guy Bolton and P.G. Wodehouse, Music by
George Gershwin, Lyrics by Ira Gershwin; Imperial Theatre,
November 8, 1926)

Oh, Kay! is one of the shows at which dinner parties will be
ending up for many months to come. An inveterate diner-out will
probably see Oh, Kay! fifteen or twenty times during the season.
It could exist entirely on its class, but it also has Gertrude Lawrence,
Oscar Shaw, Victor Moore and Gershwin music. So you see.

> --Robert C. Benchley in Life (De-
> cember 9, 1926), page 23.

* * *

Turning from the old to the new, very new indeed, we found
Oh, Kay! one of the brightest musical comedies we had seen in many
a long night. This is the piece by Guy Bolton and P.G. Wodehouse
which was specially built around the personality and beauty of Gertrude Lawrence, who has blossomed from several Charlot Revues into
a play all her own. Having left the lamented Miss Lillie languishing
somewhere in the provinces, she stormed the citadel of New York and
captured it the first night. There is a reason for this. Miss Lawrence is not only lovely to look at--that is usual enough--but she

can sing and dance as well, and, rarest of all in a musical comedy
actress, she acts. George Gershwin has written more tuneful music
in days gone by, but it is pretty enough to fill the bill and all of
it sounds new. We should have been perfectly happy if Miss Lawrence had managed to include in her performance a revival of the
famous "Limehouse Blues," but one cannot ask everything in so
sparkling an evening, and besides Mr. Charlot might object.

--Larry Barretto in The Bookman,
Vol. 64, No. 6 (February 1927),
page 730.

ON APPROVAL (Frederick Lonsdale; Gaiety Theatre, October 18,
1926)

There is nothing particularly startling about On Approval (unless it is the excessively wrinkled view of Scotland which is glimpsed
through the open door in the second act, suggesting that that section of the Scottish moors had been slept in the night before in an
armchair), but it is very nice entertainment. Mr. Lonsdale has written with his customary glibness, and has utilized what seems to be an
infallible recipe for comedy--the acrimonious hatred of one character
for another. The bitter and articulate enmity between Hugh Wakefield and Violet Kemble Cooper (in character, of course) is good for
an almost constant laugh. Wallace Eddinger and Kathlene MacDonell
are less acid but distinctly valuable. Altogether, very pleasant indeed.

--Robert C. Benchley in Life (November 11, 1926), page 23.

* * *

Two playwrights, one English, one American, of--as far as
one may be didactic about those things--equal merit and gifts, offered their respective season's plays: Frederick Lonsdale with On
Approval and George Kelly with Daisy Mayme. In the former, two
young couples, or young enough, leave London to spend several
weeks in a Scottish country house, the purpose of the hegira being
to discover whether such close quarters are conducive to matrimony.
This state of affairs provides Mr. Lonsdale with an amusing if by no
means new situation, and he makes the most of it. The lines are
light, sure fire stuff which kept the audience in gales of laughter.
We know of no playwright who can build up witty dialogue from airy
nothings so competently as Mr. Lonsdale can. He picks his words
and tosses them into the air, whence presently they descend in glittering streams which not even the mouthings of not always inspired
actors can impair. This particular cast did very well with them. As
a matter of fact we thought Violet Kemble Cooper in her shrewish
rôle ranted a bit too much, her voice at times rising to such a

scream as is rarely heard in the drawing rooms of the great; but
her blonde beauty sufficed to soothe the eyes even while the ears
were deafened. Hugh Wakefield made admirable comedy of his part
as the Duke of Bristol, and Wallace Eddinger, somewhat stouter
since the days of Captain Applejack, did well. The honors of the
evening, however, went to Kathlene MacDonell. She played her rôle
with such smooth humor as to lend conviction to the not always
credible lines. She was, in a word, completely natural. This season we are going in for naturalism. Actors and actresses who so
much as suggest that they are playing a part will find scant favor in
our eyes. James Reynolds has done marvels with one of the sets--
a drawing room with all the gilt and brocade magnificence of a Stroz-
zi palace. It is the first time in our existence that we have yearned
for one set to remain standing throughout an entire play.

> --Larry Barretto in The Bookman,
> Vol. 64, No. 5 (January 1927),
> pages 618-619.

ONCE IN A LIFETIME (Moss Hart and George S. Kaufman; Music Box
  Theatre, September 24, 1930)

Hollywood has taken plenty of beatings in its time, but without
any particularly chastening effect. If Once in a Lifetime doesn't do
some good, then the whole thing might as well be dropped and the
movie industry allowed to work out its own damnation. For Once in
a Lifetime is top in mockery.

Just where Moss Hart and George S. Kaufman got their data
about the workings of the cinema mind and hand nobody seems to
know, but it comes straight from the papier-mâché hills of Hollywood-
land in the genuine, original package. The lines are funny to the
point of being convulsing at times, but each one packs a terrific jab
with a poisoned needle and Mr. Kaufman's brief talk at the end of
the second act on what is wrong with the movies is so bitterly direct as to be just a little embarrassing. (Mr. Kaufman takes part in
his own play and gets more into just sitting in a chair and waiting
than many an old-time actor has got into a duel.)

With such sterling performers as Hugh O'Connell and Jean
Dixon (Miss Dixon still very cross) and a large cast of excellent
people to imitate the Western boulevardiers, Once in a Lifetime is
practically devastating as a satire. It is said that neither Mr. Kaufman nor Mr. Hart has ever worked in Hollywood, but one, or both,
of them evidently got as sore at the place as any old employee whose
option has not been taken up. Somebody's blood has gone into the
making of Once in a Lifetime, which is why it is so much more than
just a comedy.

> --Robert C. Benchley in The New
> Yorker (October 4, 1930), page 34.

* * *

Offered up to the gods of laughter on the stage of the Music
Box, this play has already proved itself welcome in their eyes. The
authors, Moss Hart and George S. Kaufman, have prepared a delicious tribute, and the high-priest, Sam Harris, has spared nothing,
not even ermine coats, in the splendor (albeit of the garish variety
native to Hollywood) of its presentation.

Mr. Harris has dubbed the play a "new comedy," although he
knows, as well as the audiences packing his theatre, and should
know a lot better, that it is sheer farce. That rapid tempo, so admirably sustained throughout those kaleidoscopic and innumerable
scenes--even the half-dozen doors in the studio set, kept in perpetual motion during all the second act (vive la France, if for no
other reason than discovering the importance of active doors to farce!)
belong only to farce--to say nothing of the lines, many of which are
slapstick and almost Rabelaisian in character. Satire, it is true,
abounds, but it is laid on with a heavy hand, and is hung rather on
the tricks of direction, costuming and staging, than on any inherent
subtlety in the lines. The movie queen's inelegant voice is only funny because she wears such elegant clothing, and because her retinue
is so elegantly liveried.

It would be ungracious, however, to quarrel with Mr. Harris
over the niceties of definition when he has given us such a thoroughly refreshing production. Here are personalities not unfamiliar to
the drama we have known in recent years. The stranded vaudeville
trio of fairly standard type--one of whom, painted perhaps with brush
a trifle too broad, is the good-natured "sap" dear to all audiences.
The more brainlessly he behaves, the more radiantly fortune smiles
upon him. Those who require something more solid than the excellent farcical qualities offered in this play will also find in it a love
story, to which the acting of Jean Dixon brings the same depth and
seriousness that characterized her performance in June Moon. But
this is in all half-light, made subsidiary to the flashes of an uproarious farce whooping its way successfully through three acts and
seven scenes.

The gifted Mr. Kaufman, not content merely to collaborate in
the writing of Once in a Lifetime, and to stage it, manages to act in
it as well. His impersonation of the weary playwright, driven to
nervous prostration through months of waiting on the imperial wishes
of the czar of Hollywood, is whimsically delightful.

The movies are delicious satirical meat, which the authors have
served up most humorously--even if the meal drags a bit at the end.
Broadway now has its happy chance to even up an old score with its
ancient enemy, the cinema, and to prod it nicely. In Once in a Lifetime the laugh is on the movies.

--H.W.H. in The Commonweal, Vol.
12, No. 23 (Oct. 8, 1930), p. 584.

OUTWARD BOUND (Sutton Vane; Ritz Theatre, January 7, 1924)

   And now we come to our idea of what a play should be, Outward Bound. Not that we do not, sitting in the critical cool of the
evening, see where Outward Bound could be made a lot better than
it is, but if we had had the original idea and had carried it through
as well as Mr. Sutton Vane has done, we should feel quite satisfied
to take a farm somewhere and wait for the rest of the playwrights
to catch up to us. And it would be a good long wait, too.

   Before the play came into New York we had heard an outline
of the first act, how the passengers gathered in the smoking-room
of a liner gradually come to the realization that they are all dead and
sailing for a port unknown to any one of them. At the very telling
of it, we broke out into a rash from the excitement of the idea. We
were almost afraid to see the play, fearing that no author could carry it through.

   And it is true that Mr. Vane's play takes a dip in the middle
and comes near to finishing with an obvious examination scene when
the passengers are allocated by the visiting official in more or less
conventional groupings. But the final scene makes up for everything, and bears out the promise of the first act, than which we can
give no higher praise without bursting.

   An almost ideal cast, consisting of J.M. Kerrigan, Margalo
Gillmore, Leslie Howard, Alfred Lunt, Charlotte Granville, Lyonel
Watts, Beryl Mercer, Eugene Powers and Dudley Digges, helps to
make Outward Bound by far the most thrilling play of the year.
                              --Robert C. Benchley in Life (Jan-
                                uary 31, 1924), page 18.

                         *   *   *

   There is much to admire in Sutton Vane's Outward Bound. It
is one of those odd plays that comes along every once in a while
and that, by virtue of its general complexion of grace and skill,
persuades one theatrically that even its failings, like those of a winning child, are charming. The story is of an assortment of men and
women who find themselves somewhat puzzlingly aboard a strange
ship bound for they know not where and who gradually awaken to
the realization that they are dead and on their way to whatever heaven or hell may be like. With what seems to me to be as shrewd a
sense of dramaturgic values as has come out of the popular theatre
of England in many a day, Vane relates this tale with a constantly
surprising and enviable aptitude for foretelling his audience's every
momentary turn of mood. His melodrama, sentiment, comedy, burlesque, irony and fantasy are dovetailed with a very deft talent indeed; each falls into place with an exact click; each avoids the slightest suggestion of pigeonholing; the handling of each is perfectly

timed and with a most blithe and captivating unstudied air. If I
were a playwright, I should envy Vane his uncommon gift in this uncommon achievement of theatrical effect. At bottom, his technic may
be as old as the hills, but his particular talent lies in making it
seem fresh and hearty and engagingly new, like an old friend come
back after a long absence. The pleasure of the evening is heightened
by the knowledge that the job his theme offered him was anything
but an easy one and by the further fact that he has triumphed over
the difficulties that confronted him by taking the hardest road. The
road of melodrama, the road of sentiment, the road of fantasy, the
road of derisiveness, the road of comedy--each was open to him and
each might have found a play at the end of it. But the road to a
good play on this particular theme was not so smooth and straight,
he appreciated. One would have to hoof them all, jump now and then
from one to the other and again retrace one's footsteps as the theme
elusively turned this way and that. This Vane has done. And out
of the jigsaw he has evoked a sustained theatrical mood that marks
a popular theatrical achievement of unusual quality.

     The chief defects of the play, which actually disturb one very
little while under its pleasant spell, lie in the author's Mother Goose
point of view toward heaven and hell and in his strainful avoidance
of dramatic climaxes. On the latter subject, I have already made
discourse in another place. There I observed that the current
prevalent fashion among dramatists of regarding a good, old-fashioned,
rousing climax as something beneath dignity and artistic propriety is
far from my own peculiar taste. When a dramatic climax has been
foreshadowed and is rightly to be expected with high anticipation, it
is thoroughly disturbing and disappointing to observe the playwright
shush it off the stage and substitute for it a nonchalant, drawling
allusion to the villain's spats. An effective climax is nothing to be
ashamed of; the present-day practice of avoiding the realization of
such climaxes to their full is the rankest affectation. In the matter
of his heaven and hell, Vane makes the mistake not of failing to use
his imagination, as his critics charge, but of using it. That imagination, like the imagination of most playwrights who approach the same
subject, were better left in peace. Its agitation is productive of dissent and dissatisfaction, and almost inevitably. Unless one be possessed of a very great poetic or ironic fancy, which Vane is not,
philosophical explorations into the character of the hereafter may
best be abandoned, especially in the theatre. When they are not
abandoned, we are very likely to get such things as the Macpher-
sons' Happy Ending, which pictures heaven as a Pittsburgh million-
aire's garden party, Uncle Tom's Cabin, which pictures it as a German Christmas card, and Vane's Outward Bound, which reveals it to
be something like a William Hodge play. Had Vane left the subject
to his audience's imagination rather than to his own, his play would
have been a better theatre play. The production is extremely well
made--William Harris, Jr., has never shown finer editorial taste--
and the presenting company, with Alfred Lunt as its outstanding

figure, is from first to last excellent.

--George Jean Nathan in The American Mercury (Vol. 1, No. 3),
March 1924, pages 372-373.

PARIS (Book by Martin Brown, Music and Lyrics by Cole Porter and
E. Ray Goetz; Music Box Theatre, October 8, 1928)

Martin Brown's "musicomedy," briefly called Paris, is a pretext
to enable Miss Irene Bordoni to wear those enormous feathers which
have been esteemed beautiful in Paris vaudeville for the past thirty
years and to sing very badly Cole Porter's "Babes in the Wood,"
"Don't Look at Me That Way" and "Let's Fall in Love." These, fortunately, were also played and sung by Irving Aaronson's Commanders,
likewise "The Land of Going to Be," a tuneful number by Ray Goetz
and Walter Kollo. Everybody laughed when Miss Bordoni spoke
French rapidly, but as the audience also appreciated to the full the
real comedy of Louise Closser Hale and Arthur Margetson, one had
to smile at the prestige of a French accent and enjoy what is, on the
whole, a pleasant variation on the usual musical comedy.

--Ernest Boyd in The Bookman,
Vol. 68, No. 4 (December 1928),
page 456.

*   *   *

Compared with these serious offerings, Miss Irene Bordoni in
Paris is practically heaven. In an ordinary week it would not have
been so good. A more hackneyed play would have been impossible
to find (and apparently a great deal of hunting was done and a
great deal of bother taken to disentangle it from the hundreds of
other stories exactly like it) and there are moments in it when we
had some idea of going back and seeing if Faust really was as bad
as we thought. But these moments were not when Miss Bordoni was
on (or, at least, not many of them) and certainly not during the
singing of Mr. Cole Porter's songs. It is Mr. Porter who contributes
most to Paris and it should be a matter for local rejoicing that he has
decided to return to America and write songs for the public instead
of for a little group of fortunate ones around a piano in Paris.

If Paris were a better play, the introduction of Irving Aaronson's entire band (who just happened to drop into the apartment for
an informal rehearsal and were, by great good luck, shown up)
would be more of an intrusion. As it is, nobody cares much what
happens to the story, as everything that could happen to it happened
years ago, and so the "Commanders" help out considerably by their
ambidextrous efforts.

--Robert C. Benchley in Life (October 25, 1928), page 17.

THE PASSING SHOW OF 1921 (Book and Lyrics by Harold Atteridge,
    Music by Jean Schwartz; Winter Garden Theatre, December
    29, 1920)

   The Passing Show of 1921 is the best of the long series of annual revues that have made the Winter Garden a Broadway institution
--best in burlesque, in color, in variety. It can be recommended to
the most discriminating deacon this side of the Monogahela.

   The Howard Brothers, tireless and versatile fellows, sing and
impersonate amusingly. Willie Howard gives an imitation of Frank
Bacon that is amazingly life-like.

   Marie Dressler is funnier than ever--superlative praise, in-
deed--in a number of scenes, notably in the amusing burlesques of
The Bat, in which she is a placid and imperturbable old woman and
Spanish Love in which she is a much-loved señorita.

   Harry Watson brings his unique drollery to view in these burlesques.

   Cleveland Bronner displays his vivid sense of color in an exotic dance revue. Janet Adair and Dolly Hackett take good care of
singing assignment. Tot Qualters is a decorative jazz demonstrator.

   And there are dancers after dancers, including the rhythmic
Grace and Berkes, the supple Sammy White, the graceful Cortez and
Peggy, the attractive Mellette Sisters and the acrobatic Zambouni and
O'Hanlon. Girls, girls, girls fill the picture--and the eye. The run-
way is densely populated.

   The costumes are effectively bizarre, the settings rich and harmonious. The music is Winter Garden.
                              --Louis R. Reid in The New York
                              Dramatic Mirror, January 8,
                              1921, page 59.

THE PASSING SHOW OF 1923 (Book and Lyrics by Harold Atteridge,
    Music by Sigmund Romberg and Jean Schwartz; Winter Garden
    Theatre, June 14, 1923)

   The Winter Garden usually leaves us twenty degrees cooler
than the street, but we must admit that the new Passing Show (called
The Passing Show of 1923 in honor of the current year) is highly
satisfactory. And we won't add the usual "for a Winter Garden
show."

Especially during the first half of the performance is there an absence of the buck-eye note which has, in past years, distinguished the spectacles in the Messrs. Shubert's Refuge for Visiting Buyers. There is a minimum of jet, and the color pink, when it is used at all, is used sparingly. The costumes all seem to be new and each one made for the girl who wears it. And, although the book and lyrics are still written by Mr. Harold Atteridge, who has been responsible for the Winter Garden belles-lettres in the past, there is a touch to the present book which would indicate that Mr. Atteridge is at last in High School and getting along well with his teachers.

During the first hour or two, there are many moments of what we sensitive people call "real beauty," and a surprising number of loud laughs. We would have hotly denied that the spectacle of a man being propelled suddenly from behind into the orchestra pit could make us laugh, and yet there was nothing else to call what we did when Roy Cummings, all set to sing a sentimental ballad in the amber spotlight, received a terrific shoot from some unseen and mighty force behind the curtain in front of which he was so trustfully standing.

This has worried us quite a good deal, this hysterical reaction of ours to what we are wont to call scornfully "slap-stick." And this is how we have explained it. We do not laugh when a man is knocked over by a weak, vacillating blow which hurts him only slightly. But the mysterious tornado which hit Mr. Cummings in the back was so complete and so devastating that it crashed out of the class of slap-stick and became Art. There was fully a half-second when Mr. Cummings was not visible at all. And only a half-second before he had been so sentimental-looking and so oblivious of the impending opposition to his singing. As we remember it, one single sweet tenor note had just left his lips when the world came to an end. It must have been the enormity of the thing, the vastness of its conception and the cruel completeness of the singer's annihilation that made us laugh. Also the fact that Mr. Cummings himself is very funny.

And, of course, there is always the possibility that we are just a plain, ordinary low-brow. We never thought of that.

In every revue there must be a number in which a tall, statuesque lady, wearing a large hat and singing soprano, stands by the proscenium and renders a song (with much 'cello work in the orchestra) the words of which seem to be, roughly: "Wua-fua, wua-fua, fle-e-e flua-a-a wua-a-a-a." The title is usually "Love's Garden of Roses" or "When Grandma Was a Girl Scout," and the chorus walk up and down behind the singer making appropriate movements. No one ever hears the words. No one ever remembers the music. It is just "a number." Ah, well! Life is like that for many of us, isn't it, my dear Lady Hatherington? It is the tragedy of living.... I don't know what makes me this way to-night. Come, let us go into the card-room.

Aside from Roy Cummings, there are Barnett Parker and the Georges--Hassell and Jessel--to aid in the merry-making, and James Watts, who always has an unpleasant effect on something inside us. It surely must be more than coincidence that he is usually entrusted with the repellent features of a show. And the second half of the Winter Garden show is not without its repellent features. In fact, there are times when you might think that you were right back in The Passing Shows of 1920-19 or -18. They even bring out the jet and throw the spot-light on it.

Helen Shipman manages very nicely to keep up the tone at the head of the Ladies' Department of the performance, and Walter Woolf, in spite of his endorsement of Mineralava in the back of the program, has a good male voice and uses it well. It was thought by some that in his Rose song he had left a little of the beauty-clay on his face by mistake, but it turned out to be merely an extra-fecund set of side-burns of the Neo-Valentino school.

Relations between this country and England should be enormously strengthened by the spectacular scene in Westminster Abbey, representing the more public features of the marriage of Princess Mary. The management has done very well by the Queen and her daughter in selecting two of the prettiest young ladies of the chorus to play the parts, but King George and Viscount Lascelles seem to have been made up from old photographs of Rutherford B. Hayes and General Custer respectively. Nat Nazarro, Jr., plays the Prince of Wales, and the whole thing is very elegant.

--Robert C. Benchley in <u>Life</u>
(July 5, 1923), page 20.

*   *   *

Competing--very obviously competing--with <u>George White's Scandals</u> is the newest Winter Garden show designed by J.J. Shubert--<u>The Passing Show of 1923</u>. Both these entertainments, at some stage or other of rehearsal, had borrowed heavily from Parisian revues, and from the same revues. As first conceived, no less than five numbers were identical: a mirror scene, a curtain of semi-nudes far below Ziegfeld's current offering in taste and beauty, a rose episode, a chandelier decorated with chorus girls.

The Winter Garden show, having a lead of half a week or so, brought all four numbers into town. White displayed the first three to much more advantage. Just to make resemblance doubly sure, the Shubert entertainment borrowed an idea from a very old Scandals-- the translating of a foreign playlet into Yiddish-American by a man watching it from a box--and for good measure it threw in another illustrated ballad such as graced <u>The Greenwich Village Follies</u> in Jack Hazard's song about returning to good old Alaska.

Trade papers and dramatic editors have luxuriated in descrip-

tions of the race to town of these two revues laden with identical
scenes. The Shuberts, controlling the booking of out-of-town theaters, deftly succeeded in putting The Scandals in a house from
which it could not escape, while they cancelled the announced engagement of the Passing Show in Philadelphia and rushed it into the
Winter Garden.

The total result was the display by the Shuberts on a Thursday of the three aforementioned scenes which White showed off on
the following Monday. White, incommoded further by having to drop
two other episodes which the Shuberts used, waxed wrathy over
what was really the funniest joke in either revue--the fact that his
rivals had neglected to explain that the "stolen" numbers really belonged to a producer in Paris.

The current Passing Show is blessed with no such comics as
Allen, Dooley, and Patricola, but it has a fine actor in George Has-
sell, a very fair soubrette in Helen Shipman, an excellent singer in
Walter Woolf (which The Scandals have not), a number of good if not
funny dancers of the acrobatic sort, and much more taste and much
more speed than any previous Shubert production.

By and large the current Passing Show is a Winter Garden
show. It is expansive and expensive, violent and vaudevillian. Its
chief failing on the opening night was a decline from the Shubert
standard of amusing personalities; since then Phil Baker has been
drafted to raise the level of amusement. Its chief virtues lie in two
other departures from past performances at the Winter Garden. The
Passing Show has decidedly more pep and speed in the stage direction than any of the series, and it has more beauty and good taste
in costumes and settings than the Shuberts have exhibited even in
their exceptionally well-handled Viennese operettas.
                              --Kenneth Macgowan in Shadowland
                              (September, 1923), page 52.

THE PASSING SHOW OF 1924 (Book and Lyrics by Harold Atteridge,
    Music by Sigmund Romberg and Jean Schwartz; Winter Garden
    Theatre, September 3, 1924)

Compared with The Greenwich Village Follies and The Ritz Revue, The Passing Show at the Winter Garden, although better than
its predecessors, is pictorially just nothing. It has its moments, it
is true, but for the most part its effects are very woolworth. It
has James Barton, however, and anything that has James Barton has
a lot.
                              --Robert C. Benchley in Life (Oc-
                              tober 9, 1924), page 18.

THE PLAY'S THE THING (Ferenc Molnar, adapted by P.G. Wodehouse; Henry Miller Theatre, November 3, 1926)

Nobody is cute in The Play's the Thing; so there is no particular disgrace attached to enjoying it, yet it really shouldn't be as
amusing as it is. Molnar has written a very phony little comedy, shot
full of the old play-within-a-play hop to keep it on its feet, with another of those wise old butlers making cryptic remarks about life,
and he ought, by all rights, to have nothing at all to show for it.
Yet, thanks to the lines (many of them obviously Mr. P.G. Wodehouse's) and to the delicious playing of a delicious role by Reginald
Owen, the whole thing amounts to a highly amusing session.

We say that some of the lines are obviously those of the adapter, Mr. Wodehouse. Certainly he wrote the following:

> Mr. Blinn (to Mr. Nairn, the butler): What made you so
>   late?
> Mr. Nairn: I fell downstairs, sir.
> Mr. Blinn: That oughtn't to have taken you long.

It will probably be pointed out to us to-morrow that Mr. Wodehouse had nothing to do with these lines and that they are the ones
that Molnar is proudest of having written. Well, they sound like
Wodehouse, anyway.

And, having mentioned Mr. Blinn and Mr. Nairn, we may say
that they are excellent. We always expect this of Mr. Blinn, but we
should never have thought that another of those dialectic philosophers
in livery could be made bearable. Mr. Nairn does even more than
this--he makes him a delight, aided again by somebody's lines.
Young Mr. Crandall, whom we shall always remember as saying good-
by to Young Woodley in the doorway, also aids in the general work
of making a very nice evening out of nothing.
                        --Robert C. Benchley in Life (No-
                            vember 25, 1926), page 23.

THE PLOUGH AND THE STARS (Sean O'Casey; Hudson Theatre, November 28, 1927)

Quite naturally the reappearance of the Irish Players, this time
in a repertoire of Sean O'Casey's plays, created considerable advance
interest. So much has been heard of O'Casey's work on the stages
of Dublin and London and so little of it has been seen over here--
that one heard everywhere the question, "How will O'Casey's plays
emerge when played by his native group of actors?"

The first answer to this question came with the initial production of The Plough and the Stars, a play of the Dublin tenements during the historic Easter uprising of 1916. Into the merits of this play, as a true reflection of conditions in Ireland at that time, there is no use entering. Opinions will differ considerably on this historical aspect, but they can hardly differ on the dramatic intensity of the play itself. The present production, in many respects, is crude. The scenery is very unpretentious, and many important opportunities for effects in staging have been either lost or overlooked. But the acting is of the kind that creates its own illusion, independent of stage trappings. From the rich and boisterous comedy of Arthur Sinclair, as Fluther Good, a carpenter, to the poignant tragedy of Sheila Richards as Nora Clitheroe, or the more brutal intensity of Sara Allgood as the fruit vendor, Bessie Burgess, the acting of one and all has that unconscious spontaneity which makes for the finest theatre and the most realistic illusion. The carrying of this general excellence even to the minor parts is one of the conspicuous merits of this production at the Hudson.

It has been said that The Plough and the Stars gets off to a very slow start. So far as plot is concerned this is true, but the plot is the least important aspect of this play. As in the Theatre Guild's production of Porgy, one feels here the drama of background events even more strongly than the story of the particular people on the stage. It has about it the primal elements of a folk play. It is an account of passion and prejudice, of persecution, of humorous bravery, of reckless audacity and of the meannesses and weaknesses of humanity under the stress of terror. It is a play salted with quick humor even in the midst of crushing tragedy. Under these circumstances I feel that Mr. O'Casey has done well to use the first two-thirds of his play to create a broad and vivid portrait of the human elements around which the tragedy is gathering. He has let us see the birth pains of modern Ireland through the eyes of a dozen or more characters. Through them we gather the sense of multitude, of bigness and of infinite variation. If the play as a whole is not a masterpiece, it has at least been touched by the strokes of a master. If many will find it objectionable, they will at least find it hard to question the absolute dramatic sincerity of the author.

> --Richard Dana Skinner in The
> Commonweal, Vol. 7, No. 6 (De-
> cember 14, 1927), page 816.

POPPY (Book and Lyrics by Dorothy Donnelly, Music by Stephen Jones and Arthur Samuels; Apollo Theatre, September 3, 1923)

This department's enthusiasm for Madge Kennedy as a comedienne is common talk from Shanghai to Marseilles. And now that

Poppy has brought it to the attention of the world for the first time that she also has a charming voice and a graceful facility at stepping, there doesn't seem to be much left for us to do but just quietly explode and be gathered up with the rest of those unfortunates in the world's history who have died of love.

As if this were not enough for one musical comedy to effect, Poppy also brings W.C. Fields out of pantomime into a long and intricate speaking-rôle which he handles with all the ease and skill that he has in the past bestowed on billiard balls and cigar boxes. We are now ready to affix our seal to a proclamation declaring him eligible for any honors that he may care to attain in the musical comedy field from now on. He certainly has his particular area all to himself.

Perhaps somewhere into the above there has crept a hint that we think that Miss Kennedy and Mr. Fields are good. Such is exactly the case. We don't know how good Poppy would be without them, but then we don't have to speculate on that point. It has them. But there are some lines in the book that we are sure would coagulate if spoken by any one less adept than Miss Kennedy. And there are many perfect lines spoken by Mr. Fields that we are equally sure would never have been spoken at all had Mr. Fields not been playing the rôle. So much for the book.

It would have been almost more than we could bear to have Miss Luella Gear in the cast in addition to Miss Kennedy, but Miss Gear is given practically nothing to do to display her remarkable comedy gifts. In spite of this, she manages to display them, and the two song hits of the piece, "Mary" and "Alibi Baby," are safe in her keeping.

The score of Poppy was written by Stephen Jones and Arthur Samuels. Audiences have been listening to Mr. Jones' music for several seasons without knowing his name, for he has hitherto devoted his talents to orchestrating the tunes of other composers. All those who have ever bought their favorite song-hit in the lobby only to find out, on trying it over on the home-piano, that it was a thin, one-finger version of what they had heard in the theatre, will understand what the orchestration does for a good tune. Mr. Jones stands a good chance of coming into his own with Poppy.
                                        --Robert C. Benchley in Life
                                    (September 20, 1923), page 18.

PORGY (Dorothy and Du Bose Heyward; Guild Theatre, October 10, 1927)

The Theatre Guild opened its fall season with a complete de-

parture from all of its traditions. No members of the now famous
"acting company" could be espied on the stage. Nor was the invisible hand of an old-line Guild director to be seen. Instead an expert group of Negro players filled the stage--a stage made vivid with
the beauty of rags and tumult by Cleon Throckmorton's settings.
And the story of Porgy the gambler, beggar, murderer and crippled
knight-errant of Catfish Row was unfolded to the beat and direction
of Rouben Mamoulian--an entire newcomer to New York in the magic
of welding a play from a script and a score of almost unknown actors.

Mr. Mamoulian received, and deserved, a high and unusual
tribute from many of the first-night critics. However much the character of Porgy himself may have dominated Du Bose Heyward's book,
the play achieves its drama from mass feeling and mob action. Porgy
dwindles to the proportions of one instrument among many which carry the theme of Negro life in the crowded fishing tenements of
Charleston, South Carolina. His simplicity, his frank rascality, his
moments of grandeur, his confused vision of his limited universe--
these all become in the play the summing-up of forces eddying about
him, a reflection, too, and almost pale at times, of the whole passion
of a race. Mr. Mamoulian has taken the play in exactly these terms
and given it the heightened drama of a people rather than of persons. The result may be disappointing to those who wish to have
reproduced in the theatre the precise emotions and relation of interests they gathered from the book. But to those catching their im-
pressions fresh from the play--without preconceptions or elusive
hopes--the Guild production will flash with the ardor and the sultry
magnificence of folk melodrama.

Here and there the effort of the novelist and of his wife,
Dorothy Heyward, who helped him with the dramatization, to retain
the original personal strength of Porgy somewhat arrests the sweep
of the folk drama. This is no perfect play--nor does it rise at all
times above the level of a concrete realism which robs it of much of
its epic importance. It often uses verbal "shockers" instead of more
universal expressions of hate, love and despair. But these are the
occasional faults of a work whose larger proportions have the dignity
of eternal tragedy.

When Porgy was first being talked of as a possible play, I remember hearing discussions of the difficulty of assembling a competent
Negro cast. One argument held that the emotional qualities of the
Negro made him a born actor; another that these same qualities were
very dangerous to a successful production, because of the fact that
natural emotions often fail to carry across the footlights as well as
competently simulated, or synthetic, emotions. Whatever the theo-
retical value of this latter argument, Mr. Mamoulian has shown that,
with expert handling, the Negro can and does project the simpler
human passions with astonishing directness and stark power. Porgy
is an exceptionally well-acted play.

Rose MacClendon and Frank Wilson are, of course, both experienced artists. Much of the beauty of In Abraham's Bosom was
due to their finely graded performances. Wilson now plays Porgy,
lending to the part all the perception and understanding of a true
creative talent. Miss MacClendon as the God-fearing Serena once
more exhibits that fine restraint which first came to public notice in
Deep River. Evelyn Ellis, who plays Crown's Bess, I do not recall
having seen before. She raises her part to a level of considerable
distinction, and the same is true of Jack Carter as Crown. This
dark, hulking, heaven-defying figure creates many memorable moments in the theatre. The minor parts are all well taken, with a
pleasing sincerity and simplicity and, when needed, with a rich
sense of comedy.

The play is unpleasant in many details. It could hardly be
otherwise, granted its material, unless a far greater skill were employed to give universal strength to local realism. But I feel sure
that when all details are forgotten, one impression will live long, and
that is the surging tragedy of a race expressed in the spirituals, in
the mass hysteria, and in the occasional uncanny silences which
achieve theatric magnificence under the guiding hand of Mr. Mamoulian and in the settings of Mr. Throckmorton.

--Richard Dana Skinner in The
Commonweal, Vol. 6, No. 26
(November 2, 1927), page 642.

* * *

The Guild's latest offering is an American play, a dramatization of Du Bose Heyward's short novel Porgy, by the author himself
and his wife, Dorothy Heyward. There is plenty to enjoy in Porgy,
and I enjoyed it immensely: the singing, the settings, the lights
and costumes, and three or four scenes. Then there were bits of
pantomime and a good deal of first-rate dialogue. I am inclined to
attribute the moderate success of the play to these incidentals, all
of which are very pleasant.

But Porgy is a rather dull play. Perhaps I can make clear
to you (to all except those who like grand opera) what the matter
is, when I say that the play is a grand opera libretto in which most
of the dialogue is spoken rather than sung. Nearly all of the many
scenes are in reality bits of dramatized atmosphere, with little slices
of plot into which a thin thread of story is somewhat ineffectively
woven. Time and again the curtain rises on a scene full of movement
and color: there is a crap game, or a chorus singing spirituals, or
what not. After a few moments the chorus is gracefully (if obviously) disposed of, and the leading characters have what would in opera
be their duets, trios, and quartets of momentary drama.

The story of the lame beggar who wins his girl and loses her
is almost buried under a multitude of details; the local color blurs its

outlines and made me wish I were reading Mr. Heyward's story as it
was written. The dramatization of a story ought surely to add something that was not in the printed text, and something that is worth
having. What in Porgy the novelist was unable to put over (plus a
certain amount of what he did) should have been the aim of the
dramatisers. But this dramatization adds nothing save a few details
that are quite trivial, even if they are picturesque and moving.
                              --Barrett H. Clark in The Drama,
                              Vol. 18, No. 3 (December 1927),
                              pages 73-74.

R.U.R. (Karel Capek; Garrick Theatre, October 9, 1922)

        The Theatre Guild seems to be the only producing agency in
town with the ability to select plays which have novelty and dramatic
value, and which, at the same time, give a thought to some of the
Bigger and Deeper Things of Life. And, oddly enough, the Theatre
Guild makes money.

        Certainly no ardent supporter of The Bat or The Monster
could ask for a more devastating chill than that which sweeps up
and down your back in the third act of R.U.R., the first offering
of the Guild's new season. R.U.R. stands for "Rossum's Universal
Robots," the trade name for the fabricated men and women made by
Old Man Rossum and his son and the organization which they built
up around them.

        The robots look like men and women except for a certain rath-
er horrible sameness and a gigantic appearance around the chest and
arms. They were intended to do the work of the world, leaving humans free to devote themselves to culture and other luxuries. Then
someone thought of using them to fight wars. They were turned out
by the millions, and all went well until one of the scientists in charge
of the production decided to experiment a little and make them a bit
more like human beings. The result was a revolt of the robots of
the world and the almost complete extermination of the human race.

        The scene in which the last half-dozen humans are waiting in
the house surrounded by thousands of quietly approaching robots, is
terrific. And when one of the scientists, peering out through the
barricade, says with a shudder: "We shouldn't have made their
faces all alike," the effect is hardly to be borne.

        Like most of the good plays which the Guild has put on, there
is perhaps a little too much talk now and then, but it is excellent
talk, and well talked by a cast led by Basil Sydney and Kathlene
MacDonell. The symbolism of the story is obvious and, in the present depleted condition of the world, accepted by practically everyone

as true. Five years ago the Vigilantes would have run the play out of town, and, when next we want to go to war, the members of the Theatre Guild will probably be watched by Military Intelligence officers for having produced anti-war propaganda in 1922.
                                        --Robert C. Benchley in Life (No-
                                          vember 2, 1922), page 20.

THE RACKET (Bartlett Cormack; Ambassador Theatre, November 22, 1927)

I hold up for your admiration one of the best plays of its kind that has ever been written. The Racket, by Bartlett Cormack, will make it extremely hard for the old-timers to give us the same stock figures and situations that have entertained the public for nearly twenty years. Here we have doublecrossing, and stoolpigeons, inspectors and reporters, and the nice young man; even the girl, only she isn't the heroine, and no one will marry her. Mr. Cormack, who is a newcomer in the theatre (a Chicago man, I think; at least he went to the University), has beaten the other fellows at their own game. I find myself still wondering how he did the trick. The only thing he has done is to make his play credible; it seems simple enough. He has done this by making his characters real. Ah, there is the miracle. He has also done what I believe no one else has done; he has linked up the activities of his crooks and his police force with the municipal political "racket." At last, something genuine. And what a tremendous job he had explaining all the ins and outs of intrigue! You might think this would be dull, but it isn't.

Here we have the story of Captain McQuigg (played by John Cromwell), who has been transferred to a "quiet" district because he has dared to show a little independence in relation to his boss. Into the same district has come his old enemy Nick, a powerful political boss and a crook. The play tells the story of the struggle of these two men. Beginning in a most leisurely fashion, the action rises to a point of great intensity; with the fall of the curtain on act 2, you are as completely held as you are in What Price Glory. Then the play quickly unfolds in the last act. This is played chiefly by the Captain and Nick; it is a magnificent battle between two powerful men.

The details of the plot are skilfully introduced; not a character, no matter what his function, that is not truly and credibly etched. All I can say is that what I have been objecting to in crook plays is not the type, but the examples I was shown. Mr. Cormack has turned the trick. Unless he allows himself to copy the old formula without bending it to his own ends, I predict a brilliant career for him. His first play puts him into a class with the other recent "he"

dramatists who can handle the raw material of melodrama and use it
for the purpose of saying his say.
> --Barrett H. Clark in The Drama,
> Vol. 18, No. 4 (January 1928),
> page 106.

* * *

To our way of thinking the best cop-and-crook play of the
season, or several other seasons, is The Racket. This melodrama
is so real that you feel as if you had actually been covering Police
Headquarters for an evening. The author, Bartlett Cormack, is an
old newspaperman himself, and what is more, an old Chicago newspaperman, and his picture of the workings of the Chicago racket at
police headquarters and allied joints gives every indication of being
authentic, as well as highly dramatic. Certainly his picture of newspaper reporters, from the kid whose own City Desk doesn't know he
is working for the paper (Norman Foster) to the hard-boiled vet-
eran with a copy of the American Mercury in one pocket and a bottle
of Scotch in the other (Hugh O'Connell), is perfect. If we know
the veteran-type at all, he has an idea that one day soon he will
write a story for the Mercury out of a lot of dope that he has, but
somehow he never gets around to it. John Cromwell, Edward G.
Robinson and Marion Coakley also add to a cast which couldn't be
better.

Incidentally, it ought by now to be a truism that the best all-
around acting in the theatre to-day is to be found in the ranks
whose names are not in lights and probably never will be.
> --Robert C. Benchley in Life
> (December 8, 1927), page 21.

RAIN (John Colton and Clemence Randolph, based on a story by
Somerset Maugham; Maxine Elliott Theatre, November 7, 1922)

When we heard that a stage adaptation was to be made of the
bitter story by Somerset Maugham (called "Miss Thompson" when it
appeared in the Smart Set) we remarked cynically that it would probably be doctored up for the Baptist trade. And when it was announced that Jeanne Eagels, of Daddies fame, was to play the part
of the broken-down prostitute, you could have heard us laughing
harshly a block away and saying: "You see? It's going to be a se-
quel to Daddies, in which she turns out to be not a prostitute at
all, but his daughter masquerading for a lark."

Therefore, we deserved all we got in the nature of emotional
shock on the opening night of Rain, and we may say that seldom
have we experienced a more powerful thrill in the theatre than in the

last act, when the raucous sound of the old phonograph in the next
room signalled the salvation of Sadie Thompson from a horrible conversion.

The only thing that the adapters (John Colton and Clemence
Randolph) couldn't do was to make Jeanne Eagels look broken-down.
Her voice is coarse and her clothes tawdry, but, as she stands, she
is what you might call "in the pink of condition." And her performance is one of the most startlingly convincing that we have ever
seen.

Rain is not a play to take evengelically-minded people to....
On second thought, it is just the play to take them to.
--Robert C. Benchley in Life (No-
vember 30, 1922), page 18.

REBOUND (Donald Ogden Stewart; Plymouth Theatre, February 3,
1930)

Donald Ogden Stewart, the author of Rebound at the Plymouth
Theatre, is a member in more or less good standing of the Thanatopsis Literary, Luncheon, Inside-Straight and Parlor Recitation Club of
New York, of which Franklin P. Adams, Heywood Broun, George S.
Kaufman and a number of others in the same line of endeavor were
the founders. The Club is periodically in bad odor as a log-rolling
verein, but it has made one great gift to American culture. It is
father to a distinct school of humor. Unfortunately for the general
public, this humor is almost wholly oral. It consists in wringing
satire from commonplaces by pronouncing hackneyed phrases in a
certain slow, halting, apologetic, bashful manner which must be
heard to be appreciated. The secret lies in the peculiar intonation.
You or I could say, for instance, "Richard's himself again," without
raising any more than our auditor's eyebrows, but a member of the
Thanatopsis Club would pronounce the phrase so that the hearer
would feel the quotation marks and fall on his back in an agony of
laughter.

Mr. Stewart acts in his own play, and while he is on the stage
his words get themselves pronounced with the true and inimitable
accent and they are excruciatingly funny. But the other members
of the cast have not been baptized. They pronounce their lines
with the varying vocal apparatus with which they have been naturally endowed and, since the simple story of the comedy is related almost entirely in bright remarks, things very often get a little monotonous. Even as fascinating an actress as Hope Williams is a little
crushed by it all and rambles on and on in a tone of voice which
would sound to a foreigner who did not speak English as though she
had set out to count up to one billion in two hundred years.

Nevertheless, for two acts, there are enough intrinsically funny or shrewd observations on the theme of the play--how is a woman to get and hold a husband against such formidable vampires as Katherine Leslie?--to afford spasmodic bursts of laughter. Mr. Stewart has practically nothing to say, but the drollest way of saying it, and it is only the serious autopsy performed on Love in the last act that is continuously dull.

--Ralph Barton in _Life_ (June 27, 1930), page 16.

RIO RITA (Book by Guy Bolton and Fred Thompson, Music by Harry Tierney, Lyrics by Joseph McCarthy; Ziegfeld Theatre, February 2, 1927)

In _Rio Rita_ the gorgeous Mr. Ziegfeld has produced a gorgeous show in his gorgeous new theatre. No need to say what his play is all about save that the music is tuneful, the girls lovely, the sets magnificent, and the Ziegfeld Theatre itself something to be remembered. The murals are Persian in design, there are dancing rooms and lounges for intermissions, and the seats, praise be, have enough space between them and the next row so that long legged men may stretch in comfort. The Albertina Rasch girls "stopped the show" twice on our particular night, and that is something for a chorus to boast of, beautiful and agile though they may be. _Rio Rita_ is going to add many to the ranks of tired business men who make this sort of thing possible.

--Larry Barretto in _The Bookman_, Vol. 65, No. 2 (April 1927), page 209.

* * *

As for the production which opened the Ziegfeld [Theatre], we are violating no confidence in letting it out that it's name is _Rio Rita_. It is a musical comedy dealing with Mexico and will serve. The music is not so nice as one might expect from the authors of _Irene_ but no music this season (with the exception of that in _Peggy-Ann_) seems as nice as one might expect. The production (which includes the young ladies) is very beautiful. For comedy we have Miss Ada May and the Messrs. Robert Woolsey and Bert Wheeler, and when given anything at all approximating a funny line they do nobly by it. You can't expect much from lines like "It is simply magnolious!" but Messrs. Woolsey and Wheeler do contrive a very funny and sadistic slapping act just as the show is about to close.

The high spot of the evening is a Moonlight Ballet by the Albertina Rasch dancers, and this tribute comes from one to whom most ballets are so much poison. But this particular one seemed quite the loveliest we have ever seen.

A great deal of energetic soprano and tenor work is handled
by Ethelind Terry and the upstanding J. Harold Murray, and the
villainy by Vincent Serrano. The devilish motorcycle in the first
act which brings the comedians on with a barrage of gas explosions
is the work of the Indiana Motorcycle Co. of Springfield, Mass., and
we have already asked the courts for an injunction against them.

                              --Robert C. Benchley in Life
                              (February 24, 1927), page 21.

THE ROAD TO ROME (Robert Emmett Sherwood; Playhouse Theatre,
     January 31, 1927)

     We wish that gentlemen, as soon as they get to be editors of
Life, would not feel called upon to write a play. It puts this department in a very uncomfortable position. If we don't like it, we
can't very well say so, because we might be transferred to the Ran-
goon office. If we do like it, we can't very well say so, because
then we should be accused of logrolling. However, one can't say a
good word for Charles Dickens nowadays without being accused of log-
rolling; so here goes.

     Our Mr. Sherwood has written a play called The Road to Rome,
in which Miss Jane Cowl is starred and is supported by Mr. Philip
Merivale. Of it, Mr. Hammond of the New York Herald Tribune says
that it is a "good, canny show, worthy of the attention of the brightest as well as the dullest of the drama-lovers," while Mr. Woollcott
of the World calls it "a fine, nourishing, delightful evening in the
theatre," and Burns Mantle of the News, "satisfying entertainment
for adult seekers after diversion in the theatre." On the evening
of the next day Mr. Vreeland in the Telegram referred to it as "an
adult, incisive, heady entertainment on which New York may well
pride itself."

     Lest we should be accused of logrolling for Messrs. Hammond,
Woollcott, Mantle and Vreeland, we will say that, as often as not,
they are quite unreliable guides, although personally very charming.
In this case, however, we agree with them. The Road to Rome is
a good show, thank God!

                              --Robert C. Benchley in Life
                              (February 17, 1927), page 19.

                         *   *   *

     Robert Emmet Sherwood, known to thousands who read Life,
is likely to gain new audiences for himself with his play The Road
to Rome. It must have been inspired in a certain degree by The
Private Life of Helen of Troy and we wonder why John Erskine ever
let himself be caught napping. The dramatization of the book had

been announced so often that one grew weary of waiting. Possibly
the delay was due to the fact that Ethel Barrymore was not available for the part of Helen; but in the meanwhile Mr. Sherwood stole
a march. It must not be inferred that The Road to Rome is in any
sense taken from the book; but both are laid in olden days, both
concern a beautiful discontented wife who talks too much, and both
offer food for present day thought in the witty, casual speeches of
the ancients. Helen's private life is a plea for tolerance, and The
Road to Rome asks again, What price glory? Most of the asking is
done by Amytis, wife of the Dictator of Rome, who travels to Hannibal's camp outside the walls to demand what all the fighting is about.
Hannibal isn't able to answer that question, but he takes into consideration the fact that the love life of Amytis is far from complete.
The immediate result of this consideration is that Rome is saved.
Since Amytis knows it is dying of its own power anyway, we imagine
she was serving her own desires rather than her country. This is
no Mona Vanna delivering herself into the hands of the enemy for
a high purpose. The lines are sly, often risqué, and amused a
sophisticated audience. Jane Cowl as Amytis looked beautiful, and
Philip Merivale played Hannibal, the worn conqueror, with distinction.
At the end of the play Mago, his brother, reproaches him with having made his first mistake. Hannibal denies it. "I have made many
mistakes, Mago, but this is not one of them." Those who like spiced
comedy will not make a mistake either in seeing The Road to Rome.

> --Larry Barretto in The Bookman,
> Vol. 65, No. 2 (April 1927),
> pages 205-207.

ROSE-MARIE (Book and Lyrics by Otto Harbach and Oscar Hammer-
    stein II, Music by Rudolf Friml and Herbert Stothart; Imperial
    Theatre, September 2, 1924)

    We are a little late with praise for Rose-Marie, for it is al-
ready an assured success. As is customary with musical comedies
in which the score is a superior one, the book is a little too much
in evidence, but to hear Mary Ellis and Dennis King sing the music
which Messrs. Friml and Stothart have written is an experience so
far unequalled in the new season. In our expansive mood we laughed
occasionally at William Kent and, expanding even further, looked at
the program to see who staged the dances and found David Bennett
credited. His "Totem-pole" dance is one of the most effective chorus
numbers we have ever seen. In short, Mr. Hammerstein has produced to the hilt a show which deserves it.

> --Robert C. Benchley in Life (Oc-
> tober 2, 1924), page 20.

* * *

Turning to words-and-music, Rose-Marie impresses us as far and away the best musical comedy since Wildflower. It is pleasingly tuneful and colorful--and the chorus is a delight. Mary Ellis, Dennis King, William Kent, and Pearl Regay are the outstanding features of a smoothly balanced company, and the entire production is polished, unusual, and charming.

> --Stephen Vincent Benét in The Bookman, Vol. 60, No. 3 (November 1924), page 331.

THE ROYAL FAMILY (George S. Kaufman and Edna Ferber; Selwyn Theatre, December 28, 1927)

Then, to the rescue of the holiday spirit, came Miss Edna Ferber with two full-to-bursting packages, the first of them concocted in collaboration with George Kaufman. It is The Royal Family and is at the Selwyn.

The Royal Family is about as much fun as any play I have ever seen. The portrait of three generations congenitally and splendidly mad about their job, which is the theatre, it has vitality, and beauty, and pathos as well.

The play has no particular story, but flashes of many stories gleam through its lines. The curtain rises on the splendid apartment of the Cavendishes, and on an atmosphere of glamorous turmoil; telephones ringing, flowers arriving, boxes from the modistes, telegrams, breakfasts served all about and concatenated luncheons, the frenzied arrival of Anthony Cavendish, who has been in the movies and has knocked out his director and is about to jump for a steamer.

Before the play is over one knows all about the Cavendishes. How they rebel at the slaveries of the theatre, and plan to desert it (all but Fanny Cavendish, who is so old she knows better) and sometimes do desert it, but always come back. About how wild and difficult they are, but how gloriously alive.

And one understands perfectly the boredom, more awful than Paula Tanqueray's, which steals over Julie Cavendish's face when the lover to whom she has turned as a haven of refuge sketches the sheltered, plutocratic life they will live. And because one has learned that old Fanny Cavendish is too ill to go trouping again, though no one dares tell her, one watches her die drinking a toast to the great Aubrey Cavendish, with a sense that death has been as kind to her as life.

Oh, a grand play! Thank you, Miss Ferber and Mr. Kaufman. It's just what I needed.

The playing of it is not superlatively brilliant but maintains a
balanced excellence with Haidee Wright as Fanny Cavendish, Ann
Andrews as Julie, Otto Kruger as Anthony, Sylvia Field as Gwen,
and Jefferson De Angelis as Oscar Wolfe.

> --Charles Brackett in The New
> Yorker (January 7, 1928), page
> 19.

* * *

And then, as if to make things easier for us, two more personal friends, Miss Edna Ferber and Mr. George Kaufman, come a-
long with a swell comedy, The Royal Family, and all we have to do
is to point to the daily reviewers' estimates of it to show that we
were not biased in our delight at it.

It may very well be that, unless you are conversant with the
peculiarities and shop-talk of theatrical people, some of the dialogue
in The Royal Family will not send you into the guffaws it sent us,
for the play deals with the home life of a family of stage folk, founded
now and again on a very definite family group high in our national
theatrical roll of honor. But there is plenty of good, everyday
comedy in it, and several performances, notably those of Haidee
Wright as the regal grandmother, Ann Andrews as the lady star,
Otto Kruger as the bounding brother, and Jefferson De Angelis as
the general manager for the whole damned family, with Sylvia Field
and Orlando Daly thrown in as less recognizable but none the less
effective characters, which ought to make it a delightful show for
everybody.

> --Robert C. Benchley in Life (Jan-
> uary 19, 1928), page 21.

SACRED AND PROFANE LOVE (Arnold Bennett; Morosco Theatre,
    February 23, 1920)

Arnold Bennett's Five Towns reached the American stage last
Monday night in an episode play adapted from the novel, Sacred and
Profane Love. Constance and Sophia, the epic figures of The Old
Wives' Tale; Clayhanger, Hilda Lessways, Carlotta Peel are all familiar
to American readers, but it is Carlotta in the person of Elsie Fergu-
son who makes her first appearance in dramatic form.

And on the stage Carlotta becomes quite as appealing, though
not as engrossing a figure as she was in the book. She is a remarkable study in feminine psychology--first an impressionable English girl, with all the curiosity of girlhood, seeking to analyze her
soul struggle that has been caused by her mad infatuation for a
famous pianist, who is especially gifted in interpreting Chopin; later

a mature woman of the world, conscious of the uncanny knowledge
of life which her relation with the pianist has brought her.

Though Carlotta comes upon new experiences--as a novelist
she has won wide renown--it is her love for the pianist that remains
her dominant interest in life. She is poignantly aware of it when she
learns that he has become a morphine-wrecked derelict in Paris, and
she goes to rescue him and bring him back to his former self and
glory. And, of course, she succeeds. Then with a sardonic glance
to the box-office, Mr. Bennett shows his passionate friends deciding
to follow the conventions and live happily ever after.

The performance seems ironically keyed to the unevenness of
the play. One finds rough and smooth spots, naturalness and theatrical ranting, subtlety and heavy-handed portraits. One might
gather the impression that Mr. Payne's direction was not as auto-
cratic as it should have been.

Miss Ferguson--beautiful as ever to behold--was at her best
as the young girl of the first act. Here she endowed the part with
the youthful spontaneity, wholesomeness and peculiar British mannerisms required. In the later scenes her tones frequently took on a
pulpit cadence which marred the effect of her characterization. A
little more repression and naturalness in that remarkable voice of
hers and she might have scored another Outcast triumph. Jose Ruben
gave an excellent portrait of the pianist, making up in the morphine-
crazed scenes in realism and vividness what he lacked in distinction,
when he first appeared as the celebrated Chopin player. Renee de
Monvil gave an interesting sketch of a Parisian. Peggy Harvey was
a typical English flapper. J. Sebastian Smith, Olive Oliver, Maud
Milton, Alexander Onslow and A. Romaine Callender were adequate
in their respective parts.

A party of very young girls, seemingly from some advanced
school, occupied the vantage point of a stage box and drank in Mr.
Bennett's discussion of sexual relations with a sophisticated air that
would probably not be found in their grandmothers.

> --Louis R. Reid in The New York
> Dramatic Mirror (February 28,
> 1920), pages 362-363.

SAINT JOAN (George Bernard Shaw; Garrick Theatre, December 28,
1923)

It is the ingratitude of criticism that it can never forgive established genius for being anything less than complete genius. Like
a sharp-shooter, it hides behind a rock on the upward trail waiting,
and not without an occasional smirk, for genius to slip on a stray

pebble and descend ever so slightly from the heights. Genius is the
one thing in the world that can never afford to be even itself; it
must ever progressively be more than itself. The artist who has
painted a great picture or chiseled out a great statue or composed a
great symphony or written a great play must next paint a greater
picture or chisel out a greater statue or compose a greater symphony
or write a greater play. If he does not, criticism will wag its head
in doubt, and speculate on its earlier high estimate of him, and even
now and again, base ingrate!, laugh derisively. This modicum of
derisive laughter is now heard once more in certain quarters in the
instance of George Bernard Shaw and his latest work, Saint Joan,
and in these certain quarters and among these deplorable and igno-
minious scoffers I regret to report that I find myself. For though
the genius who has given us the greatest modern English ironic historical drama and one of the greatest of modern English comedies and
the best of all modern English satirical farces and the most intelligent of modern English dialectic fantasies has been gradually slipping
down, down the golden trail in the last decade and with his comparatively feeble one act plays like The Inca of Jerusalem and ten act
plays like Heartbreak House and two hundred and seventy-five act
plays like Back to Methusaleh has gathered behind the mountainside
rock an increasing number of skeptical francs-tireurs, there have
been, and are still, those of us who look to him stubbornly and
steadfastly to duplicate and even augment the dramatic gifts that
these years ago were so dazzlingly his. But each new year with its
new manuscript brings a new disappointment, and the treasures that
the man of genius has given us in the past are with an ignoble
thanklessness forgotten in the light of his more recent failures. I
say failures, although of course such a man never fails as meaner
men fail. There are streaks of diamond dust in even his shoddy.
Yet one expects--has the right of expectation that the man himself
has given us--that these streaks shall be not mere streaks. The
cobra eyes of criticism ever fasten their deadly glare upon the
artist who has already realized himself.

Thus, Shaw's Saint Joan, though it is a work far above the
general, fails to satisfy us. From a lesser genius, it might pass
muster--at least to a degree. From the hand of Shaw, it comes as
an affaire flambée. We have had the Drinkwater chronicle play, and
now we have a Vegetarian one. It is relatively undernourished; it
cries for Old Tawny and red meat. It is as literal as the inscription
on an envelope; the incidents of history with which it concerns itself are sieved through an indubitable imagination whose holes in
this instance are so large that the incidents remain much as they
were before. One looks for brilliant illumination and one finds but
pretty, unsatisfying candle light.

This Saint Joan seems to me to be for the major portion as affectation on Shaw's part to prove late in his career to a doubting
world that he has, after all, a heart. Why Shaw should want to convince the world that he has a sympathetic heart baffles me quite as

if Darwin or Huxley or Einstein had wished or would wish similarly
to convince the world of the fact in their own cases. But age ever
grows sentimental, and Shaw, whose genius lay in tonic cynicism and
disillusion, has grown comfortably sweet. Relatively so, true enough,
but the genius of incredulity and dissent cannot compromise with
the angels and survive. Yet one cannot convince one's self that this
late compromise on Shaw's part is not very largely another instance
of his sagacious showmanship, or in other words, conscious hokum.
Shaw is undoubtedly just selling his soulfulness to the box-office
devil. The sentiment of his rare Cleopatra was wise, and not without
its leaven of irony, and very truly beautiful. The sentiment of his
Joan of Arc is the bald sentiment of a wartime soapbox plea for
money to buy milk for French babies. It is effective in an open
and shut way, but its artistic integrity is suspect. Now and again
in the course of his play, Shaw, with the ghost of the Shaw of
fifteen years ago mocking him, becomes for a moment himself again,
and we get a flash of the old-time quick mind playing its smiling
skepticism in counterpoint to the Rubinstein "Melody in F" dramatic
motif. But splendid though these isolated moments are--the speeches
of the Archbishop of Rheims in the second episode and of the bench
of the Inquisition in the episode before the last are Shaw at his
best--they yet paradoxically, because of the confusion of the sentimental and rational keys, weaken considerably the texture of the
drama as a whole. The greatest love scene in all the drama of all
the world, a scene of tenderness and passion and glory all compact,
would fall promptly to pieces were the heroine to hiccough or the
hero, embarrassingly finding an alien particle in his mouth, to spit.
Shaw's hiccoughing is amusing and his expectorations are corrective
and prophylactic, but they do not jibe with the story of Joan as he
has set out to tell it and as actually he has told it. The story of
Joan is perhaps not a story for the theatre of Shaw, after all. It is
a fairy tale pure and simple, or it is nothing--an inspiring and lovely fairy tale for the drunken old philosophers who are the children
of the world. It vanishes before the clear and searching light of the
mind as a fairy vanishes before the clear and searching light of
dawn and day. It is a tale for the night of the imagination, and
such a tale is not for the pen of a Shaw. It is a tale for a Rostand,
or a Barrie at his best, or maybe for some Molnar. If irony creeps
into it, that irony should be an irony that springs not from the mind
but from the heart.

Speaking of Shaw's Joan from the purely theatrical rather than
from the library point of view, I cannot persuade myself that such
an essentially inferior--very, very inferior--play as Moreau's on the
same subject does not constitute a much more persuasive and convincing spectacle. It takes all for granted, and it accordingly sweeps
the necessary theatrical emotions up into its arms. It may be a very
poor play, but it never falters in its grim, artistically pitiable, passion. Shaw, to the contrary, has sung his dramatic "Marseillaise"
with a trace of British accent. The melody is there, still vibrant
and still thrilling, but with too many disturbing suggestions of Pic-

cadilly. It moves, yet we do not move. It thinks when we would
feel; it is literal when we would soar into the clouds of fancy; it is
humorous, with a Krausmeyer's Alley-species of humor--as in the
handling of the episode of the eggs in the first act--when we do not
wish to be humorous. The old Shaw jokes on the dunderheadedness
and insularity of the English somehow do not seem to belong here;
the George V. Hobart dream allegory of the epilogue is the old de-
risory Shaw making an obviously desperate last jump for the step of
the rearmost car as the train is quickly pulling out and away from
him; the episode of Joan kneeling, sword aloft, head bathed by the
spotlight man, before proceeding on her way to lift the siege of Orleans is the stained-glass stuff of the old Stair and Havlin circuit.
When Shaw is literal, his literality lacks vital simplicity; when he is
fanciful, as in the epilogue, his fancy is more literal still.

The Theatre Guild's presentation of the play is a poor one.
The groupings are amateurishly contrived; the direction is frequently
so lopsided, what with the characters quartered either wholly on the
left or right side of the stage, that the stage itself seems imminently
about to be resolved into a see-saw; movement is lacking; the manuscript is made static. Several of the actors are excellent, notably
Mr. Albert Bruning as the Archbishop, Mr. A.H. Van Buren as the
Earl of Warwick and Mr. Henry Travers and Ian Maclaren as the Chap-
lain of Stogumber and Bishop of Beauvais respectively. Miss Winifred Lenihan, however, is so unequal to the heroic demands of the
rôle of Joan that the rest of the cast is plainly concerned with laboriously playing down to her. She may convince the Theatre Guild management that she could save the armies of France but not for a moment does she convince the actors who play the leaders of that army
or, more important still, the folks out front. Her fire is a small blaze
at Sargent's Dramatic School; her voice--"a hearty, coaxing voice,
very confident, very appealing, very hard to resist," thus Shaw de-
scribes it--is dry, and coaxing and appealing only with the mechanical formality of a player-piano. Several of the minor moments she
manages nicely; in scenes calling for cold directness and chill reserve she is competent; but otherwise she lacks, and lacks entirely,
the warm spark that must set aflame such a rôle as this one.

--George Jean Nathan in The American Mercury (Vol. 1, No. 2),
February 1924, pages 241-243.

SALLY (Book by Guy Bolton, Lyrics by Clifford Grey, Music by
Jerome Kern; New Amsterdam Theatre, December 21, 1920)

Sally has a biographical value. It represents the rise of Marilyn Miller in the reign of Florenz the Second. Miss Miller has long
been a gay and graceful and fascinating exponent of the dance. She
has now achieved the distinction of stellardom. The honor is deserving.

Just as Miss Miller has been elevated from the ranks so Sally presents the gradual progress of a Greenwich Village Bohemian of a certain dancing skill to Ziegfeldian eminence at the New Amsterdam. It is a refreshing and novel version of the respectable old tale "from rags to riches," though the rags in this particular case are not unwelcome so strong is the pride of Bohemianism.

But Sally has dreams far beyond Greenwich Village. They extend to Forty-second Street, in fact. And when her big opportunity comes she is quick to grasp it. She realizes her dreams. She is a Ziegfeld star. She becomes the most conspicuous figure in the Ziegfeld domain. And when you stop to consider the figures in this domain literally you have a man's job on your eyes.

Miss Miller as Sally was never more captivating, never more airy in her grace, never more refreshing in youth. Handsprings are the order of the day when one attempts to pay her tribute. She danced divinely--and divinely is the only expression, as even the gods of the daily papers admit--and her performance is one of the daintiest things of an unusual season. Great is Florenz and Marilyn is his profit.

But risking an anti-climax there are other attractive features in Sally. There is, for example, Leon Errol, with his capital sense of the grotesque, dancing in comic contrast to Miss Miller. He was always amusing.

Walter Catlett, fresh from English conquests, is also present-- droll and imperturbable as ever, and with a bag of new tricks. Mary Hay exhibits her vivid personality--an ingratiating person in the role of an Irish Bohemian. The pictorial Dolores stalks through various scenes. Stanley Ridges and Irving Fisher take care capably of the sentimental song assignments.

And there are numerous young women of superlative beauty, bearing such names as Vivian Vernon, Gladys Montgomery and Barbara Dean.

The music is in the familiarly tinkly vein of Kerr, while Victor Herbert's ballet accompaniment is charmingly melodious. Guy Bolton performed a creditable task with the book.

But Sally is Marilyn Miller from her head to her toes--and her toes were always visible, for the New Amsterdam stage was raised above the footlights for the occasion.

> --Louis R. Reid in The New York
> Dramatic Mirror (December 25,
> 1920), page 1241.

* * *

There isn't much that needs to be added to Sally at the New
Amsterdam. Marilyn Miller takes care of the dancing and Leon Errol
handles the falling with great artistry. Jerome Kern has done what
Jerome Kern always used to do by the music. And Victor Herbert
has added a ballet.

This line-up in itself is enough to guarantee an advance sale
without the aid of a single quotation from the critics.

When you consider that Joseph Urban did the scenery and Mr.
Ziegfeld the producing, you will realize why it looks like a long, hard
winter for the New Amsterdam ushers.

> --Robert C. Benchley in Life (Janu-
> ary 6, 1921), page 25.

SATURDAY'S CHILDREN (Maxwell Anderson; Booth Theatre, January
6, 1927)

Maxwell Anderson, one of the authors of What Price Glory?,
author of Outside Looking In, and co-author of two other plays most
of us have forgotten, has written in Saturday's Children (Actors'
Theatre) a very neat and satisfying comedy after the manner of
Frank Craven's The First Year. Essentially, it is the old, old story
of a boy and girl who marry in haste and repent in Harlem. Neither
one of them really wants marriage, but the girl is "nice" and the
boy "decent." So they do as others do. The romance of sex is soon
dimmed by the troubles of keeping a flat on $160 a month. Quarrels
ensue, and they separate. But the sex impulse is too strong for
them, and they become reconciled. Mr. Anderson's treatment of the
idea differs from Mr. Craven's, because Mr. Anderson is more of a
philosopher. Indeed, he has so much to tell us that he introduces
the character of the girl's father, who is just a raisonneur, in order
to preach a little sermon to us. I will say that his words of wisdom
are both just and delightful, though wholly subversive of public morality. (I suggest that our guardians of other people's morals raid
Saturday's Children on these grounds.)

I am inclined to think that many critics who overpraised the
play for its philosophic depth were deceived by what Mr. Halevy
said, taking that to be what ought to have been shown dramatically
by the play itself.

But I must give the dramatist credit for writing intelligently
about a situation which so far in our theatre has been regarded almost without exception as a purely romantic matter. In uniting his
young people at the end, he takes great care to show us that they
are not reconciled for life; only that they are brought together by
sex attraction. He does not solve their problem for them, first be-

cause that is not his business, and second probably because he can't
do it.

> --Barrett H. Clark in The Drama,
> Vol. 17, No. 7 (April 1927), page
> 200.

SCANDALS see GEORGE WHITE'S SCANDALS

SECRETS (Rudolf Besier and May Edgington; Fulton Theatre, December 25, 1922)

Old stuff and bad shooting made bearable by Margaret Lawrence.
> --Robert C. Benchley in Life (February 1, 1923), page 21.

SEVENTH HEAVEN (Austin Strong; Booth Theatre, October 30, 1922)

We now know how it feels to be advised to see a play by enthusiastic rooters and then to go and see it. We missed seeing Seventh Heaven when it opened. Shortly after we began getting letters from readers asking why we hadn't reviewed it, as they considered it the best play in New York. People spoke in hushed tones about the acting of Helen Menken. We felt rather out of things.

Then last week we finally went. Perhaps we had heard too much about it. Perhaps we were tired. Whatever the reason, it seemed to us to be just about the most artificial, impossible thing we have seen this year. Without even the excuse of being translated from the French, it is written in that wooden scroll-work style which seems necessary to indicate that the characters are Parisians. Every once in a while someone says "le bon Dieu" or perhaps just "the bon Dieu" to lend Gallic flavor, and one character tells of someone "who lives across the rue from us." If he had been just a little more French he might have said "across the rue from nous." The situations are cut out of the same piece of linoleum as the language.

And since Miss Menken is now too well established as one of our most remarkable young actresses for any word of ours to trouble her, we may say that if her "big scene" in the second act is great acting, then anyone who can scream, wave her arms, and push over a table, is a great actress. That is, provided there is a band playing a French marching song outside.
> --Robert C. Benchley in Life (February 1, 1923), page 20.

SEX (Jane Mast; Daly's Theatre, April 26, 1926)

On the morning following the opening of the play entitled, with commendable candor, <u>Sex</u>, the newspapers were brief and a trifle pettish in their dismissal of it. "Cheap," "dull," "vulgar" and "tiresome" were a few of the descriptive adjectives used by the assistant dramatic critics who went 'way up to Sixty-third St. to cover it. Things looked pretty black for a Mr. C. William Morganstern, who had given himself the distinction of "presenting" the drama.

That night, there being nothing else to write about, we thought that we might trek up to see <u>Sex</u>, if, indeed, it was still running after its castigation in the press. We hate to sit in a half-empty theatre, but there might be a couple of good moral notes that we could strike on the subject; so up we ambled.

At the corner of Central Park West and Sixty-third St., we ran into a line of people which seemed to be extending in the general direction of Daly's Theatre. At first we thought that Mr. C. William Morganstern was being inserted in the stocks by the authorities, but the line was directed more at the box-office than at the public pillory, and what was more, the people standing in line were clutching, not complimentary passes, but good, green dollar bills. In other words, <u>Sex</u>, one of the most banal of plays, was a whacking hit, solely because the papers had said that it was "vulgar" and "bold" and because some one had the genius to think of its name.

And we feel that the Filipinos aren't yet quite ready for us to let them govern themselves.

The sudden rush to see <u>Sex</u> is not confined to the canaille. The agencies are hot after tickets and each night soft-purring limousines roll up with theatre parties of gentry, out "just for a lark." There must be <u>something</u> in this sex business, after all, to interest so many people.

As a matter of fact, <u>Sex</u> is no more startling and no more shocking and certainly no more reprehensible than a half-dozen others which have graced the local boards this winter. So far as one can judge, it was written with no more of an eye to the box-office than was <u>The Shanghai Gesture</u> or <u>Lulu Belle</u>. All three may claim that they are sincere pictures of that particular stratum of life which they represent, and certainly, once you have your characters talk as such characters really talk, you can not maintain that you are a sincere realist and the other man is a gross panderer to public depravity. Once you write a sex play, you must take your place with the other writers of sex plays and accept your royalties without wincing.

<u>Sex</u> is technically a much worse piece of work than <u>The Shang-</u>

hai Gesture and Lulu Belle, and is nowhere near dirty enough to pay you for getting up a dinner party of nice people to go to it, but we see no reason why it should come in for any eyebrow-lifting.

--Robert C. Benchley in Life (May 20, 1926), page 23.

* * *

Since you insist--or don't you?--on knowing a little about all that comes to town, there is no reason why mention should not be made of something called Sex, which has begun to play at Daly's. But let it be just a mention. As the title implies, it has nothing to do with sex. It is simply a poor balderdash of street sweepings and cabaret sentimentality, unexpurgated in tone, singing, sobbing and writhing as hard as it can to work on the biological facts of life and thus gain junior membership in the Yea-bo-Belasco school of drama.

How anything so undressed in its intentions can manage to be also so dreary is the chief wonder of Sex. Mae West, who plays the principal and most overheated part in it, is suspected of having written it, too. I know not, nor care. Sex would turn any Mr. Casanova into a Mrs. Grundy.

--G.W.G.* in The New Yorker (May 8, 1926), page 26.

THE SHANGHAI GESTURE (John Colton; Martin Beck Theatre, February 1, 1926)

There can be no question about it, life does have its physical side. And we, in the theatre, must face it, willy-nilly. (By the way, what ever became of that Willy Pogany case?)

Broadway in the past few weeks has met the situation squarely. The conspiracy of silence concerning sex matters which has existed for so long has been broken and at last we know where we stand. There is a differentiation between the sexes and the groups are called "male" and "female."

Mr. Woods has chosen to bring the message in one form with The Shanghai Gesture, Mr. Belasco in another with Lulu Belle. The methods are respectively those of the peep-show and the panorama.

In The Shanghai Gesture we see the various phases of commercial love on the Chinese curb market. Practically nothing is spared and one wonders if, after all, man isn't just an animal. (We must

*The New Yorker records indicate the writer was G.W. Gabriel.

take that matter up for discussion sometime.) The motif of the play
is one of a wronged woman's vengeance, and as every one in the
world likes to hear some one else get a good bawling out, the scene
in which Florence Reed makes the gesture from which the play de-
rives its name--if you could call a laying-about with vicious right-
and left-hooks to the jaw a gesture--is pretty sure to draw out tremendous applause and send audiences away in considerable of a twit-
ter.

The thing begins to assume just a touch of a stunt when the
Britisher who was to blame for everything finds that not only has he
one daughter as an inmate of Mother Goddam's establishment, but
two, which is certainly Nemesis running wild. The tragedy of the
Britisher's position is a little lightened for the audience by the fact
that McKay Morris, who plays the rôle, wears a dress-suit which is
just a teenty-weenty bit large for him.

However, The Shanghai Gesture accomplishes what it sets out
to do, and consequently seats are very difficult to buy.

--Robert C. Benchley in Life
(March 4, 1926), page 21.

* * *

For those who don't care for the morality of The Constant
Wife, there is always The Shanghai Gesture, as strictly moral a play
as I know. Virtue is rewarded and vice punished as swiftly as in
the Rollo books.

--Barrett H. Clark in The Drama,
Vol. 17, No. 4 (January 1927),
page 106.

SHOW BOAT (Book and Lyrics by Oscar Hammerstein II, Music by
    Jerome Kern, based on the novel by Edna Ferber; Ziegfeld The-
    atre, December 27, 1927)

Miss Ferber's other contribution* is at the Ziegfeld Theatre,
where her novel, Show Boat, appears made into a musical comedy by
Oscar Hammerstein II, and a musical comedy which, even though so
heralded by Philadelphia, I found thoroughly satisfactory.

Almost the whole torrential story has been put on the stage,
though the Grim Reaper has been carefully omitted from the dramatis
personae. Its rushing movement, its clearly defined characters, and
its general exuberance keep it from being lost, as it might well have

---

*Along with The Royal Family.

been with a triple A score by Jerome Kern, beautiful Ziegfeld settings, a beautiful Ziegfeld chorus, and a spirited negro one, to dis-
tract one's attention.

I can't imagine anyone's being disappointed at Show Boat except the out-of-town buyer who demands that a Ziegfeld show be a
fashion parade, or the pathological wise-crack addict.

The cast is pretty good, with Norma Terris a sweet Magnolia,
and Helen Morgan a lovely Julie. Bursting out of that parsimonious
phrase is Edna May Oliver as Parthy Ann Hawks. Charles Winninger
is rather better as Cap'n Andy than I have ever seen him, and
Howard Marsh, who sings Gaylord Ravenel, maintains more control
of his hands than he has in his recent appearances, though his fa-
cial muscles have an elasticity I felt was a mistake in a cast including
Francis X. Mahoney, the superb Rubber Face.

> --Charles Brackett in The New
> Yorker (January 7, 1928), pages
> 19-20.

* * *

Mr. Ziegfeld has a valuable genius for bringing his shows into
town with glowing prestige from the road try-out. The news from
Show Boat previous to its New York opening was that it was the
most remarkable show in the world. It is not quite that, especially
during its second act, but it is pretty swell entertainment just the
same. Charles Winninger, Helen Morgan, Norma Terris, Puck and
White and a company of Negro singers headed by Jules Bledsoe, and
that mysterious quality which Mr. Ziegfeld is able to inject into all
his shows, good or bad, make Show Boat worth at least a try at getting seats.

> --Robert C. Benchley in Life (Jan-
> uary 12, 1928), page 21.

SHOW GIRL (Book by William Anthony McGuire, Music by George
    Gershwin, Lyrics by Ira Gershwin and Gus Kahn; Ziegfeld The-
    atre, July 2, 1929)

I did not see Ruby Keeler (Mrs. Al Jolson) in the leading rôle
in Show Girl, having been bye-bye for several weeks. But I saw
her successor, Dorothy Stone, swing into the part gracefully after a
few days' rehearsal, and she fitted it like a glove or anything you
think up.

Theatrical environment has left its mark on this talented daughter of the equally talented Fred Stone. She has simplicity, charm and
an indefinable sweetness--an unbeatable trinity of talents these decadent days.

I wish also publicly to apologize to the Messrs. Clayton, Jackson and Durante. In a recent syndicated paragraph I said that they mistook noise for humor. I had heard their deafening café clowning in the intimacy of a night club and they had me snapping at my shoe laces.

Under the Ziegfeldian magic they stand out starkly as the funniest harlequins I have seen since Bert Lahr unloosed his jack-ass laugh a year ago. Especially Durante! Clayton and Jackson are merely able foils. It is all jovial commonness, the maddest horseplay, but so engaging I found myself watching them again the next night.

Durante has an unbelievably huge beak--"Snozzle" they call him in the play--but he does not have to depend solely upon his funny smeller for laughs. If I know anything about the theatre, which is becoming increasingly debatable, this low, vulgar person has positive genius.

With a voice like a buzz-saw hitting knots he puts over a song in a way no one else has since Al Jolson calloused his off knee wah-wah-ing to "Mammy." I refer you to his ditty "I Ups at Him," which has for its coarse theme a Broadway type of pathological lollipop, and yet I dare the most finicky to hear it and suppress a rousing chuckle.

The utter madness of this cock-eyed trio dominates the show. They appear as three property men and in one scene where Durante out-wynnes Ed Wynne in funny hats I have never heard such explosive laughter in the theatre.

Show Girl has no coherent plot. I imagine Ziegfeld merely used the title and tossed McEvoy's amusing book in one of his pink-beribboned waste baskets. It opens on the front lawn of a colonial mansion. It develops to be the dress rehearsal of a play and a stage director suddenly breaks up the stirring beauty to give the ladies of the ensemble merry hallelujah.

This offers an excellent opportunity to introduce Clayton, Jackson and Durante as the mad property men. The rest of the first act is a quick succession of scenes such as a Western Union Desk, a penthouse apartment, a street scene in Flatbush and the Club Caprice in New York.

The second act shows the façade--like a sail bellying the breeze --of the Ziegfeld Theatre. What a marvelous self-exploiter, this irrepressible Ziggy! The play deals more with Ziegfeld and his theatrical activities than with the tribulations of a show-girl but with the adroit skill that is fascinating.

The high spot of the second act is the scene "An American in Paris," which is a musical description by George Gershwin of a tour-

ist's experiences in the City of Lights. The score deftly suggests
the honk of the kitten-powered taxis acrawl on the boulevard, the
ancient queer streets, the velvety dignity of the Bois and the gaiety
of wine, women and song.

Threaded into the hodgepodge of scenes is the frail and hackneyed story of Dixie Dugan (Dorothy Stone), the little Flatbush girl
who made good in the city and had her name etched in lights in the
Broadway heavens.

Not to be overlooked in the array of talent is Eddie Foy, Jr.,
as the loosely gaited greeting-card salesman whose quick stepping
stopped the show as did his fleeting grimace which gave the familiar
old mouth curl of his beloved Dad.

Then there was that girl who never smiles, the divine dancer
Harriet Hoctor, who floated out from the wings airily like a puffball
and had several of us down-front antiquarians adjusting our ties and
running our fingers slyly through our thinning hair.

Show Girl is not Rio Rita nor Show Boat nor even Whoopee,
but it is about as fine entertainment as you'll find in town these hot
nights. It hasn't a song hit or the usual startling Ziegfeld stage
effects and I for one could get along without so many repetitious and
insinuating "yeahs" in the dialogue. Yet it has Dorothy Stone and
Clayton, Jackson and Durante should be enough for anyone.
                                   --Robert C. Benchley in Life (Au-
                                   gust 30, 1929), page 22.

THE SHOW-OFF (George Kelly; Playhouse Theatre, February 5, 1924)

It is getting a little monotonous, this hailing each week a fresh
comedy of American home-life as the best since The First Year. We
wish now that we had saved the First Year reference for The Show-
Off.

The Show-Off is by the author of The Torch-Bearers, and this
makes George Kelly pretty nearly our favorite American playwright.
His new play is not so continuously hilarious as The Torch-Bearers,
but it is a better play. And the way in which everyday small-talk
and idioms are strung together, with scarcely a wise crack or a gag-
line to lend artificial brilliance, is just about as smooth a piece of
work as we ever remember seeing, even from the pen of Mr. Frank
Craven.

The Show-Off also adds another to the season's long list of unusual characterizations. Mr. Aubrey Piper, as played by Louis John
Bartels, is a type so accurately observed and so uncannily brought

to life that at times you want to cry through the sheer joy of recognition. We have had nervy boys on the stage before, and we have
had slangy, back-slipping four-flushers, but Messrs. Kelly and Bartels have put something into Aubrey Piper that awakens something
new in you. It is a combination of blood-lust and perverted sympathy which you may not have felt for any one since 1910, or 1903,
or even 1898, when you yourself knew an Aubrey Piper in the flesh
and may or may not have relieved your feelings by pushing his nose
in with your thumb. The Aubrey Piper of to-day, as depicted by
Mr. Bartels, is much more blatant than at any other time in the world-
history of Pipers, because of the modern influence of the Personality
Plus courses and the Go-Getter school of business procedure. His
clichés (everything is "all washed up and signed on the dotted-line"
with this "bimbo from North Philly") are more vivid, and his opportunities for Big Talk are enhanced a thousandfold with the advent of
the automobile and the wonders of modern science. His cheery hailing of his mother-in-law as "Little Mother" and "Mother Fisher" alone
would mark him as a great creation.

The support, or rather, opposition given Mr. Bartels by his
"Little Mother" (Helen Lowell) is equally splendid, and Juliette Crosby
and Regina Wallace are both finely veracious in their portrayal of the
pitifully gypped sisters in matrimony. We note on the program that
Mr. Kelly directed the show as well as wrote it. Now we are sure
that he is the White Hope of American comedy, for better direction
we have seldom seen.

--Robert C. Benchley in Life
(February 21, 1924), page 18.

* * *

When the curtain went up on George Kelly's The Show-Off
and disclosed the suburban sitting-room with the walnut centre table
draped with a fringed tidy, the armchair upholstered in nondescript
velvet and the cheap brass chandelier, I said to myself: here is
still another of the attempts to duplicate Craven's The First Year,
and prepared myself for the worst. There was nothing in the first
fifteen minutes of the play to make me change my prefatory attitude.
These minutes were given over to a recitation by two characters of
a series of usual and immediately recognizable bromides which, according to the next morning's newspapers, constituted remarkable
powers of observation on the part of the author. (In New York, a
remarkable observation consists merely of the talent for hitting off
the more obvious and superficial characteristics of a dramatic character. Thus, any old woman who keeps on mouthing such familiar
sayings as "What a small world it is, after all!" or "My rheumatics
is troubling me again; it's a-going to rain," is uniformly greeted as
a well-rounded character made sharply photographic by the playwright's "observation.") A few more minutes went by, and down the
hills of Angostura still the tide of perceived stencils rolled. Then
something happened. There was a loud, reverberating, barbershop

laugh off stage and a moment later it entered in the person of a character named Aubrey Piper, and a moment later Kelly's play took on life and shrewd humor and some very real observation. Did I say the play? If I did, I am foolish, for the play did nothing of the kind. But the character of Aubrey Piper did, and in the doing caused the play to fade gracefully and unnoticed into the background, after the manner of an oil painting in a window full of tin-types.

This Aubrey of the belted overcoat and the latest Kuppenheimer modes, with his Mr. Simms of Seattle handshake, oppressively expansive nature, egregious prevarications and glowing regard for himself, is, for all the leaven of burlesque which the author has injected into him, as authentic and honestly entertaining a character as the native drama has given birth to. Jimmy Gilley in Bought and Paid For, the fat boy in George Cohan's Broadway Jones who won't smoke cigarettes because they soften the brain, the coon in George Ade's County Chairman objecting to certain cigars because they are rolled "too severe," the young boy in Tarkington's Intimate Strangers, this Aubrey Piper--in such as these flows some of the best blood of American drama. If our dramatists were as expert in drama as they frequently are in dramatic character, the American theatre would be rich indeed. Kelly, for example, has achieved this excellent Aubrey, but not much more. His dramatic method is largely the method of the vaudeville sketch: five minutes of jokes followed by five minutes of drama, and repeat. There is no get-together. Again, his invention is crude. When, for example, a father dies in the hospital and the family rushes off to his bedside, he keeps the more loving of the daughters at home for no other reason save that he has to keep her at home or stop his play. Still again, he rings down on nothing more tangful than the ancient E.E. Rose-Winchell Smith success of the million dollar invention. But the Mons. Aubrey thumbs his nose derisively at his creator's other shortcomings and blinds the audience to them. A thoroughly amusing figure. And played by a vaudeville actor, Louis John Bartels, to perfection.

> --George Jean Nathan in The Amer-
> ican Mercury (Vol. 1, No. 4),
> April 1924, pages 500-501.

THE SILVER CORD (Sidney Howard; John Golden Theatre; December 20, 1926)

After all our worry about taking Ned McCobb's Daughter off to alternate with The Silver Cord, it turns out that The Silver Cord is quite as good a play as Ned McCobb's Daughter. In it, Sidney Howard has written a fine and intensely interesting story of fanatic mother-love, which gives him the unique distinction of having two of the best plays on Broadway at the present moment.

While the problem presented would have been a bit more thrilling had the mother been a little less explicitly classified as a downright Bad Influence, this was offset in our mind by the fact that the
young wife, who proudly designated herself as a sort of "scientific
Nemesis," was almost as sinister a figure as the mother. Perhaps Mr.
Howard did not intend her to be, but personally we would almost
have preferred to be coddled by a doting mother to having the "arid
wastes" of our mind worked upon for the rest of our life by a lady
scientist who wanted to "bring us out." To our way of thinking,
David let himself in for a pretty slim time in New York with Christina
and her buddies in the Rockefeller Institute. If he was the kind of
architect we suspect he was, he would have done much better to let
his mother set him up in Phelps Manor and leave those comfortable
"arid wastes" in his mind alone. A "scientific Nemesis" is no fun to
have around the house. Both women seemed to us to be pretty terrible people.

The high grade of The Silver Cord as a play is enhanced by a
performance which leaves little to be desired. Laura Hope Crews as
the mother, Elizabeth Risdon as the militantly modern wife, Margalo
Gillmore in several superb moments as the jilted fiancée (and here
again we protest that it was much better that she and Robert did not
marry, Robert being what he was), Elliot Cabot as the refreshingly
arid son, and Earle Larimore as the mother's boy, all deserve higher
praise than we can give them in this space. The Silver Cord is
certainly something to be seen and acrimoniously debated.
                                        --Robert C. Benchley in Life (Jan-
                                            uary 6, 1927), page 21.

                            *   *   *

It seems to be a Sidney Howard year. Last month the Theatre
Guild produced his Ned McCobb's Daughter, and following closely on
that event the same organization offered The Silver Cord. While the
former was in many ways admirable and found favor, this new piece
bids fair to be a hit, and it is by all odds the better of the two.
The Silver Cord is that tenuous bond between mother and child which,
often unbroken at birth, continues through the later years growing
in strength until it has the power of a cable and is about as inescapable. In the good old fashioned days we used to call it apron
strings, thereby saving sensibilities and lending an atmosphere of
the kitchen rather than the clinic to the subjects; but times have
changed and outworn metaphors must be changed with them. In this
play Mr. Howard has leaned heavily on Freud and his contemporaries.
The result is altogether excellent. The only trouble with Mrs. Phelps
was that she loved her sons too much. That seems almost a virtue,
but the playwright promptly goes about making a most damning case
against the poor woman. She coddled them to a degree that was
nauseous, she planned their lives serenely if not sensibly, and she
interfered with their love affairs to such an extent that she nearly
created a tragedy. David, the eldest, had to go to Europe to find

a wife, and his brother Robert was having hard sledding with his fiancée when the married pair returned to the old homestead on a visit which they had intended to be brief, but which the mother intended to be permanent. In the space of one short evening she showed her new daughter-in-law her place and broke off the engagement between Hester and Robert. More than that, she engulfed both sons in such an ocean of mawkish love that by some hocus-pocus they came to believe she was the finest and most self sacrificing woman who ever gave a dose of soothing syrup. She admitted that the boys were the proudest jewels in her maternal crown, and it was not until poor little Hester floundered into the duck pond in her efforts to escape this Cornelia and her Gracchi that Christina, the wife of David, turned and rent her mother-in-law in fine style. Even then Mrs. Phelps won half a victory, for while David was borne off to New York and a new life, Robert elected to remain behind, the victim of his mother's devotion.

Mrs. Phelps is brilliantly played by Laura Hope Crews who must revel in this rôle, so rich is it. Her acting is unerring, sophisticated and witty, and when in the end she makes her speech of rebuttal against Christina one is tempted to believe she has the better of the argument, so convincing is she. Elizabeth Risdon is admirable as the daughter-in-law, and Margalo Gillmore gives a poignantly lovely performance as Hester. We feel like cheering for this young actress. Miscast in Ned McCobb's Daughter, she here has a part which shows what she can do, and that is a great deal. Elliot Cabot as David and Earle Larimore as Robert do not have quite so happy a time of it. It is difficult to portray men as weaklings and at the same time make them good fellows, which was obviously the playwright's intention. In particular we were sorry for poor Mr. Larimore who had to go around arranging flowers in vases and then stand off to judge the effect, indicating thereby that he had the leanings of an interior decorator, whatever they may be. Some of the verisimilitude of the play has been sacrificed for sheer farce, especially when Christina comes into her husband's bedroom and his mother hustles him into a wrapper while the bride stands with downcast eyes. Elliot Cabot in striped pajamas is not such a fascinating sight as to cause instant havoc in the heart of maid or matron, but evidently his stage mother thought him so. That the play presents a living problem, however, is evidenced by the fact that we began making a list of ladies we could not take to it. It was considerable and consisted entirely of married women with children. Were it not for the lesson that it teaches we should advise advertising The Silver Cord as "For Men Only."

--Larry Barretto in The Bookman,
Vol. 65, No. 1 (March 1927),
pages 70-71.

THE SILVER TASSIE (Sean O'Casey; Irish Theatre, October 24, 1929)

What with the panic and postponements, there is but one theatrical opening to report this week. I am not referring to the panic
in Wall Street (I've got some heart), but to the panic that grips the
throat of a producer when he looks upon his work on the sixth day
in Atlantic City and finds that it is not so hot. There are too many
good plays running to risk bringing in an indifferent one, unless it
can be brought in wearing false whiskers on a night when there are
so many other openings that it won't be pointed at rudely, or unless
the producer happens to be The Irish Theatre, Inc., with a racial
appetite for suffering and injustice.

I can sit through Irish drama with the same ferocious glee that
one feels when one bites down hard on an aching tooth, or that an
Irishman feels when he thinks of Ireland, provided the curtain goes
up on a dismal kitchen in a cottage in Galway, or Donegal, or any
county outside of traitor Ulster. Old Michael must be sitting at a
table in the centre of the stage pretending to be eating something
from a bowl which is obviously as empty as the last fifteen rows of
the orchestra. Old Maurya, his wife, must be shuffling back and
forth, between the table and a painted stove, raising her two hands
from her two hips now and then to paw the air with them to stress
a point in her flowing complaint about things in general. Old Michael, on the other hand, never says anything but: "Ay!" To keep
the play going, Old Maurya occasionally stops to peer through the
window at the back and wonder when Cathleen will be after coming
back from the fair with that young spalpeen of a Larry. At the left,
sitting among the electric light bulbs in the footlight trough, there
must be an idiot boy with a flute. He is the author's Mouthpiece
and he delivers himself of the philosophic burden of the play in the
voice of one who would rather have been born Chauncey Olcott than
himself.

From that point on, I can sit out in front and like it, in a
way. I don't much care what happens after that, so long as the
thing doesn't turn expressionistic on me. When the actors begin
prancing about the stage and chanting unborn sentences in unison
to express the ghastly futility of this and that, I begin to be a nui-
sance to the people sitting around me. I fidget something disgrace-
ful. At The Irish Theatre's The Silver Tassie the other night, during the second act when a batch of soldiers were intoning the author's
words in what might have been Gaelic for all I was getting out of it,
I suddenly went rigid all over at a moment when my feet were planted
firmly in the back of a seat in row B, which resulted in my tearing
row C from its screws and pitching myself, Peggy Joyce and a young
man in a tail coat (could he have been the author, dressed that way
in case?) into row D behind us.

There doesn't occur to me any good reason for allowing what
has, for the past hundred years, been called "modern art" to pene-
trate behind the footlights. It is all very well for new forms to creep
into painting. Painting died of old age and pernicious anaemia about

1880, and it took all the -isms going to get the breath of life back
into the old girl's carcass. What Bouguereau and Meissonier carried
to the grave, it required a whole mob of Cézannes, Rousseaus, Sis-
leys, Monets, Renoirs, Matisses and Picassos to revive and set up in
business again. But the drama did not die. It is still blustering
along, as tough and apple-cheeked as ever. Look at Street Scene
or Strictly Dishonorable to see what can be done with just plain,
ordinary writing--in America--this year--in spite of the talkies and
all the other influences for evil.

     Scenery, it appears, can go as "modern" as it likes. The set-
ting in the second act of The Silver Tassie and a trick with the
shadow of a lamp shade in the third act are tremendously impressive.
But when the actors, who are, after a manner, human beings, cease
to act like human beings in the second act of this opus, they become
excessively arty and foolish--so arty and foolish, indeed, that it
casts a blight over the excellent and realistic third and fourth acts
of the piece which permits you not for a single minute to forget that
you are sitting in a theatre in Greenwich Village, across the street
from Ye Olde Pinke Horse-Blankette Inne.
                         --Ralph Barton in Life (November
                         15, 1929), page 24.

SIMPLE SIMON (Book by Ed Wynn and Guy Bolton, Music by Richard
     Rodgers, Lyrics by Lorenz Hart; Ziegfeld Theatre, February
     18, 1930)

     This is the third attempt to work something about Simple Simon
into this page. And now that I stop to think about it, I think, and
think, and can't remember anything but Harriet Hoctor, in pinks,
leaping bewitchingly over the hurdles in the most stirring and beautiful ballet I've seen for three years and six months (name and ad-
dress on request). In fact, I am likely to go off into a day-dream
about Miss Hoctor in the middle of conversations.

     Ed Wynn, of course, is funny. I start laughing at him when
I read in the paper that he is coming to town and go on laughing
through the advance notices and the pictures in the rotogravure sec-
tions, and laugh all the way to the theatre. And when he comes
out and tells a lot of old jokes that I succeeded, when I grew old
enough, in inducing my father not to tell any more, I laugh just the
same. Ed Wynn is funny. It doesn't matter what he does. I wish
he'd had more of his fool inventions in this show, but that doesn't
matter, either. He is as funny as they come, and there's that.

     Simple Simon, being a Ziegfeld baby, is, naturally, superbly
mounted and the girls are all pretty.
                         --Ralph Barton in Life (March 28,
                         1930), page 18.

SIX CHARACTERS IN SEARCH OF AN AUTHOR (Luigi Pirandello;
    Princess Theatre, October 30, 1922)

     Those of us who have been moaning about the lack of original-
ity in the theatre have been given a run for our passes this month.
Mr. Pemberton with Six Characters in Search of an Author, Mr.
Brady with The World We Live In, and Mr. Tyler with The 49ers
have seemed to say through their clenched teeth: "You want something that hasn't been done before, do you? Well, take that, and
that, and that!"

     Six Characters in Search of an Author is a translation from the
Italian of Luigi Pirandello, and is a fascinating combination of George
M. Cohan and Plato. To the bare stage of the theatre where a company is gathered for rehearsal come six characters fresh from the
imagination of an author who has disowned them. They seek expression through the actors. They ask to be born, and specify their
conditions. (This description is rapidly getting involved, and I
haven't the slightest idea how it is going to end, but it can't be any
more complicated than the play itself.)

     Well, anyway, the actors try to put on the play, and play-
wrights who have seen their works "adapted" by managers and "interpreted" by actors will sit in savage delight through the massacre.
In the end the manager decides that the thing is too sombre and re-
hearsals are begun on another piece. The six characters, or what
remains of them, start off again on their search for adequate expression. And the audience reels to its feet, groggy but with the curious sensation of having been doing some intensive thinking on its
own hook, and, what is more, enjoying it hugely. Six Characters
in Search of an Author is nothing to go to direct from a children's
party, with paper caps on your heads, but a good dose of meta-
physics never hurt anyone, and this is about as pleasant a way to
take it as you will ever find.
                              --Robert C. Benchley in Life (No-
                                vember 23, 1922), page 18.

THE SONG AND DANCE MAN (George M. Cohan; Hudson Theatre, De-
    cember 31, 1923)

     Mr. Cohan, having made his annual five-star announcement of
his impending retirement from the theatre, enters town with two productions, just by way of showing us what we shall be missing next
year and in the long years to come. We wish we might be able to
say that, even if he really stuck to his threat, he wouldn't be
missed, but we can't. There is no one living who could take two
such banal pieces of work as The Song and Dance Man and The Rise

of Rosie O'Reilly and turn them into goldfish as Mr. Cohan has done.
There is no one lving who has the gift of de-bunking that he has.

The Song and Dance Man is made by the personal presence of
Mr. Cohan in the flesh. As a play, it could end satisfactorily at the
curtain to each scene. It has one funny line ("The worst thing I
wish for you is that you fall asleep and wake up with a Swedish dialect"), but a great many lines which seem funny at the time, thanks
to the author's reading of them. This, by the way, in direct refuta-
tion of our contention last week, in speaking of Petrova, that an author's presence in his own play detracts from the illusion. Here it
is the third week in 1924, and we have been proved wrong eleven
times already.

Much as Mr. Cohan would be missed in person, his influence
in kidding at large would be missed even more. Without his touch,
The Rise of Rosie O'Reilly would be terrible. Even with it, it is
barely distinguishable from The O'Brien Girl and Little Nellie Kelly.

Is it possible that Mr. Cohan has for three years been deliberately writing the same show, line for line, step for step, with
the secret purpose of showing what can be done to the American
public? After The Tavern, we are willing to endow him with anything.
                              --Robert C. Benchley in Life (Janu-
                                ary 17, 1924), page 18.

STRANGE INTERLUDE (Eugene O'Neill; John Golden Theatre, Janu-
    ary 30, 1928)

Two years ago Eugene O'Neill startled us somewhat by reverting
to the use of masks in his play The Great God Brown. Of course he
did not go back to any known tradition in the use of masks, and
adopted the interesting if somewhat confusing method of having the
masks follow the outlines of the actors' faces. Moreover the masks
were used only on occasions to indicate the difference between one's
outward attitude toward the world and reality and one's inner state
of mind. In his latest play, Strange Interlude, O'Neill has startled
us in somewhat similar fashion by reverting to the use of the aside.
His stage characters enjoy the privilege of a double dialogue, part of
it expressing the thoughts they are willing to show to the world, and
part of it expressing only their innermost feelings. This is a technical novelty which, in the opinion of many of the critics, adds enormously to the scope of the drama, giving to the play the benefit,
generally reserved only to novels, of describing motives as well as
speech and action. On the other hand there are many who believe
that really skilful playwriting and acting enable an audience to grasp
inner motives quite as clearly as when they are enunciated after this
O'Neill method.

This much is certain, that Mr. O'Neill has managed to contrive a dramatic story of absorbing interest, and that he has no difficulty in holding the attention of the audience for five hours, and across the stretch of a dinner intermission, as against the two and one-half hours permitted to the average playwright. In spite of this, I am not convinced that he has achieved, in the full sense, a great play. Strange Interlude probes deeply and terribly into the recesses of a neurotic mind, as summed up in the character of Nina Leeds. It probes also into many other types of mind, and as a work of intuitive psychology, it is undoubtedly a monumental achievement. But to regard it as a great play, stated in the terms of the theatre, is somewhat like regarding a piece of statuary as a great piece of sculpture because the brush of a painter has added to it the color of life. Such a statue might be a great work of art, in the sense that it combines the finest qualities of two of the arts, but it might be neither a great statue nor a great painting.

We admit this distinction readily enough in the case of opera. Richard Wagner attempted to fuse the arts of the drama and of music and, being unwilling to have his works spoken of as opera, solved the problem simply by calling them "music dramas." Under this name we are often willing to call them great works of art, with a general inclination to admit that the music is greater than the dramas themselves. But we do not say, for example, that Parsifal is a great play, although its interest and its emotional intensity are vastly heightened by the musical score. For this reason I think it is a great mistake and a distinct injustice to other dramatists to speak of Mr. O'Neill's combination of two separate arts as a great play—to call it possibly the greatest play produced by the American theatre. He has combined the arts of the novelist and the playwright and given us what, for want of a better description, we can only call a dramatic novel. And in this particular example, the element of the novel achieves higher and greater proportions than the element of the play, just as the music of Wagner achieves a greatness lacking in his dramas alone.

Certainly there can be no objection to creating this new form of expression, and when it is handled with the power and ruthless searching of O'Neill's mind, the resultant whole deserves presentation. But although the fusion of the arts can be a fine thing in itself, it is very misleading to assume that the separate arts have ceased to exist, or that henceforth no play can be truly great which does not make use of the art of the novel as well. The bald truth is that Mr. O'Neill has covered a great deal of second-rate playwriting by some very intensive use of the novelist's privileges. In spite of certain obvious faults, Sidney Howard's The Silver Cord is a far finer play than the dramatic elements of Strange Interlude considered alone. Yet the final product of O'Neill's pen, provided you do not think of it solely as a play, is vastly more absorbing and exciting than anything Sidney Howard has written.

What O'Neill has really done is to take a rather morbid story of mediocre people and give it an almost universal importance by a careful side exposition of the motives, conscious and unconscious, that are guiding his characters. These asides are vastly more interesting than anything in the dialogue proper of the play. They touch upon experiences common to nearly all mankind. It is as if O'Neill were applying a sort of spiritual X-ray to the souls of his characters. To do this it is necessary for the characters, every few moments, to remain absolutely stationary and, in a tone quite different from the ordinary dialogue, speak out the truth which they are concealing from each other. A good actor would probably tell you that at least half of these concealed emotions could be expressed through gesture, or manner, or through the hundred and one tricks known to the artist. An actor might even make the suggestion that the play, with a little skilful rewriting of the main dialogue, could convey in conventional form everything which Mr. O'Neill has now placed in the asides. This, however, is rather unfair to Mr. O'Neill's intention and also to what he has actually accomplished. For in many of the asides Mr. O'Neill has made the characters reveal certain hidden depths of which they themselves are probably almost unconscious.

The human mind seems to work on at least three main levels—the thoughts it shares with the world in speech or writing, the private thoughts it reserves, and the deeper sources of action or feeling which it often strives to keep from its own consciousness because of the cruelty or the selfishness or the pride which they seem to reveal. The old-fashioned aside merely gave the audience the advantage of touching the second level. Mr. O'Neill's asides dive to the depths of the third level, the repressed thoughts, the unworthy emotions, the egotism, the pride or the possessiveness that so often stimulate us to apparently unaccountable action. It is this revelation of the semi-conscious or sub-conscious which constitutes Mr. O'Neill's unique achievement, and which will undoubtedly stand to many for the greatness of his play, whereas in fact it stands only for the keenness of his intuition as an analyst of human emotions and actions.

There is a great deal of Jung and a certain amount of Freud mixed up with the intuitions which are purely those of Mr. O'Neill. His explanation of the curious action of Nina Leeds would not find universal acceptance among all schools of modern psychology. We can imagine a cynical behaviorist remarking to himself, "Interesting if true." Thus when Nina's father dies, Mr. O'Neill assumes that the curious and unimpassioned love which she bestows upon the novelist, Charles Marsden, is a psychological transference of the love previously given to her father. On the other hand, this particular attachment might be explained on the ground that every human being desires at certain times the comfort of a love which does not ask too much in return. Or again, it might be said that Nina is merely exhibiting an automatic reaction from the intensity of her other emotional experiences. And so it is that throughout the play you have a hundred varied explanations for events, through motives which,

while intensely interesting to unravel and often approaching universal truths, are so limited by a particular psychological creed as
to lose much of their general importance. In some recent popular
murder trials we were regaled with interpretations supplied by various schools of psychologists. Each one was interesting in its own
way, but they often differed radically in their deductions from known
facts. Mr. O'Neill's asides, then, vary greatly in importance according to the particular prejudices of the audience and according to
which way you happen to account for the vagaries of human actions
under given conditions.

   The story of the play itself is comparatively simple. Nina Leeds
is engaged to a young aviator who is killed. She might have married him but for the opposition of her father. She then decides to
go into hospital nursing and gives her love promiscuously to various
crippled soldiers in the belief that she is somehow making reparation
to her dead hero. She discovers her mistake and marries Sam Evans,
a likely young man with whom she believes she can lead a normal
life undisturbed by any great passion. To her horror, however,
she discovers there is a history of persistent insanity in the Evans
family. Rather than bring another child of this tainted blood into
the world, she destroys the life that is already started and, with the
idea of satisfying Sam's craving for fatherhood, arranged to have a
child by another man named Darrell. Sam, knowing nothing of this,
and inspired by his sense of fatherhood, progresses rapidly in material things and becomes a highly successful business man, of rather
mediocre mentality. Nina, in the meantime, has fallen in love with
Darrell and years of her life thereafter are spent in trying to re-
solve the conflict between her love for him and her determination to
make Sam Evans happy at all costs. The child grows up having a
distinctive hatred for his own father and a genuine devotion for Sam
Evans, his supposed father. During all of this time Charles Marsden,
the novelist, has been always on hand, ready with comfort and unselfish devotion, but quite unable to inspire in Nina any more complete sense of love. In the end, Sam Evans dies from a stroke, Nina
and Darrell find that the passion of their youth has gone, and Nina
settles down in the sunset of her life in the tranquil companionship
of Marsden, her son having left her to marry, in spite of her frantic
efforts to hold him.

   Nina is thus meant to typify in herself the possessive and absorbing type of woman who draws to herself, and involves in her
own neurotic cravings, the lives of all she touches. It is not until
the very end of her days that she fully relinquishes the desire to
gather to herself every form of male love. The explanation which
Mr. O'Neill affords by means of the asides to this curious human en-
tanglement, is the outstanding interest of this obviously unpleasant
theme. The Theatre Guild, as usual, has bestowed the utmost skill
upon the production of this dramatic novel. Lynn Fontanne, in re-
creating the character of Nina, has achieved a height of artistry quite

beyond anything now current in the American theatre.
--Richard Dana Skinner in The
Commonweal, Vol. 7, No. 16
(February 22, 1928), pages 1098-
1099.

* * *

We might as well get this out of the way right at the start:
Eugene O'Neill's Strange Interlude is a highly important play, probably a great one, and one which is bound to mark a turning-point
of one sort or another in dramatic history.

Personally, as one who sat constantly interested from 5:15 in
the afternoon until 11 at night, with an hour's recess for dinner,
we were at first irritated to the bursting-point by the pretentious
banality of the lines, then gradually caught up by the sweep of the
thing, until, in Act 6, we were completely under its spell, and final-
ly--Mr. O'Neill having gone burlesque, as is his custom of late toward
the end of his plays--thrown back into a state for which "irritation"
would be too strong a name. The total impression on us was that
something big and fine had been slightly muffed--maybe by Mr.
O'Neill, maybe by us.

Our irritation arose from the method which the author has chos-
en to use in writing his drama--a pompous resuscitation of the old-
fashioned "aside." The reason that the play takes so long is that
each character, in addition to speaking his lines, must also speak
his thoughts. This would not be so bad if their thoughts were worth
speaking, but, for the most part, they could easily have been guessed
by any alert child in the audience. In certain scenes, notably the
one in Act 6 where the woman sits with her trinity of complementary
male units, all thinking out loud, this method justifies itself and gives
a hint of its possibilities in the future.

But throughout most of the play, especially during the first
acts, when soliloquy seems simply a lazy man's method of writing exposition (and essentially false as well, for no one thinks expository
thoughts--unless perhaps he is waking up after a hard night and is
trying to satisfy himself as to just who he is and whose house he is
in), Mr. O'Neill's "asides" are scarcely distinguishable from those of
the old-fashioned melodrama, and are certainly not much more subtle.
When Darrell enters and Nina says aloud to herself (Darrell con-
veniently waiting until she is through thinking): "My old lover ...
how well and young he looks ... now we no longer love each other
at all..." there is more than a passing similarity to the speech of
Richard Rackmorton in The Wolves of St. Agnes, where he steps to
the foots and says behind his hand: "I wonder if she suspects that
I am really her father. I will test her," and then, turning to Dora
(with slightly more bass in his tone): "Little girl, do you remember
the swans in the lake at Passy where you used to play?"

There are few of these "asides" of O'Neill's which any good
actor or actress could not indicate without speaking a word or any
good playwright get into his lines without resorting to tricks. Some
day this method will be used by an author whose characters don't
act as they think and who also has the gift of humor. That will be
something different.

There is a certain effect of having lived the lives of the characters in Strange Interlude when you finally emerge into Fifty-eighth
Street which is likely to be confused with having believed in them.
This is simply because you have been cooped up with them so long.
You can read one of Dreiser's novels--or rather, if you can, you get
the same effect, just from continued proximity. We used to feel that
we knew the characters in James Fenimore Cooper's novels, not because we liked them but because the English Department made us finish them. Any playwright who can make his audience stick with him
for five hours has an advantage over his rivals. He can impress
them by sheer tonnage.

Evidently no author except O'Neill can make an audience stick
for five hours. If Samuel Shipman had written the first act of
Stange Interlude (and he could have) the play would have been
laughed off the stage. If Mae West had written the boat-race scene
in Act 8 (and she wouldn't have) every reviewer in town would have
taken the day off to kid it. It is natural that O'Neill should command
respectful attention becaue he is our foremost playwright. It is natural that Strange Interlude should hold people in their seats, first,
because of its intrinsic interest and ambitious scope and, second
(and no less important), because of the fine performance of Lynn
Fontanne, together with those of Earle Larimore, Glenn Anders and
Tom Powers. No cast ever had a tougher job.

But since O'Neill is our foremost playwright, and since the pre-
tensions of Strange Interlude are so great, it is only natural that we
should expect it to be practically perfect. And it isn't--not by a
million miles.

                            --Robert C. Benchley in Life
                            (February 16, 1928), page 21.

STREET SCENE (Elmer Rice; Playhouse Theatre, January 10, 1929)

Street Scene would be good in any season. In this, it seems
like something by Sophocles (better, if you ask us). Mr. Rice has
placed his panorama of human joys and sorrows in front of a startlingly vivid setting by Jo Mielziner showing a shabby brownstone-front
with various apertures for the tenants to appear in from time to
time and the feeling of a hot summer day in the region of the Elevated caught to perfection. A large cast adds to the effect by per-

forming its various functions with considerable skill, and, during
the course of the drama, most of the more popular functions of city-
life are indulged in. It is about as comprehensive a summary of
mass existence as you could expect to find on one stage, and one
which is constantly interesting, oftentimes much more than that.
No season which can boast of Street Scene is without hope.

Our one suggestion to Mr. Rice (who directed his own play)
would be that the love scenes and other intimate groupings be played
in, or at the entrance to, the vestibule. On the steps they seem a
little unnatural, but a city vestibule can serve as a love grot, a
confession-box or a death-chamber without violating one tradition of
common useage. The whole spirit of Mr. Rice's fine condensation of
all life into one locale calls out for the very vestibule which is here
used only as an entrance and an exit.

However, on the steps or in the vestibule, Street Scene should
by all means be seen and William A. Brady should be given due
recognition for having produced it at a time when it was needed so
badly. For having written it, Mr. Rice should be awarded a palm.
                              --Robert C. Benchley in Life
                              (February 1, 1929), page 23.

                    *   *   *

Elmer Rice, the author of The Adding Machine, has brought into the anaemic and languishing theatre of this season a play of extraordinary sweep, power and intensity, which catches up with
amazing simplicity and sincere feeling the ragged, glowing, humorous and tragic life that pours in and out of one of those brown-
stone apartment houses hovering on the upper edge of the slum district of New York. It has its brutal moments and its coarse ones.
But they are never brutal or coarse from the sophisticated viewpoint
so many authors assume today, and behind every incident and every
character you feel the pity and the understanding of a playwright
who has glimpsed a great truth--that no matter what may be the
pressure of one's environment, the only true power to meet the life
of today must come from within the individual.

The gripping illusion of Street Scene quite beggars verbal description. You cannot convey through words alone what the theatre,
at its best, conveys by sound, color, motion and a subtly sustained
mood. Nevertheless, a brief outline of what happens is necessary to
an understanding of Mr. Rice's real achievement. The curtain rises
and shows us the front of an old-fashioned brown-stone apartment
house set in the lamplit gloom of a hot summer evening. Abraham
Kaplan is sitting in his shirt sleeves by the open window of the
ground floor apartment. The German wife of an Italian music teacher is trying to catch a breath of air from the opposite window. People are passing and repassing, bedraggled, heat-tortured persons.
A boy comes along the sidewalk on roller skates and calls to his moth-

er for an extra dime for ice cream cones. The neighbors discuss
the weather and the heat. Slowly you begin to learn who the various people are that inhabit this grim building--the burned-out, slat-
ternly widow, the Jewish radical, the Italian musician, the burly
stage hand and his wife and children on the second floor, the woman
on the third floor about to have her first baby. And so it goes, in
a slowly weaving pattern, intensely human, never overdrawn and
never failing, in depicting a type, to add to that type, a touch of
individual characterization. As the various inhabitants of the house
seek air on the street you begin to sense the possibility of drama in
their lives. Mrs. Maurrant, the stage hand's wife on the second
floor, has become pretty well exhausted in the struggle to get a kind
word from her burly husband. Her son, Willy (the boy on roller
skates) is getting definitely out of hand. Her daughter, Rose, clerk
in a real estate office, threatens to become involved with a married
man who wants to put her on the stage. The neighbors have seen
Mrs. Maurrant talking rather too often to the bill collector from the
milk company. Is she playing with fire? Frank Maurrant is growing
suspicious--his wife is growing reckless. But when the Buchanan
baby arrives on the third floor, it is Mrs. Maurrant who spends the
night with the mother and takes charge of the situation. Another
family in the building is about to be dispossessed. Life is becoming
very real and complex in this gathering place of humanity. The
Italian music teacher is proud of Columbus. The Scandinavian janitor languidly insists that Lief Ericson discovered America. Rose
Maurrant comes home late after dining and dancing with her office
manager. Her father drives her to bed.

The next morning Frank Maurrant is going to Hartford for the
try-out performance of a play. The bill collector drops by. The
children go to school. Abraham Kaplan goes off to write his everlasting articles on the economic revolution. His daughter departs to
teach school. His son, Samuel, begs Rose Maurrant to marry him and
go off somewhere and get out of it all. Rose leaves to attend the
funeral of her boss. Mrs. Maurrant lets the bill collector come to her
apartment. Frank Maurrant, much the worse for drink, comes back.
The brown stone beehive suddenly comes to life. Frank Maurrant
rushes upstairs, shots are fired, a moment later the frantic crazed
body of the milk collector crashes through the second-floor window
calling for help. He is dragged back in the room. Police. Ambulance. Crowds. Frank Maurrant escapes. Tragedy in the midst of
the commonplace. And, as one of the women remarks, "It all goes
to show that you never know when you get up in the morning what
the day holds." Rose Maurrant comes back in time to see the dying
form of her mother being carried to the ambulance. And during all
this, the sheriff and his men proceed with the business of dispos-
sessing the Hildebrand family and dumping their furniture on the
sidewalk. Life goes on.

There is a third act the same afternoon. But you can hardly
call it an act when it is merely the continuing, surging drama of

frightened, awestruck people who somehow keep right on about their
ways in the very shadow of death. Frank Maurrant is finally captured. He has a last word with his daughter. He must have been
clean out of his head, he tells her. He is not sorry for himself but
the pleading eyes of his dead wife hover before him. In various
ways the neighbors help Rose Maurrant. Tragedy has matured her
suddenly. Even her office manager becomes a sincere friend for the
moment, seeking nothing but the chance to help. Sam Kaplan tells
her of his love. He wants her to belong to him so that he can pro-
tect her. But she feels somehow that everything that has happened
is due to the fact that everyone has tried too hard to "belong" to
someone else. The world can't be met by trying to attach yourself
to outside things. You must find your strength and peace first from
within. Perhaps someday, a little later, she and Sam--? But there
you are. Rose goes off. A couple come looking for a vacant apartment. Life in the brown-stone will go on being what it has always
been.

It is perhaps hard to believe that from incidents as varied and
scattered as these, Mr. Rice could create an enthrallingly vivid sense
of reality, poignancy, cowardice, despair and courage. But he has
succeeded in an overflowing measure. It is, if you like to label
things, an intensely realistic play. No detail is omitted in the production which might lend photographic realism--even to the loose
rubber heel of the Scandinavian janitor. Yet I think anyone who
sits through this play will realize that Mr. Rice has only used realism
as a means to an end. He is telling a universal story of a city.
The same kind of things, differing only in degree, might happen
(from the newspapers we know they do happen) in the wealthiest or
in the lowliest quarters of the city. Behind a marble front, they
would happen with a less merciless exposure. That is the only difference. When all is said and done, Mr. Rice's highest achievement
is in painting this vivid panorama without creating a sense of despair.
Human beings are to be pitied for what they bring on themselves, but
they are not mere automatons crushed under the giant footsteps of
environment. Once more we come back to that brief illuminated moment when Rose Maurrant says that the force to meet life must come
from within. Suffering--yes. Despair--no. Life is pretty much
what we make it and the fault lies in ourselves if we make a poor
job of it. In spite of the brutal frankness of a few scenes, I cannot
help the feeling that the undertone of this play is honest and true.
It comes vastly nearer being "a great American play" than the much
vaunted Strange Interlude, or in fact any of those plays of recent
years which seek to explain life from the mud flats of pessimism.

The author directed the action of this play himself, and, to my
mind, has displayed something approaching genius in the handling of
the huge cast. The casting and acting approach perfection. Whether you take Leo Bulgakov as the old radical, Beulah Bondi as the
burnt-out widow, Mary Servoss as the bewildered and exhausted
Anna Maurrant, Horace Braham as the almost tragic Sam Kaplan, or

Erin O'Brien-Moore in her exquisitely sensitive portrait of Rose Maurrant, you can find only words of the highest praise. And the same holds true for even the smallest parts. The enthusiastic response of the audience is one of the best indications I have seen that the public automatically welcomes honesty and sincerity on the stage when it is coupled with masterly achievement.

> --Richard Dana Skinner in The
> Commonweal, Vol. 9, No. 12
> (January 23, 1929), pages 348-
> 349.

STRICTLY DISHONORABLE (Preston Sturges; Avon Theatre, September 18, 1929)

The very least we can do is sit down at once and write letters to our Congressmen thanking them for the Prohibition Law which made that beautiful little comedy, Strictly Dishonorable, possible.

The Puritan Conscience was all that was ever very wrong with America. It divided human activities neatly into "good" deeds and "bad" deeds, and we might never have discovered how much "good" there is in "bad" deeds, or how much "bad" there is in "good" deeds had the Puritan Conscience not committed suicide by giving us a law which we could not avoid breaking. Once the nation had risen up as one man and taken a drink--broken a law deliberately--done something "bad"--without being instantly consumed by a rain of fire from heaven, the nation began casting about for other fascinating Thou Shalt Nots to annihilate. That it should, for a while at first, annihilate Thou Shalt Nots with a clumsy recklessness was only to be expected and not to be worried about. After a few hangovers and a few hangings, these matters settle themselves down to a sane normal.

Liberated from the Puritan Conscience, the theatre went a little crazy at first with its own special sin: Thou Shalt Not No. 7. It went, in fact, pretty cheap and nasty. Then, along came Preston Sturges, out of Chicago, with his charming comedy of amour in a speakeasy and a bachelor's rooms; and, lo, an American's name, suddenly and for the first time in history, heads the list of those who know how to write of the tender business. Only the Hungarians-- an Hungarian--Molnar--can touch him. The English take amour too seriously, the French too lightly, the Germans too sentimentally, the Italians too heavily, the Spanish too violently and the Russians too dolefully. The American Mr. Sturges takes it, as it should be taken, seriously, lightly, sentimentally, heavily, violently and dolefully all at once, and adds to it a coating of good taste and good humor. He is a credit to his country.

Besides being a faultless play, Strictly Dishonorable is per-

fectly cast and magnificently directed and acted. In an imperfect
world, no one has the right to expect as much from an evening in
the theatre as it renders.

> --Ralph Barton in Life (October
> 11, 1929), page 24.

* * *

Strictly Dishonorable, a comedy by Preston Sturges, was an
immediate hit. The reception given it by press and public, not to
mention ticket agencies and speculators, is most instructive. Twenty-
four hours after the play opened, Broadway knew that Brock Pemberton had a "wow," and the day after that I know a man who paid
ten dollars for one seat.

Shortly before Mr. Sturges' play opened the Provincetown Playhouse began its new season at the Garrick with Michael Gold's Fiesta,
the press pronounced it a failure, and it is still possible to buy a
two dollar seat at the box office for two dollars.

Why? The comedy is entertaining, smoothly written and ably
acted; the serious play is not particularly entertaining, it is for
the most part turgidly written, and not very well acted. The one is
a hit, the other a flop. Yet it is my duty to say that Mr. Gold's
play is a finer thing, a nobler effort than Mr. Sturges'. I don't
say that the public ought to spurn the successful play and patronize
the unsuccessful: I merely state that in the long run such plays as
Fiesta are of the stuff that makes theatre-going something more than
a sort of esthetic cocktail.

What are these plays about? Strictly Dishonorable was called
"an almost perfect comedy" by one of our leading newspaper reviewers. It turned out to be, as I guessed it would, a conventional little piece that owed its success chiefly to its suavity: a quality both
in the play itself and in its production. It also has a cleverly expressed idea that appeals to the slightly sophisticated audiences that
are now crowding to see it. We have here the story of a nice young
girl from the South who is engaged to a disagreeable young man from
Orange, New Jersey. At a New York speakeasy they quarrel and the
girl decides to remain in the hands of the proprietor, an Italian opera
singer and a judge. Attracted by the opera singer she decides to
spend the night in his apartment after he tells her that his intentions
are "strictly dishonorable." Like ten thousand ingenues in French
farce she makes up to the would-be seducer who at the last moment
decides he is really in love with her and makes his exit just before
the curtain of the second act descends. Next morning there is comic
speculation on the part of the minor characters as to what happened
between the acts. Then the noble lead appears in time to prevent
the girl's returning to the arms of the wrong man--eleventh hour reform and all that. This, at bottom, the whole play. It's all very
agreeable and gentlemanly and amusing, and I for one would not think

of complaining either to Mr. Sturges, or Mr. Pemberton (who gave
me a good seat next to the man who paid ten dollars for his) or to
the actors. But the play is not great, nor fine, nor profound, nor
meaningful; it does not appeal to the imagination nor does it stir the
emotions. Its very perfections leave me cold, just as its delicious
dash of immorality is essentially deliberate and lacking in spontaneity.

On the other hand, Michael Gold writes with his imagination,
with perhaps too much earnestness, but without skill, and he conspicuously lacks most of the qualities of slickness that make Mr.
Sturges a sure-fire playwright. He is struggling for expression; he
is so eager to get his people and ideas before us in their essential
and truthful outlines that he forgets that even the greatest plays
must entertain. Fiesta tells of the effort of a Mexican landowner who
is inspired by the ideas of Tolstoy to make his peons self-respecting
citizens. With the ardor of the true reformer he sets up a pure
young girl on a pedestal as the incarnation of his ideal of a new Mexico, only to suffer bitter disappointment on discovering that the child
is human. The whole world seems to refuse to understand him; worse,
not to want to understand or be benefited by him.

An idea that is not new, but one that must be rewritten by
various men in various times and lands to fit new circumstances, not
for the sake of the idea (which needs no play to exemplify it), but
for the characters. In spite of his radical politics Mr. Gold possesses
the heart of an artist and his play is in no sense propaganda unless
you use the word to describe a work that sets out to prove the futility of propaganda.

Where Mr. Gold failed is in the means of telling his story. In
spite of a romantic background and picturesque minor characters, in
spite of a remarkably rich fund of folklore, dancing, music and incidental details of speech and gesture that lay easily to hand, his whole
fabric is heavy. The MS is crowded with repetitious dialogue, and
oceans of rhetoric that just misses eloquence; he has not yet learned
to conduct a scene to its inevitable point and leave it at that. In a
word, he needs training and experience. Consequently, for all of
James Light's sympathetic directing, Fiesta remained a rather dull
thing.

But because it was not complete, or perfect, or explicit, suave,
slick or effective, Fiesta is precisely the sort of work that the
Provincetown Playhouse should produce. Not, of course, because of
its shortcomings but because these shortcomings happen to be found
in a work which has within it a quality, a potential beauty worth
fostering. Mr. Gold is young, and he can learn some of the tricks
that seem to come naturally to men like Preston Sturges and George
Kaufman, George Abbott and a dozen others. The difference between
him and the clever boys is that he has something that they have not.

I am pleased to add, however, that I heard something Mr.

Sturges is reported to have said about himself that gives me hope
that he will not be satisfied to be just a successful playwright. His
next two or three plays will tell. I wish him luck.

--Barrett H. Clark in The Drama,
Vol. 20, No. 2 (November 1928),
pages 40-41.

STRIKE UP THE BAND (Book by Morrie Ryskind, Music by George
    Gershwin, Lyrics by Ira Gershwin; Times Square Theatre,
    January 14, 1930)

The book of Strike Up the Band, by Morrie Ryskind out of
George S. Kaufman, comes breath-takingly near to being too intelligent for a musical comedy. The show is sung and danced around
the story of the Horace J. Fletcher Private Memorial War, waged by
America against Switzerland to keep the world safe for the American
milk chocolate business. Satire as good as the satire in this exhibit,
directed against Big Business and containing some very caustic observations on the awful truth about the late unpleasantness in Europe,
is no laughing matter, and if it weren't for certain relieving features,
the vasty audiences at Strike Up the Band would be sitting out in
front clucking their tongues and sighing heavily for the colossal im-
becility of the human race and vowing to raise its boys to be Peace
Conference attenders.

However, the above mentioned relieving features turn the
evening into one of the gayest that can be purchased for money anywhere in town. First of all, there is George Gershwin's precise,
jaunty, swinging, superbly musicianly music to too many good songs
to list. To put down "A Typical Self-Made American," "Soon," "If
I Became the President," "He Knows Milk," "Strike Up the Band,"
"Mademoiselle from New Rochelle" and "I've Got a Crush on You,"
only makes one want to name all the others and have done with it.

To these songs, are brother Ira Gershwin's lyrics; quite as
intelligent and bitingly satirical as the book, but so nimbly and deftly fashioned that their serious import sinks in without hurting. If
they were printed in a book, I should buy it and find something
more than the accident of alphabetical arrangement in the fact that it
would be placed on my shelves next to the works of W.S. Gilbert.

It is the presence of the hilarious team of Clark and McCul-
lough that insures a violent and pleasant agony in the side for the
evening. From the moment that Bobby Clark walks out in a cloud
of flying cigars and walking sticks and begins opening up a pair of
beaming eyes in astonishment at and appreciation of the brilliance
of his own jokes, one finds it easy to forget what the dentist said
would have to be done to that second superior bicuspid and that the

Income Tax is due next month. Bobby Clark is just about my favorite musical comedy comedian and he makes Strike Up the Band just
about my favorite musical show in town.
                              --Ralph Barton in Life (February
                                 7, 1930), page 28.

THE STUDENT PRINCE (Book and Lyrics by Dorothy Donnelly, Music
    by Sigmund Romberg; Jolson Theatre, December 2, 1924)

    The Student Prince and The Love Song are in the first rank
of shows to which you would not be ashamed to take a real musician,
and they fly the Shubert banner. Here again we pause to recon-
struct our old prejudices.
                              --Robert C. Benchley in Life
                                 (March 5, 1925), page 18.

SUN UP (Lula Vollmer; Provincetown Theatre, May 25, 1923)

    Native drama of the backwoods, worth seeing if you are inter-
ested in native drama.
                              --Robert C. Benchley in Life
                                 (August 30, 1923), page 19.

SUNNY (Music by Jerome Kern, Book and Lyrics by Otto Harbach
    and Oscar Hammerstein II; New Amsterdam Theatre, September
    22, 1925)

    While we are on the subject of openings, we may say that we
are bitterly disappointed to have to report favorably on Sunny, for
the Dillingham management took us off its first-night list for that
occasion. In our resentment we bought and paid for our own seats,
determined to give our pitiless flaying apparatus full sway. Unfortunately, we could find nothing to flay. Sunny is good substantial
entertainment from beginning to end, even though our two little boys
get fifteen dollars and forty cents less of schooling on account of it.

    After all, one has merely to read the cast to see that it couldn't
be very bad: Marilyn Miller, Jack Donahue, Joseph Cawthorn, Clif-
ton Webb, Mary Hay, Esther Howard, Cliff Edwards (né Ukulele Ike),
Dorothy Francis and a young lady named Pert Kelton. Music by
Jerome Kern. Staged by Hassard Short. There's the story. It isn't
so much that Sunny is constantly good, but that it has practically no

bad spots. Our chief regret is that so smart a comedienne as Esther
Howard is again given straight work to do. Now that Ada Lewis has
gone, we haven't enough funny women on the stage to waste any.
                              --Robert C. Benchley in Life (Oc-
                                 tober 15, 1925), page 18.

                              *   *   *

    It seems that no first rate musical show is complete nowadays
without costumes and sets by James Reynolds, the most able colorist
working in the American theatre. He has contributed to Sunny
what is the best part of an expensive and pretentious entertainment,
and his settings and costumes for The Vagabond King are worth
seeing many times. Both these pieces are meeting with immense success. Sunny, starring Marilyn Miller, who is as charming as ever
and dances if possible more beautifully than she has ever done, is
so stupendous an affair that one is dazzled by cast, settings, orchestra, etc. into believing that it is better than it is. The book is plain
stupid, the music very fair, and the cast one hundred carat.
                              --Louis Bromfield in The Bookman,
                                 Vol. 62, No. 4 (December 1925),
                                 page 480.

THE SWAN (Ferenc Molnar; Cort Theatre, October 23, 1923)

    "Well, well, here we are again," as the clown in the English
Christmas pantomime always says at his first entrance. Since I
wrote last, not much has happened. The one play I looked forward
to, Molnar's Launzi, has come and gone, without setting fire to the
Harlem. But another play by Molnar, and one which I did not predict, turns out to be the most delightful of the current season. I
refer to The Swan.

    Whenever I gaze upon the acting of Miss Eva Le Gallienne I
always feel an Alexander Woollcott-like sensation coming over me. I
lose all desire to question and quibble, content that I am watching
Miss Le Gallienne act. Perhaps in one's second childhood one does become extremely susceptible to young actresses, yet I am unwilling to
admit this explanation. I think the truth is that Miss Le Gallienne
is not only a beautiful person, but she is at the same time our most
expert and intellectual player among the younger generation. Therefore, I do not know whether The Swan is a good play or not; I do
know that Miss Le Gallienne's princess in this play is all and more
than any fairy princess of my dreams, and I suspect the play of
cleverness, of gentle satire against romance, and of other ingredients
compounded to make a delectable evening. Of course the story of
princess who has to give up true love for political reasons is not

exactly new, nor is it, as an idea, profound. And yet--oh, go see
The Swan for yourselves.

> --Jack Crawford in The Drama,
> Vol. 14, No. 3 (December 1923),
> page 90.

* * *

It is a pleasure to record the advent of so satisfactory a play
as The Swan, even though we are conscious of not recording it well
enough. Once you have said that a play is the best of the new season's offerings, that Miss LeGallienne is splendid as the Princess,
Basil Rathbone excellent as the tutor, and Philip Merivale delightful
as the Prince, you have said all there is to say and in much more
conventional language than they deserve. If we hadn't already used
"excellent" in connection with Mr. Rathbone, we might use it for
Halliwell Hobbes, who plays Father Hyacinth. And there you are.

We may be able to break the monotony of a favorable review
by saying that we personally thought the tutor-hero quite a tiresome prig, one of that increasing band of heroes who feel that if
they should smile once during the performance they would violate
their extra-precious integrity of spirit, and we were very glad that
the Princess didn't marry him. Life with the gracious and gentlemanly
Prince would be much more bearable than a career of constant tripping
over the feelings of a young man who, starting out with Henley as
captain of his soul, would not be content until he had promoted himself to at least lieutenant-colonel.

This, however, is beside the point that The Swan and the
company playing it and the direction of David Burton make altogether
a delightful and, at present, incomparable entertainment.

> --Robert C. Benchley in Life (No-
> vember 15, 1923), page 20.

TARNISH (Gilbert Emery; Belmont Theatre, October 1, 1923)

Now in Tarnish it seems to us that Mr. Gilbert Emery has managed to bring home quite as old a message as that which Windows
preaches, but in a way which makes you believe that you are listening
to real people and not to the Althea Debating Society. Even the old
silk-hatted satyr, Adolph Tevis (played, to our way of thinking,
quite as he should be by Albert Gran), whose blossoming speeches
are like those of no one we have ever heard, did not offend our
sense of actuality in the slightest. We came away from Tarnish with
the feeling of having seen the most genuine play of the season so
far.

It is difficult for us to say just how good an actress Ann Harding is, owing to a failing we have of being favorably disposed toward any beautiful young woman on the stage. We _think_, however, that she has the makings of a very good actress. Tom Powers is another whose work we find it difficult to assay, because he seems such a pleasant young man personally.

Considerable credit should go to Mr. John Cromwell, who, in his second venture into producing, saw something in _Tarnish_ which many of the wise managers who know "what the public wants" passed up entirely. It is quite evident that the public wants _Tarnish_, as it is one of the first sure hits of the season.
>   --Robert C. Benchley in _Life_ (Oc-
>   tober 23, 1923), page 18.

THEY KNEW WHAT THEY WANTED (Sidney Howard; Garrick Theatre, November 24, 1924)

Mr. Howard, on the other hand, has dared much more than Mr. O'Neill in running this theme through a comedy.* There are times when you don't see for the life of you how the thing can possibly end tolerably. Yet it does, and with a great deal of distinction, too. With several scenes of industrial sociology deleted, it will be one of the few fine American things that the Theatre Guild has done.

Of course, Pauline Lord raises it to heights which make even the qualification "American" unnecessary. Her Anna Christie was undergraduate work for Amy in this play. It is just about as near a perfect performance as you are likely to see. Glenn Anders, in spite of the fact that on the opening night he was not allowed to take a curtain call (or at any rate didn't take it), contributed the next most satisfying characterization and, in every way, held up his end of the remarkable scenes with Miss Lord. This does not mean that Richard Bennett did not practically tear our heart out, but he is one of the stars and every one knows that he is good. Mr. Anders is very young and has had to live down _The Demi-Virgin_, and so his splendid performance seems a much more important piece of news. All in all, it was a big night at the Garrick.
>   --Robert C. Benchley in _Life_ (De-
>   cember 11, 1924), page 18.

* * *

*This review immediately follows a review of _Desire under the Elms_ (q.v.), which Benchley feels has a similar theme.

Sidney Howard's <u>They Knew What They Wanted</u> throws overboard much deadwood of the old theater in order that it may take on a fresh cargo of reason and common sense. Unlike the other two American plays mentioned this play moves in a spirit of comedy. The author takes a theme that has for years been treated sentimentally and handles it with a revealing sweet reasonableness. How dramatic common sense is after all! How stirring it is to recognize that white is white when for years we have been telling ourselves that white is black. Again as in O'Neill's play the fabric of the action is made up of passions and desires. But fortunately the sun shines in California. So what might have been a very bad situation comes out well in the end. What might have been a tragedy if the characters had acted like play actors, ended in comedy because they acted like sensible men and women. None of them were overly wise or heroic or saintly. But they knew what they wanted.

> --Thomas H. Dickinson in <u>Ameri-</u>
> <u>can Review</u>, Vol. 3, No. 2
> (March-April, 1925), pages 220-
> 221.

THIS YEAR OF GRACE (Noel Coward; Selwyn Theatre, November 7, 1928)

Well--the English still have the better of it when it comes to concocting and staging a so-called intimate review. A few years ago it was Charlot who introduced us to this particular type of amiable and witty entertainment (and incidentally to Beatrice Lillie and Gertrude Lawrence at the same time). The American copyists began at once to follow his lead, some of them with moderate success. The Grand Streeters had always been doing this sort of thing in a quiet way, and promptly came into greater vogue as Broadway learned to appreciate them. We began to hope that, Ziegfeld aside, we were in for a new era in reviews of wit and simplicity.

Then something happened. Charlot came back and tried to repeat his first success. He was too confident and careless. His material seemed stale. It reached out for sophistication and only got daubed with Broadway dirt. Broadway itself turned back to its old game of more and more girls and fewer and fewer clothes and less and less wit and a plethora of leering jokes. A few producers tried a compromise type of review--and failed. The refreshing breeze that Charlot brought over seemed to have died down completely. And then, of a sudden November evening, Charles B. Cochran opens up with <u>This Year of Grace</u>, and simplified showmanship comes back into its own. It is not quite as clean a wind as the first Charlot. It has distinctly decadent moments. But for sheer wit, brevity, speed and simplicity throughout the greater part of the evening, it certainly has no equal on our stage today.

Much of its success we can attribute at once to that versatile
young man, Noel Coward, who has written for it all the music, lyrics
and sketches. For the rest we can thank the inimitable clowning of
Beatrice Lillie and the expert direction of Mr. Cochran. And if we
live to be a hundred, probably none of us will ever forget a certain
waltz danced by Marjorie Moss and Georges Fontana--beyond doubt
the most deliciously poetic and perfectly executed thing of its kind
to be seen anywhere. I have seen many couples start out well, only
to end by disfiguring the very spirit of the waltz with awkward acro-
batics. I have seen others sustain a mood, but without glamour.
Moss and Fontana have here achieved something of classic loveliness
and surpassing grace and radiance. It makes one think only of the
rich groundswell of a sea under a warm moon.

But to return to the review--for the Moss-Fontana waltz is an
interlude quite by itself--the economy of Mr. Coward's wit is best
illustrated by the series of sketches he has grouped together under
the title of the Theatre Guide. We are all familiar with the rather
lengthy and sometimes amusing skits on current productions in the
average review. Compare them, then, to the following satiric comment
on Miss Le Gallienne and her Civic Repertory Theatre. It is called
Any Civic Repertory Play. The curtain rises on a black-curtained
stage, with a woman in black velvet seated despairingly at a table.
She raises her arms. She cries out--"Ah--such pain!" The curtain
drops. That is all. But where, in the name of all the muses, can
you find so much comment in so few words?

When it comes to the work of Beatrice Lillie, one is a bit bewildered in trying to dissect its qualities. She does the same things
she has been doing for the last four years--at least in gesture and
pantomime. The surface details are different, but the mechanism of
comedy and drollery is the same. Yet it strikes you as freshly as
the first time you saw it. You can only say that, like Chaplin, she
has struck certain great universals in the art of clowning which never
take on age. She strikes a perfect balance between the grotesque and
the serious, between the pathetic and the satirical.

Noel Coward also appears in the review and to very telling effect. He is, as everyone knows by this time, a capable actor. He
has a clear-cut quality of distinction, both in writing and in the
actor's technique, and above all a magnificent sense of rhythm. When
you think that he can write as intensely tragic a play as The Vortex,
and act its leading rôle with poignant conviction; that he can write
the entire musical score for the present review, all the sketches and
all the lyrics, dance capably, clown effectively and be a polished and
humorous master of ceremonies as well; you have a fair picture of
one of the most versatile talents of our day. This Year of Grace
is not a perfect prescription, in the sense that it has no objectionable
moments, but it distinctly does include some of the finest elements of

the intimate review yet seen in New York.

                    --Richard Dana Skinner in The
                      Commonweal, Vol. 9, No. 3 (No-
                      vember 21, 1928), page 75.

* * *

Ever since the disbanding of the old Charlot troupe several years ago, the incomparable Beatrice Lillie has been saddled with Anne Caldwell librettos of various kinds and has been forced to sit more or less idly by and watch her ex-team-mate, Miss Gertrude Lawrence (also incomparable in her own field), flutter past in the golden hits of Messrs. Aarons and Freedley. It is now Miss Lillie's turn to laugh coyly from over her fan, for Noel Coward has provided her with This Year of Grace, a lay-out after her own (and the public's) heart, while Miss Lawrence finds herself in the awkward position of carrying a very wet albatross by the name of Treasure Girl.

Noel Coward has proved himself nothing short of a wonder-man in the concoction of This Year of Grace, for which he has written the book, music and lyrics, besides taking part in it himself. It is the kind of revue that one might dream of writing for a completely civilized world and, so long as people crowd in to see it as they are doing now, we are prepared to retract everything we have ever said against Mankind. If Mankind wishes, we will even indorse it--blindfolded. But unless someone in America is able to do something that approximates Mr. Coward's feat, we shall always feel that it was a mistake to break away from England back there in 1775.

After years of reciting Miss Caldwell's and other natives' lines it must seem like heaven to Miss Lillie to find herself back in the "bus rush," or singing "Britannia Rules the Waves" in the world's low-water mark in bathing suits, or executing a gorgeous burlesque of Miss Lawrence herself in "I Can't Think." To sing quietly through a number like "World Weary," confident that one of the biggest laughs in the theatre is waiting at the finish, must be a very comfortable feeling. And, incidentally, Miss Lillie sings the quiet part of this song well enough almost to get by with it as a straight number, for, as a result possibly of her chastening experience with American-made books, she has acquired a calm, almost a sadness, which does much to enhance her comedy. Since the first Charlot revue so many local young ladies have taken to using her intonations and gestures in private conversation that she does well to leave the more obvious of them to her imitators.

Perhaps we have already indicated that we hold Mr. Coward's talents in high esteem. We have not, however, mentioned the finesse of his own personal performance in such recitations as the outline of the plot of the ballet, "The Legend OF the Lily OF the Valley," or the singing of his own macabre number, "Dance, Little Lady," which latter vivid attack on society is probably in for frequent and clumsy imitation in future revues.

We should like to point out, however (and God help us for
mentioning good English to an Englishman), that the meticulous,
though quite natural, pronunciation of the word "dance" on the part
of the chorus only accentuates the slight irregularity of such a sentence as "Teach Me to Dahnce Like Grandma Dahnced." If one is
going to pronounce it "dahnce" (as one very probably should pronounce it), one should also say "as Grandma dahnced." It fits in
a little better with careful usage.

However, the only credit which America can take in the whole
remarkable evening's entertainment is the sensational waltzing of
Moss and Fontana--and they probably came originally from somewhere
else.

>   --Robert C. Benchley in Life (No-
>   vember 30, 1928), page 11.

TIP-TOES (Book by Guy Bolton and Fred Thompson, Music by
    George Gershwin, Lyrics by Ira Gershwin; Liberty Theatre, De-
    cember 28, 1925)

Tip-Toes trips its way with considerable charm, excellent music, and adequate dancing through Florida scenery. Perhaps it is
one of the ills that the "Florida boom" carries in its train, that the
public, surfeited with colorful advertisements of that land of eternal
youth, should be compelled to watch the curtains of current musical
comedies roll up, disclosing tropical trees and expensive southern-
resort hotels. So it is with Tip-Toes, and so it was with The Florida Girl.

But aside from the banality of the Florida landscape, already
too familiar to that dwindling minority of our population that has
never even been to Florida, and also aside from the too prolonged
sustaining of humorous situations which are not especially humorous
to start with, Tip-Toes is agreeable.

Diminutive Queenie Smith more than makes up for what she
lacks in stature in a personality and freshness quite individual. Andrew Tombes and Harry Watson, Junior, as her partners in the vaudeville trio which has all sorts of amusing adventures, provoke sufficient spontaneous laughter to send away, at the final curtain, a pleasantly cheered audience. George Gershwin's music in "Looking for a
Boy," "Sweet and Low Down," "That Certain Feeling," and "These
Charming People" (who can resist the satire or the plausibility of
"if these people can be charming, we can be charming too"?) is delightful.

>   --H.W. in The Commonweal, Vol.
>   3, No. 11 (January 30, 1926),
>   page 301.

TO THE LADIES (George S. Kaufman and Marc Connelly; Liberty Theatre, February 20, 1922)

   George S. Kaufman and Marc Connelly took their <u>Dulcy</u> and
wrote her--or him--as a man. Then they took or remembered or hit
upon a variation of <u>What Every Woman Knows</u> and <u>The First Year</u>.
And wrote a play that is in many respects finer and certainly more
amusing than all three.

   <u>To the Ladies</u>. But please do not let me lessen the glory that
should be theirs. There is a wholly new idea in it. Yes a dozen
new ideas. And a hundred twists and turns in the dialogue which
are simply masterful. The resemblance to the other plays I point
out only because of the aid they give me in describing the play.

   Whether you think that it is the male <u>Dulcy</u> or a satire on the
magazine readers who believe even in the ads or a dramatization of
banquets or a play in which the big idea is women's work in business via thinking for husbands--it doesn't matter much what you
think the play is about. The important thing is that nothing so
satirical, so well built, so amusing and so pointed has come to town
in many a season.

   The gift which these authors have is not only the gift for idea
and construction. Their chief gift is comment. And by comment I
mean a sort of comment on their work. Any number of deft touches
which do not seem to be lugged in. And all laughs. Laughs which
are not of the theatre. That is, laughs which come from the sharpest
of observations of life.

   Otto Kruger didn't seem to be acting. And when an actor
makes you forget his work and see only the character, he has no
little achievement to his credit. Helen Hayes had a few effective moments but there is too much straining in her work. Isabel Irving
was superb. I know of no performance this season which compares
with what she does to sustain the interest for the other actors.
Equally fine was George Howell. His business man was real. His
last act sheepishness was acting. Acting.

   Have I neglected to tell the story? It can't be told. Isn't
that splendid? There should be more plays in which the "story"
couldn't be told.
                              --S. J. Kaufman in <u>The New York</u>
                                <u>Dramatic Mirror</u> (April 1922),
                                page 115.

                         * * *

   After having proved to everyone's satisfaction in <u>Dulcy</u> that the
woman who tries to help her husband in his business is a national

pest, Messrs. Kaufman and Connelly, the authors, now throw off
their cynical masks and step gallantly to the footlights with To the
Ladies in which they prove (also to everyone's satisfaction) that
women who help their husbands are the backbone of the nation's
business. You may take your choice.

Personally, our choice would be with the grimmer message of
Dulcy, especially as it calls for less serious connubial cooing than the
other, but at the end of the second act of To the Ladies, we were
willing to believe anything. This scene, which shows the head-table
at a banquet of the John Kincaid's Sons Piano Co., is unquestionably
the most original bit of comedy in town.

Even for those fortunates whom life has never dragged down
to attendance at a business banquet, this scene will have the fascina-
tion of true novelty. For the rest of us it is pitiless in its reality.
Everything is there, from the turgid speeches and the bantering of
the toastmaster to the waiters clattering off with the remains of the
squab bonne femme and the man who hopes to sell copies of the flash-
light photograph taken earlier in the evening. Russia has never
turned out drama more uncompromising in its adherence to the fright-
ful, sordid facts of life.

If only one banquet scene could be preserved for future generations out of all the files of drama, our vote would stand as follows: First choice--banquet scene from To the Ladies! Second
choice--banquet scene from Macbeth.

The rest of To the Ladies is just good, old-fashioned home-
made bread, in which you are constantly biting on delightful raisins
of sophisticated observation and satire which seem as if they belonged
in a cake. For writers who are such devastating kidders of hokum
in business, the authors of To the Ladies have been shameless in
the amount of hokum they have kneaded into their present play.
To ears attuned to the constantly recurring notes of incomparable
irony with which the three acts are filled, it seems incredible to hear
the young bride croon in all seriousness that being poor together is
not so bad after all, as it gives so many opportunities to make little
sacrifices for one another.

And someone must answer to his Maker for burdening Miss
Helen Hayes with an entirely gratuitous Southern accent, as if there
wasn't trouble enough in the world as it is. Miss Hayes has an up-
hill fight against an excess of sweetness anyway, without taking on
a Mobile drawl. It is greatly to her credit, therefore, that she
comes through To the Ladies with a plucky victory. And as for Otto
Kruger, all we can say is that at the last meeting of this department
he was elected its favorite juvenile.

The preceding acid remarks about To the Ladies must not be
taken as implying any lack of merit in the show. They simply were

inserted to avoid the charge of playing favorites with Messrs. Kaufman and Connelly, who, as our readers know, are a couple of <u>Life</u> boys who have made good. Mr. Kaufman was the lucky winner of <u>Life</u>'s Clean Fun Prize for the best Life Line thrown out a couple of months ago, and Mr. Connelly is the author of the famous Joseph L. Gonnick series on Business Efficiency. In fact, Mr. Gonnick himself appears in the flesh in <u>To the Ladies</u> in the character of John Kincaid (George Howell), president of the Kincaid Piano Co. His motto is, "The Kincaid Piano is the Heart of the Home." If you have been following Mr. Gonnick's articles, you should be particularly sure to see <u>To the Ladies</u>.

--Robert C. Benchley in <u>Life</u>
(March 9, 1922), page 18.

TOPSY AND EVA (Book by Catherine Chisholm Cushing, Music and Lyrics by the Duncan Sisters; Sam H. Harris Theatre, December 23, 1924)

The Duncan Sisters, our favorite two-part singers, in what is left of <u>Uncle Tom's Cabin</u>.

--Robert C. Benchley in <u>Life</u>
(March 19, 1925), page 19.

THE TRIAL OF MARY DUGAN (Bayard Veiller; National Theatre, September 19, 1927)

The author of <u>Within the Law</u> and <u>The Thirteenth Chair</u>, Mr. Bayard Veiller, has demonstrated once more his splendid sense of the theatre in <u>The Trial of Mary Dugan</u>. This time he has done rather more than write a good play. He has accomplished what very few dramatists could hope to do--he has created absorbing theatrical entertainment with no other machinery or action than that found in a court room during a murder trial. When the audience enters the theatre, the stage is already set to represent a session of the New York Supreme Court, and long before the play begins, scrub-women, policemen, reporters and other court hangers-on, wander about the scene in the desultory manner so familiar to anyone who has served on a jury trial. The gradual darkening of the house lights is the only indication that the play is about to begin. The audience itself represents the jury box.

With this novel beginning, the action of the play picks up quickly and holds with great intensity to the last moment. The break between acts is handled quite naturally through two adjournments of the court forced by incidents in the trial itself. The defendant in

this case is one Mary Dugan, recently of the Follies, who is alleged
to have stabbed and killed Edgar Rice, a man politely referred to by
one of the witnesses as her "sugar daddy." The way in which the
dramatic action develops through the unexpected revelation of several
of the witnesses is a masterpiece of stage technique. And the moment at which Mary's brother, Jimmie Dugan, discharges her attorney
and takes the case into his own hands is one not easily forgotten.
As the play involves all the elements of a mystery story, it would
be obviously unfair to give the solution.

There is only one fault to find with this play and that is its
obvious effort to sentimentalize the character and past life of Mary
Dugan herself. There were moments when one feared that her entire
career would be painted in a rosy glow of wronged innocence. Mr.
Veiller, however, came very near to saving the situation when he had
Mary Dugan admit that luxuries could after a time become almost necessities in one's life. But there is very little in the story to match
the relentless candor of such a character as Madame X.

This play has been staged by Mr. A.H. Van Buren and is a
masterpiece of expert casting and intelligent direction. Arthur Hohl,
as the district attorney, shows the sincerity of his performance by
making himself thoroughly and heartily disliked. The parts of the
various witnesses are not only characterized in the lines of the play
but invariably well acted as brief and succinct portraits. The chief
emotional burden falls, of course, upon Rex Cherryman, as Jimmie
Dugan, and upon Ann Harding, as Mary. Miss Harding has improved
notably in her restraint since her rather theatric performance in The
Woman Disputed last year. Mr. Cherryman's work is finely shaded
and full of manly sincerity. This story is obviously one of falsified
values, but of great theatrical quality.
                                        --Richard Dana Skinner in The
                                        Commonweal, Vol. 6, No. 24
                                        (October 19, 1927), page 584.

                              *   *   *

In these pages I have often complained of the dullness of our
crook and mystery plays: the same old formulas, the same old dum-
mies instead of people, the endless references to double-crossing,
dicks, stoolpigeons and bumping-off--these bore me to tears. With
few exceptions the dramatis personae are highly conventionalized
stock figures, like the characters in the old Italian Comedy of Masks.
All any playwright need do is to take a set of them from any play
of this category that has preceded him, and work them into his plot.
Take one murder to begin with, skilfully conceal the identity of the
criminal, mix up two "dicks," Inspector Burke, a funny cop, the girl,
the man, have everyone call up Spring 3100 at least nine times in
every act, use six "rods," and play hide-and-seek for two hours and
a quarter. Make the audience fix the crimes on every member of the
cast in turn, and at fourteen minutes to eleven discover the real

murderer, precisely the one man who seemed least likely to have
committed it.

Once in a while--as in Badges--a playwright will try to gal-
vanize one of his characters to life, and the public will think they
have seen something new. As indeed they will.

Such reflections passed through my mind as I watched two
mystery plays a few days ago. The first of these was The Trial of
Mary Dugan, by Bayard Veiller. Mr. Veiller's melodramas are rather
more skilfully contrived than the ordinary runs, and somewhat more
credible. His first success was Within the Law, produced nearly
fifteen years ago. Then came The Thirteenth Chair. The Trial of
Mary Dugan is conceded to be a most ingenious affair. To begin
with, the entire action takes place in a court-room; this alone is something of a stunt, for of course the principal happenings have all occurred off-stage before the play begins. The dramatist's skill is
proved in his ability to carry through his story entertainingly. Here
we have the little girl whose attractive young brother defends her
by telling the truth before judge and jury. To make a thing of this
sort at all credible is a triumph, but a still greater triumph is in
stating a truth that has, I think, never been so put into a melodrama before; the little girl (who is the "heroine") is not a bit nice,
and she confesses the sordid story of her life without excuses. Besides, her brother forces her to relate all the unsavory details, for
the purpose of clearing her of the charge of murder. There is in
the character of Mary more than a dash of authenticity. Here is a
"fallen" woman who is neither sentimentalized, nor otherwise falsified,
and at the end she does not even marry a nice young man, nor promise to reform. She is at the same time not vicious, nor especially
unhappy; in short, she is very much like thousands of other human
beings. But what would have happened to the play if the attractive
Ann Harding had not been defended by the fresh and rosy-cheeked
Rex Cherryman, I cannot say.

Outside the character of Mary Dugan, there was no one who
was in the least credible. Now, I am not putting the blame either
on Mr. Veiller or on the type of play he is writing: there is a place
for the crook and mystery play, just as there is a place for detective
stories, and those who like either are at perfect liberty to do so. It
is not my business to criticize adversely any dramatist for not writing
the kind of play I think worth writing, so long as he does his job
well. I can only say that I am occasionally bored by a form of writing, though it is doubtless entertaining in its limited way. But I
do wish that someone would come along, and while using the old
formula, would give me something that had teeth in it.

--Barrett H. Clark in The Drama,
Vol. 18, No. 4 (January 1928),
page 105.

THE VAGABOND KING (Music by Rudolf Friml, Book and Lyrics by
    Brian Hooker and W.H. Post; Casino Theatre, September 21,
    1925)

    One of the first things that we have to do in this bright new
1925 is clean up the big pile of musical comedies which have been
accumulating ever since September. (Oh, all right, 1926 then!)

    This season has been marked by the predominance of good mu-
sical shows over good legitimate productions, the return of old-
fashioned harmony, the emergence of literate lyric-writers, and the
large number of musical comedies to which one can take the children
without having to ask them what the sex references mean.

    Following The Student Prince of last season and this, The
Vagabond King and Princess Flavia have brought back with a clatter
of swords and a zum-zum of basses the old-time thigh-slapping, stein-
raising operetta, with male choruses and trilling sopranos, loud laughter from the villagers, and comical mix-ups resulting from Prince
Udolpho's making believe that he is a poor peasant lad, or a poor
peasant lad's making believe he is Prince Udolpho. Personally, we
are never stirred to anything more than an approving nod by these
swashbuckling romantic comic operas, chiefly because the books are
so deadly and the comedians so explosive, but it is good to know that
part-singing is coming in again and that you can take the folks to a
musical show without apologizing afterward.
                                —Robert C. Benchley in Life (Jan-
                                    uary 7, 1926), page 20.

VANITIES see EARL CARROLL'S VANITIES

THE VARYING SHORE (Zoë Akins; Hudson Theatre, December 5,
    1921)

    The Varying Shore is just another tune on the same Akins
theme. And it would seem to suggest that she has but one string
to her bow. Declassée and The Varying Shore are much alike not-
withstanding that the persons concerned are from different parts of
the world. Each has practically the same problem. Each deals in
much the same way.

    And if you come back at me with, "But what's the objection to
that?", my answer at once, "None." But the Akins talent, I think,
can do another idea. Another story. Another viewpoint. What, for
example, can she do with a man's story? Let us see.

But to the new play. It tells a story backwards. Instead of telling the story so that we are interested in what will happen next, the method is that of what has happened before that, and so on. In such a sort of technique there is a great deal of suspense and cleverness, but only at the very end does it fail because the prologue and the epilogue are the same. We have forgotten what happened in act one by the time the epilogue arrives. In other words, in the epilogue the two characters are aged, say, seventy. In the third act they are aged sixteen. In the second act say twenty-five. And in the third act about forty. In this way we become somewhat confused. Still the epilogue doesn't matter so much since we know the end all the time. And doubtless that is why Miss Akins wrote it that way. She sensed what others would call an unhappy ending and so she wrote the end at the beginning.

A girl gives herself to a young Virginian. And when she learns he does not love her she runs away. That's act three. In act two she leaves another man for the same reason. In act one the man who is about to marry her decides it is too risky for his position. And all through is a beau who has been constant. Tell the story the other way (act one, act two and act three) and it is as the play is done.

The story is interesting and often dramatic but rarely is the drama very vital. The scenes are all so very long. Far too long. There seems to be constant repetition and only the ablest sort of direction could have made it hold. Too much comment.

Miss Ferguson was occasionally magnificent and often very monotonous. And the fault was as much hers as Miss Akins' lines. A voice which is as individual as hers must be used with the greatest possible care and thought to avoid the voice seeming to be always in the same key. An actress who can do what she did at the end of act three is an able actress.

The cast with few exceptions was splendid. Rollo Peters was a triumph. He will certainly go far. Paul Everton, Geraldine O'Brien, James Crane in a too small part, Charles Francis, Wright Kramer-- acting of the finest.

Again Sam Forrest proves what a craftsman he is. I know of very few men who could have made this play move as it did.

> --S. Jay Kaufman in The New York
> Dramatic Mirror, December 10,
> 1921, page 845.

* * *

The Varying Shore is the only production lucky enough to get in under the wire this week. It is a rather uneven play by Zoë Akins, with Elsie Ferguson as its star. What is probably the worst prologue since Drinkwater's <u>Mary Stuart</u> gives the performance a wet, heavy track for a getaway, and an equally bad epilogue sends you out with the feeling of having seen an awfully good show in the High School hall.

But in between there are scenes of considerable interest, enhanced by the regal grace of Miss Ferguson, and a novel arrangement of acts whereby we watch the heroine go backward, from old age to youth, in her refined but illicit career, makes <u>The Varying Shore</u> at least worth something more than the ordinary. And this in spite of the fact that early in the play Miss Akins has one of her characters hazard the simile that "Life is like a race." But perhaps that was considered new stuff in 1870.

--Robert C. Benchley in <u>Life</u> (December 22, 1921), page 18.

THE VORTEX (Noel Coward; Henry Miller Theatre, September 16, 1925)

Mr. Noel Coward, who really <u>is</u> English (Mr. Arlen is Turkish or something and the "Michael Arlen" is merely a pseudonymph),* is not so much impressed by the glamour of British citizenship. In <u>The Vortex</u> his English society sinners are just as drab and pitiful as the society sinners of Norway or America, and they work together to make a bitter and moving play. In a far better season than this one, <u>The Vortex</u> would stand out, for Mr. Coward has humor and a sense of drama, in addition to which he can act (he plays his own leading rôle). This gives him about three legs on the season's cup. If only for the curtain to the second act, and the final scene between mother and son (which, far from being the happy ending that some seem to think it, is, by inference, singularly wise and sad), <u>The Vortex</u> should not be missed.

--Robert C. Benchley in <u>Life</u> (October 8, 1925), page 20.

*   *   *

This play with which the much discussed Noel Coward has flashed into the American scene, exhibits a curious combination of theatrical strength with dramatic weakness. In fact, I have seldom seen a play illustrating with sharper outline the difference between these qualities; the theatrical, that which gives life and emotional energy to certain specific scenes, and the dramatic, that which lends enduring value or significance to the play as a whole.

---

*This review immediately followed a review of Michael Arlen's <u>The Green Hat</u> (q.v.).

Several scenes in The Vortex have an extraordinarily fine theatrical quality. In the hands of good actors, they establish an emotional power of rare intensity. But the theme upon which the dramatic importance of the whole play must rest is confused, inconclu-
sive, and in one essential point, weak.

The story will help to explain this point. Florence Lancaster
is a mother trying to retain her youth in the process of making
much younger men fall in love with her. Her grown son, Nicky, returns with his fiancée, Bunty, from a long sojourn in Paris, to find
his father a broken old man, and his mother an absurd figure, with
dyed hair and artificially young manners, leading by a string a boy,
Tom Veryan, no older than Nicky, himself. At first he does not
sense the full import of the situation. But when Bunty blithely
shifts her affections to Tom, and Nicky overhears the ensuing scene
in which his mother debases herself by appealing to Tom to remain
with her, the scales suddenly fall from his eyes.

In the last act, Nicky comes to his mother's bedroom. There
mother and son face each other with their masks torn off. Nicky, it
seems, has become a drug fiend. He realizes that in his own way he
is no better than his mother. They have each made wrecks of their
lives. In this hour of crisis and mutual disclosure, what can they
do to prevent catastrophe? The curtain falls on mother and son, in
each others arms, blindly searching for strength, beseeching the help
that neither is sure can be found from the other.

Obviously the close of the second act and the entire third act
provide the emotional quality which makes splendid theatre. You would
find the same quality if you overheard a street quarrel between a
drunken husband and his wife. But genuine dramatic interest demands something more. It demands a correspondence to some great
truth of life, without the obvious intervention of the dramatist's own
theories. Unfortunately Mr. Coward has injected into his play the
theory that both mother and son are victims of "circumstances," of
the "vortex of modern life which makes rottenness so easy." He is
not content to leave it that they are both weak-willed, and to let
the catastrophe work itself out from that as a starting point. He
would have it that forces larger than themselves have conspired
against them; and here is where the play preaches a pessimism far
beyond the testimony of human experience. Neither character seeks
from within the strength to start over again--because neither sees
clearly that the beginning of the tragedy came from within. To say
that our particular modern life makes rottenness easy, is to give the
lie to the testimony of centuries, which says that in all times and all
conditions of mankind, it has been infinitely easier to fall than to
rise. A play whose motivation is tacked down to the special conditions of a day--and falsely tacked down, at that--cannot hope to attain that universal importance which is the key to genuine dramatic
power. The Vortex states a problem falsely, and then offers no solution. It has deliberately shifted the moral responsibility to un-

reality--to an imaginary being that simply has no separate moral ex-
istence--to society.

> --Richard Dana Skinner in The
> Commonweal, Vol. 2, No. 22
> (October 7, 1925), page 537.

THE WANDERING JEW (E. Temple Thurston; Knickerbocker Theatre,
    October 20, 1921)

I wonder if Mr. Belasco had anything to do with it, The Wandering Jew. The only Belasco touch, so far as I could see, was
the speed of the performance. Not, please understand, that I mean
to minimize Mr. Latham's credit. But as in a Hopkins or a Cohan or
a Belasco production there are always distinct evidences of the work
of these men.

The Wandering Jew isn't a play. It's a series of plays. A
series of episodes. Each sufficient in itself. Each dramatic and compelling. And written so that it must find a tremendous interest in
Jew and Gentile. At the outset the Jew is cursed with everlasting
life. Then follow a series of persecutions down the ages until the
Spanish Inquisition is reached. There his soul sees the light of
Christ and he dies. In the bald telling no notion of the beauty.
And seeing the light of Christ is not propaganda for converting Jews
to Christianity. The Jew is always saying that Christ is a Jew and
that he is the only Christian. E. Temple Thurston, who wrote it,
has, it should be added, made the suspense a matter of just how it
would all end. Of just how the Jew would be made to look upon the
face of Christ. And to do this without making it propaganda is no
little feat, as you will see when you see the play.

There are bound to be comparisons with Ben Hur, but this
has no scenic effects to lure the crowd. Its effects are rather more
of story and acting. And that will be its appeal.

Of the acting it seemed to me that the best was Howard Lang
in two characters. The difference between his work and that of
Tyrone Power--who acts the title rôle--is that Mr. Power seems always to be reading lines and never to be thinking about them. That
is, we do not see him think as we do Mr. Lang. In the final scene
he has less of this abstraction, but it is his physical rather than his
mental or spiritual side that carries his performance.

Helen Ware had all too little to do. Merely one death scene.
Albert Brunning, too, was wasted. Sidney Herbert is always excellent. And Belle Bennett the night's triumph.

> --S. Jay Kaufman in The New York
> Dramatic Mirror (November 5,
> 1921), page 665.

* * *

The Wandering Jew is pretty dull. It has lots of people, lots
of scenery, and gives every indication of having been an expensive
thing for Messrs. Belasco and Erlanger to produce, but along about
nine o'clock you begin to wonder what the next stage-setting is going
to look like. It is the same speculative interest in the scenery of the
next act which buoys me up through some operas and most Shakespearean performances.

And the time has passed when a spectacle can knock audiences
cold simply by being a spectacle. John Murray Anderson and Mr.
Ziegfeld have changed all that. Something more than money has
got to be put into scenery in order to make it distinctive to-day.
Even money and ordinary good taste will not do it. Perhaps "imagination" is not too strong a word for what is needed. Fifteen years
ago The Wandering Jew would have struck people blind with its
splendor, but to-day they are impressed with it in much the same degree as they are impressed by the Hotel Touraine in Boston.

This is not to say that The Wandering Jew is badly done. It
is done about as well as it could be. But what's the sense in people
going about talking in blank verse anyway? It sounds silly.
                         --Robert C. Benchley in Life (No-
                           vember 17, 1921), page 18.

WATERLOO BRIDGE (Robert Emmett Sherwood; Fulton Theatre, Janu-
     ary 6, 1930)

With his latest play, Waterloo Bridge, the author of The Road
to Rome, Robert Emmet Sherwood, emerges from George Bernard Shaw's
whiskers a full-fledged playwright on his own. Furthermore, he
emerges as one in whose work there is an under-rumble of real dramatic power. He manages to make his spectators sit with their
mouths a little open, oblivious of their surroundings, with the delicious sensation running up and down their spines that something
overwhelming is about to happen. The theatre was invented to house
this sensation and it offers no better entertainment to its customers.

Nothing overwhelming ever quite happens in Waterloo Bridge.
It is a simple war-time story of a guileless youth in the Canadian
Army who meets a street-walker on her beat, falls in love with her,
continues to love her even after he finds out the worst, and leaves
her with the menace of reform hanging over her head. Mr. Sherwood has been obliged to string a good many words between the
peaks of action, and sometimes they sag a little when the peaks are
too widely separated; but they are all very intelligent words and

they are feelingly pronounced by Glenn Hunter, June Walker and an excellent cast.

> --Ralph Barton in Life (January
> 17, 1930), page 20.

WHAT PRICE GLORY? (Maxwell Anderson and Lawrence Stallings;
  Plymouth Theatre, September 3, 1924)

What Price Glory? by Lawrence Stallings and Maxwell Anderson is the sensational success of the season. There is about a popular sensation something that imposes upon the critic a certain caution. A play is seldom as good as it is said to be in the first heat of enthusiasm. What Price Glory? is in fact a remarkably good play whose popularity is due partly to its merits and largely to a variety of circumstances that have little to do with its merit. Even the merits of the play are of a type that might easily have failed of recognition had the elements not been mixed for the occasion. There are few subjects about which more romantic lies are told than about war. And there is no time at which the unromantic truth is more acceptable than just after the lies have been nailed by experience. The authors of this play were fortunate that their play appeared at a moment at which the audience was ready for a cooling draft on war. It does not follow that this play tells the truth, the whole truth and nothing but the truth on war. In its way it too is romantic. Nor does this play tell the whole truth about the A.E.F. There is a great deal of truth about the American troops in France that this play does not tell, and some things that it tells are in my humble opinion untrue. But if What Price Glory? is not an authoritative disquisition on war it is none the less a noteworthy play. At one blow the authors have freed themselves of the tyrannies of plot, suspense, manipulated action and climax. There is no story to speak of, no motive of romantic love; woman appears in only one character; no villains are foiled and punished; no heroes are rewarded. The authors play no favorites and the audience at no time finds its sympathies deeply concerned with anyone of the characters. It is through these facts rather than in spite of them that the play achieves its highest virtues. For the play is firmly knit and closely observed. It is robust and realistic. It moves with an inexhaustible store of energy and good spirits. Such lusty vigor as is displayed in this play is a rare quality. There is in What Price Glory? a Balzacian quality of robustness that is the mark of imagination at its best. Art demands the observant eye, the instructed brain. It also demands muscle.

> --Thomas H. Dickinson in American Review, Vol. 3, No. 2
> (March-April, 1925), page 220.

THE WHITE PEACOCK (Olga Petrova; Comedy Theatre, December 26,
    1921)

    Olga Petrova, who has of late been appearing in the films and
on the vaudeville stage, returned to the legitimate, at the Monday
holiday matinee, in a new florid romance of which she is the author,
producer, and star, all in one. Her talent is undeniable, and her
personal appearance is a great asset. She is thrillingly beautiful,
and moves with a grace that is superb.

    The play itself, which caused sedate Boston to fret a little, is
a gaudy type of melodrama, full of grand opera hysterics and comic
opera costumes. The action takes place in Seville, which at the start
calls for bright colorings. Revette di Ribera y Santallos, played
with intensity by Mme. Petrova, is discovered trailing about her bedroom attired in a gorgeous gown of blue-green broacde, which she
soon abandons for a more comfortable sleeping dress with a train
several yards long. A handsome stranger in a Don Jose costume enters via the window, and--the rest is about what you expect after
reading The Sheik! He has really escaped from the jail, but looks
like a prince in disguise. Revette is involved in a scandal, but at
eleven o'clock she lands forever and respectably in the hero's arms,
with only a bullet wound and internal injuries for her trouble.

    Mme. Petrova moves majestically and gorgeously throughout the
play, and succeeds in making it entertaining, at least pictorially.
Malcolm Fassett and E.L. Fernandez are two excellent players who
contribute much to the performance. It is an interesting evening, and
there are doubtless plenty of people to flock to see this colorful play.

                              --Homer Dwight in The New York
                                Dramatic Mirror, December 31,
                                1921, page 999.

                        * * *

    Madame Olga Petrova has done handsomely for herself in The
White Peacock, which she wrote for her own use. It is full of eye-
work, and Madame Petrova flashes an intensely wicked iris, to say
nothing of throwing the letter "r" about like so much listerine.

    But full as The White Peacock is of Spanish hokumaño and
chile con carnal, the always intelligent personality of Madame Petrova
glides through the play, projecting such lines as she has with an
effectiveness that promises a great deal for the night when she first
appears in a real part.

                              --Robert C. Benchley in Life (Jan-
                                uary 19, 1922), page 18.

THE WHOLE TOWN'S TALKING (John Emerson and Anita Loos; Bijou
     Theatre, August 29, 1923)

     If we were surprised at seeing Bruce McRae in an open-and-
shut farce with music,* imagine our emotions on finding that the
feverish little party dashing in and out of the room in The Whole
Town's Talking was the quiet, repressed Grant Mitchell. Not that
Mr. Mitchell doesn't run in and out, and even climb up on chande-
liers, very well indeed. It just seemed funny, that's all.

     Probably John Emerson and Anita Loos, who wrote the play,
had a very large and definite public in mind when they put it together. They are too clever a team to strike out aimlessly. But the public that they will reach in their synthetic first act is not the public
that will enjoy the amusing Brother Elk scene in the last act, although both publics will probably enjoy the fight in the dark.
Which makes quite a good assortment of publics, when you come right
down to it. And almost any public will appreciate the fact that Miss
Catherine Owen is beautiful. Any public, that is, with what is known
as the Public Eye.
                                   --Robert C. Benchley in Life (Sep-
                                        tember 20, 1923), page 18.

WHOOPEE (William Anthony McGuire; New Amsterdam Theatre, De-
     cember 4, 1928)

     Although Whoopee is not a moving picture, I venture to mention
it on this page because Mr. [Robert] Benchley was in Hollywood making talkies at the time of its opening, and I can see no reason why
our loyal readers should have to wait for him to announce that
Whoopee is one of Mr. Ziegfeld's grandest shows, in which several
undraped ladies appear riding on glorified Shetland ponies, and in
which that comical fellow, Eddie Cantor, sings a song containing the
line,

          "It's not the chorus girl's voice
          That gets her big Rolls-Royce --
          It's making whoopee!"
                                   --Robert E. Sherwood in Life (De-
                                        cember 21, 1928), page 22.

                         *   *   *

*A reference to Little Miss Bluebeard, in which Bruce McRae co-
starred with Irene Bordoni.

There are certain ventures in the American theatre which aren't ventures at all. As soon as somebody says "Let's do it," they are as good as sold out three months in advance. Directly the names "Florenz Ziegfeld" and "Eddie Cantor" were placed in juxtaposition in the press-agent's advance notices, and the New Amsterdam Theatre specified as their meeting-place, a man would have been a fool to plan on getting in to see the show before the ice is out of Forty-Second Street.

It wouldn't have made any difference if Whoopee had been a bad show (which it isn't). It was foreordained to success. In the first place, it has the aura of success in its horoscope, and, in the second place, even a bad show with Eddie Cantor would be good entertainment. So it would be difficult to see how Mr. Ziegfeld could lose, unless he played the entire show with the lights out or in another theatre from the one to which he had sold tickets. Even then people might enjoy themselves just because they had bought tickets to a Ziegfeld show with Eddie Cantor in it. Such is the power of the Will to Laugh.

Mr. Cantor is no child of fortune, born with a silver gag in his mouth. He has not achieved this impregnable position overnight. No one can begrudge him his present pretty sitting-position, for he has earned it through years of hard work, each year improving on the model of the year before, until now it is difficult to believe that this wide-eyed master of clowning is the same tiny black boy who used to dart back and forth clapping his hands and singing sex songs for the Shuberts.

Mr. Cantor's first step toward his present perfection was when he took the white horn-rimmed glasses away from those terrified eyes and gave his Levantine features a chance to work in the light unhampered by burnt cork. He need worry no more about further improving his stuff. In the words of the camera-man, he can "hold it." It is just right.

Need we add the customary salute to Mr. Ziegfeld for a perfect production of Whoopee?

--Robert C. Benchley in Life (January 4, 1929), page 21.

WHY NOT? (Jesse Lynch Williams; 48th Street Theatre, December 25, 1922)

A high comedy of conventions inspirited by a brilliant dialogue and a commendable esprit de corps. A quadrangle situation with much excellent satire on the laws relating to marriage and divorce,

and the canons of the church as they affect monogamy. Tom Powers
distinguishes himself as the poet-butler.

--Pierre Loving in The Drama,
Vol. 13, No. 6 (March 1923),
page 213.

WILD BIRDS (Dan Totheroh; Cherry Lane Playhouse, April 9, 1925)

Some very delicate and beautiful writing, much deep artistry
and a great deal of poignant and fine acting, have gone into this
play by Dan Totheroh--a new playwright whose sense of tragedy is
no less profound than Eugene O'Neill's, while possessing a greater
refinement, a much higher spirituality, and a richer spirit of song.
The Cherry Lane Playhouse has given Wild Birds a production which
more than merits all the praise the critics have bestowed on it.

Unlike the expressionistic drama of Walter Hasenclever, Beyond,
in which nearly all semblance of reality was stripped away, leaving
only certain deep and essential thoughts and emotions to be expressed,
Wild Birds has a surface reality. It is a play with a distinct plot,
a specific locality, a time and a dialect. You can accept it as realistic drama, well conceived, swiftly moving and at times quaveringly
beautiful. But Mr. Totheroh is striving for something more. He
has chosen his characters as symbols of the life-struggle itself. Into
each one he has breathed a certain universal quality--almost as if he
were to say--"this child, Mazie, is innocence; this poor half-wit,
Sandy, with the wisdom of the serpent, is Eros; and this wandering
farm hand, Marshall, is the truth of life whom many men seek and
few encounter."

There is, in fact, a program note which likens the play to a
modern Morality--but I feel that most people, if they wish to look at
all beneath the surface drama, will prefer to gather their own meaning from it. That great master of English prose, Arthur Machen,
has pointed out with singular clearness how often the full implication
of an artist's work is unknown, even to the artist himself, at the time
of creative effort; and that it is often years later before he can look
back and gather into himself the full beauty, the stark tragedy, or
the infinite pathos of what he has done.

In Wild Birds, if I am not mistaken, Mr. Totheroh is striving
to express that age-old struggle of the human soul toward a spiritual
re-birth--the great paradox of the double victory; of death over material life, and of spiritual life over material death. The two pathetic
young characters about whom he weaves his story, after a bewildered
search through the cross currents of hate, brute force, and mis-
guided passion surrounding them, succumb to a mistaken love; only
to find death in the end. But for each of them it is a death of

purgation--a death that reveals also a truth beyond, which neither was capable of seeing while in the midst of the tumult. If, in portraying this struggle, Mr. Totheroh seems himself to be groping for his answer--if, as one suspects, he stumbles upon his final truth instead of working toward it with clear vision--and if, in selecting physical death, and in one case suicide, as his all too-easy solution-- the literal effect of his play seems to belie its spiritual intent; these are faults of incompleteness rather than of that perverted direction one feels so often in the work of O'Neill. There is here the swing and cadence of real tragedy; the beauty of search, if not of full attainment; and the singing note of sincerity. Whatever the popular success of his play, Mr. Totheroh has unquestionably taken his place as an artist of high calibre and rich promise.

A word should be added concerning the acting. In this respect I have rarely, if ever, seen so well-balanced a performance-- one in which each actor seemed to draw inspiration from the poetry of the author. But Mildred MacLeod and Donald Duff, as the two young unfortunates about whom the action turns, achieved a rare perfection of sensitive understanding. Where all were excellent, they were perhaps, preëminent.

> --Richard Dana Skinner in The
> Commonweal, Vol. 2, No. 1 (May
> 13, 1925), page 23.

WILDFLOWER (Book and Lyrics by Otto Harbach and Oscar Hammerstein II, Music by Herbert Stothart and Vincent Youmans; Casino Theatre, February 7, 1923)

Wildflower seemed to us to be one of the best musical shows of the season, in spite of what the newspaper boys thought of it. True, the book isn't much, but if you're going in for books you might as well stay at home and tell stories every evening. The music, written by Herbert Stothart and Vincent Youmans, while it may not be so high-class as that of Caroline, is just about eight times more interesting and novel, and has been so skillfully orchestrated that it makes the Caroline score sound like Ten Exercises for Tiny Fingers. While Edith Day is not one of our thirty favorite leading ladies, she does very nicely as the Wildflower, and Olin Howland succeeds in carrying the none-too-brilliant comedy along with him into the territory of genuine pathos at times. Mr. Hammerstein has again shown that he knows where to find eighteen girls who combine good looks with evidences of human intelligence, to take part in his very lively dance numbers.

> --Robert C. Benchley in Life
> (March 1, 1923), page 18.

YOU AND I (Philip Barry; Belmont Theatre, February 19, 1923)

        You and I, Philip Barry's brilliant comedy, the Harvard Prize
Play of 1922, does not sharply criticize American life but it comments
upon it, forcibly. That Mr. Barry, himself, gave over a profitable
engagement with the advertisers to become one of the playwrights,
whose living is at best precarious, is well known. This, then, is
the problem he presents: the business man who does not find an
expression for his creative imagination in his own business; who has,
perhaps for financial reasons, stifled some creative urge in youth.
In Mr. Barry's play, Maitland White betrays his own heart in living
his own problem over again with his own son. It is a poignant
theme. Barry has handled it deftly and not too heavily. His dialogue, which, as played by a superb cast whose business was to
squeeze every laugh out of the play, seemed spotty when one heard
it at the Belmont Theatre. It reads more smoothly. It is the usual
talk of nice people, in a Mt. Kisco, Westchester County setting.
There is cleverness in this play, and a good deal of underlying wisdom. It is authentic and it is competent. I find that it does not
progress so unflinchingly to its conclusion as does Icebound. It is
just a little tricked out and padded. Its excellent slang dialogue
dates it. However, these are minor considerations, are they not?
You will enjoy reading this play. Here is a wise speech from a successful novelist; but I wonder if Mr. Barry doesn't know that successful novelists though they may talk this way, never feel it?

        No, Matey. I suppose I should have, if I could honestly
        feel that art--true art-- was the gainer for my sacrifice.
        But a popular novelist! Oh--don't you suppose I know what
        my stuff is worth? (He continues with deep feeling.) I
        give you my word--there's no such hell on earth as that of
        the man who knows himself doomed to mediocrity in the work
        he loves--whatever it may be. You love painting--you think
        you could paint great pictures. Well--go on thinking--but
        don't try it. No! No!--You've done well in business--be
        wise, and stick to it.
                                --John Farrar in The Bookman,
                                Vol. 58, No. 1 (September 1923),
                                pages 58-59.

YOUNG WOODLEY (John Van Druten; Belmont Theatre, November 2,
    1925)

        There is a play concerning the struggle of adolescence before
the newly discovered monster of sex which succeeds in every respect
where The Glass Slipper fails. We refer to Young Woodley, in which
Glenn Hunter is starring after three years away from New York.

This comedy came under the ban in England, where it was forbidden
production for no reason that we can see except that it concerns
English schoolboys. Possibly in England schoolboys never fall in
love with their masters' wives, and sex is ignored until graduation.
At any rate, the play had to come to America for a showing and presumably the day was saved at Eton and Harrow. Mr. Hunter ought
to receive a vote of thanks for the beautiful restraint with which he
plays Woodley. In a rôle which teems with laughs for the vulgar, he
ignores them every one, acting his part as if he had a message to
give, which of course he has. We wondered how many parents in
the orchestra might be squirming uneasily at the thought of their own
misunderstood sons, and how many men might be remembering with a
sigh the agonies of their own calf love. The author has built up a
comedy as delicate and graceful as it is true. Indeed, its truth must
be apparent if one can sit without boredom through an evening listening to the half formed opinions of eighteen year old boys on love.
It is slightly inconsistent in a play which is entirely English, and
apparently so cast, to have Glenn Hunter, who is altogether New
York State in accent and intonation as the star. But Hunter's breathless, husky voice, and his skill in using it, would carry him over
difficulties far greater than this. Young Woodley is delightful.

                                             --Larry Barretto in The Bookman,
                                                Vol. 62, No. 5 (January 1926),
                                                pages 595-596.

                                  *   *   *

        John Van Druten, the author of this play, is a young English
schoolmaster, who writes with a great deal of tender understanding
of the eager and heartrending emotional gropings of a sensitive boy
on the borderland of manhood. It is a very frank play--laying completely bare the mind of the adolescent schoolboy as it is, and not
at all as many writers have idealized it. These boys are asking the
eternal questions of youth, some in cleanliness of spirit, some with
coarseness and cynicism. Because of the emphasis on this material,
it is essentially a play for more mature audiences, for those who
earnestly wish to recapture their understanding of troubled youth,
rather than for those who, regardless of age, are still entangled in
the confusion of youth's problem. The lift and beauty of the last
act might be entirely missed by those already too preoccupied with
the childish view of sex--and without the implications of that last
act, the play is one that would simply drive in the nail of morbidity
more deeply. This should be stated in all fairness to the censor who
barred it from the English stage. It is not a play for any and every
audience.

        Briefly, it tells the story of a boy approaching eighteen who,
rebelling against the coarser instincts of his companions, falls in love
with the young wife of his schoolmaster. Shy, awkward, sensitive,
gifted with the soul of a poet, Young Woodley falls into the trap of
his own idealizations, and turns the fullness of his growing emotions

toward the one person who seems to understand him. Unfortunately
for him, she reciprocates his love--a rebellion on her part, too,
against the cold, prosaic mentality of the man she has married. The
end of the play shows us the gradual maturing of both, and the
turning to good account of a situation that might have led to tragedy
--the boy setting his teeth into the realities of life and its responsi-
bilities, the wife after one mistake from which Woodley has a most un-
happy--and I think unnecessary--reaction, too wise to break his ideal
by insisting that her love was not real, but summoning him to the
renunciation and the strength upon which can be built the tower of
freedom and of manhood.

There is a firmness and a right mindedness behind this play
so conspicuously lacking in Shaw's Candida. Where Candida sends
Marchbanks away simply because she is still in love with her husband,
Mrs. Simmons sends Woodley into the world of men because she knows
that any other course would mean his destruction and in spite of all
the clamor of her own soul for the things her husband can never
give her. She weaves no sophistries about "conventions." Instead,
she conquers herself and in doing so gives Woodley his chance to
build fine things through suffering.

So in spite of all erotic material in which the play deals, and
at times to excess, it manages to come to grips with the finer realities and the beauty that life holds for those prepared to build on
its hardships. This theme has received an extraordinarily sensitive
and understanding treatment at the hands of Glenn Hunter and
Helen Gahagan. Of the two parts, Miss Gahagan's, as Mrs. Simmons,
is the more difficult, because the more complex, and the more acutely
restrained. Perhaps the highest tribute paid to her ever-increasing
art as an actress is the fact that the attention of all critics has been
focused on Mr. Hunter's amazingly poignant portrait of Woodley. Yet
one false note in Miss Gahagan's work would have utterly marred
this portrait. To a limited and understanding audience, this play, as
now acted, will be for the most part lyric and courageous. To others,
it might be either dangerously morbid or cynically grotesque. A
slightly greater restraint might have made it acceptable to many more.

--Richard Dana Skinner in The
Commonweal, Vol. 3, No. 2 (November 18, 1925), page 51.

ZIEGFELD FOLLIES OF 1920 (Dialogue, Lyrics and Music by Irving
    Berlin, Victor Herbert, Gene Buck, Dave Stamper, James Mont-
    gomery, Joseph McCarthy, Harry Tierney, George V. Hobart,
    and W.C. Fields; New Amsterdam Theatre, June 22, 1920)

The Ziegfeld Follies of 1920 maintains the traditions of the Follies of other years in extravagant beauty of production, in variety

and ingenuity of song and dance, in a host of comic entertainers and
what Tody Hamilton used to call "a gorgeous galaxy of girls." But
the new revue does not line up to its tradition of the almost continuous appearance of this galaxy.

After all, the national reputation of the Follies has been established upon that institution, Girl. The patrons of this year's revue seek Girl, and are given Comedian.

The beauty standards are as high as ever they were in individual
chorus girl as in the scenic aspects of the production. Mr. Ziegfeld,
like John Murray Anderson, has torn a leaf from Gordon Craig's note-
book, and has substituted rich and colorful draperies for the canvas
settings of yesterday. And Ben Ali Haggin has contributed some
strikingly effective ensemble groupings.

Charles Winninger manages to extract some comedy out of pretty poor material. Fannie Brice figures often in various vampire and
ballet numbers. She is at her best in an automobile skit, in which
she has the assistance of the droll Mr. Fields. Van and Schenck are
a harmonious success, Carl Randall dances with his usual abandon,
John Steel sings often and well, Ray Dooley offers her familiar baby-
carriage travesty, Mary Eaton is a graceful figure, De Lyle Alda
sings effectively and looks as stunning as ever, and Bernard Granville dances with his customary zest, and the newcomer, Jack Donahue, offers some amusing eccentric steps.

> --Louis R. Reid in The New York
> Dramatic Mirror (June 26, 1920),
> page 1289.

ZIEGFELD FOLLIES OF 1921 (Dialogue and Lyrics by Channing Pol-
lock, Gene Buck, Willard Mack, Ralph Spence, Buddy De Sylva,
Music by Victor Herbert, Rudolf Friml, Dave Stamper; Globe
Theatre, June 21, 1921)

However much we may moan for the days of funny librettos
and tuneful scores and complain in a high treble that they don't have
any shows today like The Yankee Consul, The Red Mill, or The Ar-
cadians, there is one thing that the present array of productions is
rich in beyond the wildest dreams of the theatre-goer of fifteen years
ago. Perhaps "Beauty" is not too strong a word for what we mean.

The beauty of the setting, costuming and ensembles of even the
most unpretentious present-day revue makes the extravaganza of
The Wizard of Oz period look like something on a wedding-cake in a
Third Avenue window. Take a man and his wife whose first baby was
born in 1905 and who since then haven't been able to get anyone to
stay with the children long enough to allow for a trip to the theatre,

and put them suddenly in seats M-101-102 at a John Murray Anderson production or any one of the more artistic of modern revues, and they would unquestionably believe themselves to be in Heaven. It is doubtful if even Heaven can boast of such good taste and delicacy of touch in the matter of decoration and ensemble numbers. I somehow have a feeling that Heaven looks as if it might have been staged by the Shuberts.

Chief among those producers who are spoiling us with more beauty than we deserve comes Mr. Ziegfeld. Each year his _Follies_ seem to have reached the point of saturation with sheer visual exquisiteness, and then the next production comes along and sets a new mark. Just what can be done next year to surpass James Reynolds' "The Birthday of the Dauphin" which opens the second act of this year's _Follies_ is is impossible to imagine. But it probably will be done.

And as a general thing I am not one to murmur ecstatically over those big spectacular numbers in which a succession of chorus-girls, each dressed to represent some flower, come on and offer themselves to the Queen Bee to be made into a gigantic wreath for the wedding of the Humming-Bird and the Ruby-Throated Grossbeak. It's all right for the first three or four minutes but it takes them all so long to get on and get their message across that by the time the wreath or the wedding-cake, or whatever it is, is half built, you feel that if a Dooley doesn't fall through the roof soon you will scream.

It was a temptation, therefore, to stay out in front of the Globe Theatre finishing that "Between-the-Acts Little Cigar" until "The Birthday of the Dauphin" was well under way. In case it should also be a temptation to you, this is to warn you not to yield to it.

At the risk, however, of being socially ostracized, it must be admitted that, so far as the Ben Ali Haggin tableaux are concerned, this department is willing to go on record as using the word "ham." Much the same effect used to be got in the old days by what were known as "living pictures," and if you were to see the same thing thrown on a screen from a magic lantern you would look around for the words to the chorus of "You're the Sweetest Little Girl of All," expecting everyone to join in singing. It would not surprise us in the least to see a Ben Ali Haggin group slowly fade out and another picture slowly come in showing a man in a robin's-egg blue coat, pink trousers, and a straw-hat on the back of his head, leaning over a yellow gate and kissing a girl in a light green frock and sun-bonnet. But, of course, that is an entirely personal reaction.

This year's _Follies_ is full of good comedy, which is somewhat of an innovation. There is in the first place Fannie Brice, our favorite actress in emotional roles. No matter how unimportant the material with which Miss Brice has to work, it takes on a new value in her hands. And here some of her material is good in itself, which makes a combination justifying any claim that may be made that she is the funniest woman on the American stage. To hear her version of "Kiss Me Again" (which is the version of almost everyone who tries to sing it to himself after all these years, viz.: the words "kiss me again" repeated over and over to fit in with the music), is, as the advertisements say, to be convinced.

W.C. Fields, who hitherto has shared with Joe Jackson the distinction of making pantomime funny, is now given an opportunity to speak, and, unless these old senses have lost their cunning, he is on the high road to being one of our best all-around comedians. A little skit entitled "Off To The Country," which he wrote himself, depicting the troubles of a family trying to board a subway train, is enough to give him the Pulitzer Prize for next year. It is a comforting thought that each year there will always be Mr. Fields with something of his own that can be relied upon.

That is perhaps the trouble with Raymond Hitchcock in the present production. He has too little of his own to work with. He has to open the show with a deadly thing written by someone else in which he apostrophizes the Statue of Liberty on the sin of Prohibition. In fact, all the Prohibition jokes in the performance are tied around Mr. Hitchcock's neck. Once in a while he breaks loose and you feel the old glow spreading through your system that only he can rouse, but only occasionally. You wish that more people would come in late so that he could have more opportunity to introduce them to the orchestra leader. These are Mr. Hitchcock's perfect moments.

And then there is Ray Dooley who is always pleasing as the raucous little girl, Charles O'Donnell, the piano tuner who wrecks the room and the nerves of the spectators without ever striking a note and Van and Schenck whose voices meld like a hundred aces in a series of unusually good songs.

And, oh yes, every once in a while some young ladies come on the stage. They look all right, too.
                              --Robert C. Benchley in _Life_ (July
                                 14, 1921), page 18.

                           *   *   *

There is always an atmosphere of reverence as the faithful gather at a _Follies_ show. There is the affable spirit of kinship which one finds at big football games and other pleasant annual rites where everyone's anticipation is sharpened by the reflection that there are hundreds of dismal souls outside who would like to be present. When the curtain goes up there is, on the stage, an air of serenity and dignity as befits a National Institution. There is no noisy striving to whip up enthusiasm, no reaching out over the footlights. A _Follies_ show is like a Follies girl, a bit disdainfully conscious of her

charm, accepting your admiration as a matter of course. We have
the feeling, as the numbers follow one after the other, that what we
see has been selected and arranged to express one man's idea of
what is beautiful and what is funny. Everything has been toned to
meet a distinctly personal taste. This, we are sure, is one secret
of Mr. Ziegfeld's success. He merely pleases himself. He hopes you
may also be pleased, as a connoisseur, taking you about among his
treasures, hopes hospitably that you may care for the things he
likes.

Mr. Ziegfeld has ridden his hobby for a number of years, and
his sense of the beautiful is fully conceived. It is a voluptuous
beauty that he fancies--the beauty of bold, rich color and lovely
bodies. In his current exhibit he illustrates "The Legend of the
Cyclamen Tree" with two pictures. The first, done in pale gold and
blue, gives his idea of what Persia should have been like in the
twelfth century. The second is a desert scene with vivid sky and
a huge splash of scarlet tapestry. Ben Ali Haggin contributes two
of his exotic tableaux. There is a picture called "The Bridge on the
Seine," in heavy shades of blue. And so on. Some of the pictures
are interpreted in song, some are not; but in every case the appeal
is to the eye. Mr. Ziegfeld prefers to appeal to the eye also when
he wants you to laugh. So this year we encounter Charles O'Donnell, the silent piano tuner, who becomes hopelessly entangled with
a stepladder without saying a word. William C. Fields (who does
funny things much better than he says them) finds himself in a characteristic predicament. This time he tries to get off to the country,
by subway, with his wife (Fanny Brice), two infants (Raymond Hitchcock and Ray Dooley), his victrola, his guitar, his bird cage, his
fishing outfit, and the other things people take with them when they
go to the country on the subway.

Other Follies have been more tuneful, others have been much
funnier, but none has quite achieved the beauty of the present one.
And it is beauty--beauty for its own sake--that Mr. Ziegfeld seems
to care most about in his chef d'oeuvre. When we consider that he
makes his sleek, overfed public care about it also, he almost assumes
the dignity of a Force.

--Kenneth Andrews in The Bookman,
Vol. 54, No. 1 (September 1921),
pages 52-53.

ZIEGFELD FOLLIES OF 1922 (Music by Victor Herbert, Louis A.
    Hirsch and Dave Stamper, Book and Lyrics by Ring Lardner,
    Gene Buck and Ralph Spence; New Amsterdam Theatre, June 5,
    1922)

Mr. Ziegfeld's having reduced the price of admission to his

Follies this year makes it a little harder to be nasty about the show.
It is worth less than it was last year, but as you are asked to pay
less, it really brings you right back to where you started from.
Except that, by the time you are through with the ticket agency,
you will have spent a tidy sum, and a tidy sum of any size seems
too much for what is offered. Here again, however, Mr. Ziegfeld's
having sent this department free seats cramps our vituperativeness
in this respect.

        Leaving money out of the question, then, let us see what there
is to pay you for your time.

        It is customary to say that the Follies are beautiful to look at.
All right, they are beautiful, especially the scenes and costumes designed by young Mr. James Reynolds. The girls, too, are pictorially
effective, although they never look very clubby. I may be funny
that way, but I like a little radiation of some sort in my beauty, and
the Follies show-girls radiate at about the same degree Fahrenheit as
Cleopatra's Needle. That's one reason I never went after Dolores
stronger. She must have wondered what on earth was the matter
with me that I never called her up or wrote to her.

        Granted that the Follies are gorgeous to look at, then. After
an hour or so your eyes get numb, and from then on Mr. William A.
Brady might as well be producing the show. Unfortunately you can't
do as you do with Nature whenever your eyes get tired of looking
at the Grand Cañon or the Engadine Valley--stoop over and look up-
side down between your knees. The seats at the New Amsterdam
would never allow for that. You can tip your head at right angles
and get a new sort of view that way, but you are likely to be misunderstood by the people behind you and asked to leave the theatre.

        We now come to the comedy. Right away it should be said that
the absence of Fannie Brice and W.C. Fields started us out with a
bias against the show. It didn't seem right to call it The Follies
without them. We sat there, fairly glowing with ill-will from the time
the curtain went up, and not even Will Rogers could make us feel
that the gap had been filled.

        Now Will Rogers' own mother couldn't have cared more for him
than we do, and we will laugh at practically anything he says, because he says it so ingratiatingly. But fifteen minutes of Will Rogers,
delightful as they are, can't make up for those golden hours of the
dear past when Fannie Brice sang and Fields fretted over the Ford in
company with the grimly silent little man in the duster.

        Great sobs shook our frame at these memories while we sat and
listened to Mr. Gallagher and Mr. Shean sing about belligerent wives
raising lumps on their husbands' heads, women getting the vote, and
Prohibition. (Incidentally, it seems incredible that two comedians
could start out with such a comic idea as that which forms the basis

of the Gallagher and Shean song and reduce it so utterly to a banality by the introduction of a five-and-ten-cent store lyric.)

Further tears, and real ones, were shed during the "Burlesk-
Ballet" participated in by Nervo and Knox. Not that they didn't do
it well enough, but that dance was a Dooley dance, and each time
there was a crash of falling bodies we expected to see the little, impassive Dooley rise from the wreckage and glide heavily onward.
But the little, impassive Dooley is dead, and we rather resent anyone else's trying to take his place--for a while, at any rate.

Ring Lardner has written a couple of skits for the show which
do much to make the comedy bearable, especially the scene at the
ball grounds in which Andrew Toombes and Will Rogers give startling
representations of a couple of Yanks warming up. But when you consider all that you have to sit through before and after you come to
the Lardner and Rogers episodes in the way of young ladies stepping
to the footlights and reciting sweetly, "I am Miss Calculate" and "I
am Miss Demeanor," drunken dancing, Hula-Hula girls shaking themselves in the manner which was calculated to throw the male element
into a frenzy back in the days when "I'll tell the world" was new
slang, with musical numbers entitled, "Throw Me a Kiss," "South Sea
Moon," "Bring on the Girls" and "Hello, Hello, Hello!" you realize
that, after all, there is nothing like canoeing for a summer evening.

--Robert C. Benchley in <u>Life</u>
(June 29, 1922), page 18.

* * *

The process of glorifying the American girl, which Mr. Ziegfeld undertook in his last season's <u>Follies</u>, has hardly been acceler-
ated by the addition of Eddie Cantor to the show, and yet the show
itself has been speeded up enormously thereby. Whatever Mr. Cantor has not, he certainly has pace.

There are really two Eddie Cantors, and if you will draw your
chairs up very close, we will tell you about them. First, there is
the black-face comedian, who darts about like something on top of a
pond, singing songs which may or may not be funny but which are
always nothing for Grandma to hear at her age. For years this
Eddie Cantor meant considerably less than nothing to us as entertainment.

Then last year at the Winter Garden, he washed up, and in
place of the neurotic Negro appeared a Jewish boy with large, bewildered eyes and mild manner, an apologetic calm superseding the
offensive assurance, and, oddly enough, a considerably more sanitary
batch of songs and jokes.

Both Eddie Cantors are in the <u>Follies</u> this summer and you can
take your choice. Ours is the Jewish boy, especially in the scene

with the traffic policeman, where his eagerness to conciliate and his
humility in the face of a terrific injustice borders on high tragedy.

A great many of our thinkers are disturbed at the popularity
of Mr. Cantor's song, "Yes, We Have No Bananas." They see in it
a sign of national disintegration. It is pointed to as one of the evil
results of Prohibition or the Gulf Stream. Several leading citizens
are thinking of leaving the country.

To this department it is the most encouraging lyric that has
caught public fancy in our memory. In an age when we seemed sunk
in a bromide mixture of spurious Mammy sentimentality and Silver
Lining treacle, along comes a song which is utterly mad, almost
gloriously so. And a public which had gone on for years having its
opinions and enthusiasms flattened out for it in the shape of matrices
before daring to accept them, suddenly leaps at this bit of flaming
insanity and waves it aloft.

It is true, we were a little sorry when we found that in the
verse of the song the immortal phrase, "Yes, we have no bananas,"
is specifically attributed to a certain fruiterer and that it arose from
a confusion in learning English rather than from a native madness.
But nine-tenths of the people who sing the song do not know this.
To them it is simply a shouting denial of the unities of speech and
thought, an espousal of a New Idea, and incidentally an easy song
to sing in a crowd. A nation which will take up with a song like
this is not nearly so much of a fool as it looks.

And then, just as we are in this exalted spirit of pride in our
countrymen's behavior in a national crisis, the Messrs. Gallagher and
Shean come on and receive tumultuous approval for their song, which
offers the old Egyptian sayings that having one's wife in Paris is
like taking a sandwich to a banquet and that bare knees make the
girls look shorter but the man look longer. There has probably never
been a more illegitimate lyric written than that which entrances thousands nightly from the lips of Gallagher and Shean. That it can be
as popular as it is is a sure sign of our national disintegration. It
shows what Prohibition has done to our American fibre. If it continues to flourish we are seriously considering leaving the country
altogether.

Other additions to the summer edition of the Follies are Ann
Pennington and Brooke Johns, featuring Miss Pennington's knees
and Mr. Johns' teeth in a pleasant manner. For some reason the most
beautiful number of the original edition, the Sicilian scene, has been
omitted, but Ben Ali Haggin's art calendar groups have been re-
tained. These "living-pictures," which is what we used to call them
in our church entertainments, are now known as "pastels," and are
several degrees above that other feature of the Follies which has also
been tenderly kept, the Radio number. If any New Yorker were to
see this number produced in a small city, he would hail it as typical

ham and just what you might expect once you got off Broadway.
Under Mr. Ziegfeld's spell it becomes one of his several hundred
last words in modern stage effects. Which doesn't keep it from being
ham, however.

On the whole, the additions to the show have helped, in spite
of the great gap left by Will Rogers. And, as everyone who comes
to New York insists on seeing the Follies whether they are good or
not, we might as well admit that it is about the best thing for them
to do, at that.

--Robert C. Benchley in _Life_ (July
26, 1923), page 18.

ZIEGFELD FOLLIES OF 1924 (Lyrics by Gene Buck and Joseph J.
  McCarthy, Music by Victor Herbert, Raymond Hubbell, Dave
  Stamper, Harry Tierney, and Dr. Albert Szirmai; New Amster-
  dam Theatre, June 24, 1924)

As Will Rogers said on the opening night, the difference between a good Follies and a bad Follies shows up in the gross receipts
on the season to the tune of about $1.80. It doesn't make much dif-
ference to the public whether the Follies are good or bad. They are
Follies. It is this charming trait in the American people, this shut-
eye acceptance of anything so long as it has the right name, that
makes it so easy to sell them bad liquor, bad styles, and bad Presi-
dents.

There really isn't any need, then, for Mr. Ziegfeld to worry
much whether or not the critics like his shows. So long as he brings
on plenty of young ladies and keeps all the lamps burning in the
Ziegfeld Follies sign on the front of the theatre, he can count on his
constituency. So long as it is a recognized factor in New York sales-
manship to take a visiting prospect to dinner and then to the Follies,
the critics can go and chase one another around the Central Park
Reservoir.

The new Follies, as a matter of fact, is a big improvement over
last year's, which is saying just about as little as it is possible to
say and still be articulate. It has nothing that is actively bad in it.
It is true, a sincere examination fails to disclose many things that are
actively good, but perhaps that would be a little too much to expect.
The eye is pretty continuously pleased, the seats are comfortable,
and the New Amsterdam Theatre is within easy reach of both railway
terminals and the subway stations. Things might be worse.

The case of Will Rogers is unique in entertainment circles.
Although for entirely different reasons, he, like the Follies itself,
does not have to be very good. That is, his material does not have

to be very good. So tremendous is the unassuming charm of this
native that he can say almost anything and you are suffused with a
warm glow of goodwill toward him. In spite of the fact that he receives a large sum for his services, and that he, like any other actor, deliberately steps before you with the avowed intention of amusing you, there is something so unprofessional and casual about his
manner that even the mildest of his cracks are acceptable.

And, of course, when he is at his best, as he is with his old
rope and chewing equipment, he is as keen a political satirist as the
country has ever had. No show which contains Will Rogers can be
said to be unimportant.

"Unimportant," however, would be a good word for much of
the current show. In fact, it is difficult to remember much about
it without consulting the program. Before we turn to this form of
cribbing, we will, just for the fun of it (and a pretty pass our
civilization has come to when this can be classed as fun), recall as
many outstanding features of the galaxy as we are able to as we sit
here before the fire dreaming through the pipe-smoke.

First, and most vivid of all, is the success of Mr. Tom Lewis'
inchoate speech, always a success so far as we are concerned. In
it, no sentence is ever finished, no thought ever brought to its frui-
tion, and yet the general effect is at least equal in lucidity to that of
most of the speeches with which the radio was burdened during the
recent conventions.

Then the Empire and Tiller Girls in their remarkable exhibition
of keeping step.

And the finale to the first act, the title of which we forget,
but which might well have been called "Illicit Dalliance Through the
Ages," in which such famous ladies as Eve, Cleopatra, Guinevere,
Eloise, Nell Gwynn and Lady Hamilton come down the steps dressed
in delectable shades of salmon and old rose and stand about waiting
for the curtain to come down.

There is also an effective rearrangement of old-time Victor
Herbert numbers which sends the blood coursing through long-unused
channels of the hearts of those who were at the height of their cal-
low romantic movement when "Absinthe Frappé" and "I Can't Do That
Sum" were new.... Ah, me! Those days! Those girls! Many of
them mothers now. Dear, dear!

As for the rest of the Follies, we must consult the program.
On the second thought, perhaps we had better not. Mr. Ziegfeld
sent us seats for the opening this time, and the least that we can do
in return is let it go at this.

                                        --Robert C. Benchley in Life (July
                                          17, 1924), page 18.

* * *

In the new Fall edition of Mr. Ziegfeld's <u>Follies</u> there would
seem to be a news story of magnificent proportions. It is surprising
that the press-department has not already caught its possibilities.
We refer to what was apparently the Great Lilliputian Terror in Russia
a few years ago. The fact that no word of it had reached America
before only shows how little real news has come out of that country
since the war.

In this new edition there is what is billed as "Celebrated Russian Troupe of Lilliputians of Mr. Ratoucheff." Before the performance of a very dull pantomime, Mr. Ratoucheff himself (who adds up
to about two feet six inches in good heavy woolen socks) comes before the curtain and makes a speech in which he craves the indulgence of the audience because his troupe does not spik English.
Your indulgence in this respect is not heavily taxed, however, as
they work entirely in pantomime anyway. It really is gratuitous in
Mr. Ratoucheff to give away their secret, unless it is that he wants
to make sure that you understand that these are no mere local Lilliputians out on a lark.

But the big punch in Mr. Ratoucheff's speech does not lie
here. In the course of his explanation as to why his celebrated
troupe finds itself on these over-hospitable shores, he lets drop,
with characteristic Russian casualness, the fact that they were driven
out of their native land by the "present unhappy situation." Of all
the monstrous things that have been laid at the door of the Bolshevik
government, nothing has shaped up quite so gigantic in Machiavellian
devilry as this deliberate route of Mr. Ratoucheff's celebrated troupe
of Lilliputians.

What a night that must have been in Red Russia! One can almost visualize it, even without more details from the plucky Mr.
Ratoucheff. Lenin, at the height of his strength and power, consulting with his lieutenants under the walls of the Kremlin in the icy
moonlight of the Russian night. He whispers nervously, for he is
about to undertake a coup on which hangs the success or failure of
the Red Régime. "Men," he says, "to-night Soviet Russia meets her
test. To-night we drive Mr. Ratoucheff's celebrated troupe of Lilliputians out of the country or we ourselves go under. A bas les
Lilliputians! They constitute the sole remaining menace to the Red
government."

And then begins the memorable scene on the Nevskii Prospekt,
the fighting Lilliputians, led by Mr. Ratoucheff, gamely struggling
against tremendous odds until finally, charged by the Soviet horsemen,
they give up the unequal fight and book passage on the <u>Berengaria</u>.
The red hordes had won, but in Mr. Ratoucheff's breast there still
flames the spirit of Romanoff Russia, and as he stands there on his
tiny pedestal in the excessively uninspired pantomime entitled "Story

of the Paris Night," he registers all the emotions, from grief and
anger to German measles, with an intensity and fervor which must
make the spirit of Lenin, wherever it is, wince at the futility of his
attempt to stamp out the dauntless fire of the Ratoucheffs.

Incidentally, we will gladly serve on a committee of five to
draw up plans whereby the quota on Lilliputian actors can be reduced to practically nothing. Failing to restrict the quota, if the Ku
Klux Klan will include thespian midgets in their list of undesirables
we will promise to take out a two-weeks' guest card in the order.
We could do an awful lot in two weeks.

As for the rest of Mr. Ziegfeld's new edition, we must admit
that, compared with his "bull-dog edition" which was on the streets
last June, it is a very pleasant show. Nothing startling, but pleasant. Lupino Lane seems funnier than he did at first and Miss Pennington, while disclosing nothing in the way of talent that wasn't
disclosed several seasons ago, still manages to hold her own, which
is eminently satisfactory. We have already gone on record concerning
Will Rogers, who could carry along a much worse show than the
Follies all by himself.

As a special added attraction, Mitty and Tillio, the dancers,
have been brought in. They are all right, but it would seem that
one thing that our revues do not need at the present moment is another pair of naked dancers who hurl themselves at each other in
rhythmic wrestling and exit with the gentleman carrying the lady
high above his head. This Bernarr Macfadden school of dancing has
its points, but sometimes we long for the old days when Mrs. [Irene]
Castle used to come out with all her clothes on and do a waltz.
                                --Robert C. Benchley in Life (No-
                                   vember 20, 1924), page 20.

                              *   *   *

Through the inscrutable working of Fate, the comedy sketches
which were originally a part of J.P. McEvoy's The Comic Supplement
(foundered off Newark, N.J., February, 1925) have been inserted
into the new edition of the Follies, making the show funnier than it
has been since--well, since W.C. Fields was in it before.

Given an act like "A Back Porch," with Miss Ray Dooley, the
Baby Peggy of the spoken drama, to work with him (if you can call
it working with), and W.C. Fields is just about as grand as a comedian could possibly be. We ask for nothing better in this life.

Incidentally, we are happy to be able to report for once that,
in direct competition with an English revue sketch, our own dear land
comes off so far ahead as to be almost insulting. This sketch of Mr.
Field's, "A Back Porch," challenges comparison at every point with a
similar idea in the sainted Charlot's Revue, a scene in which a man

tries to snatch a few minutes' sleep in the face of domestic interruptions. The American version, in the writing, business, setting and
costuming, stands out like The Miracle in comparison with Ben Hur.

The costuming, in particular, takes a couple of good long jumps
ahead of anything that has ever been done in a revue before. This,
too, is a salvaged feature from The Comic Supplement and is the work
of John Held, Jr., the artist. Even if you didn't see the credit to
Mr. Held on the program, you would know that he designed the ladies' costumes, because of the three inches of open space between
the top of the stockings and the--whatever they are. Just as today
you can always spot a Rubens or Botticelli girl, art students of the
future will learn to recognize those three inevitable inches as the
sure mark of a genuine Held.

We don't want to devote too much attention to the pictorial side
of the new Follies, when we need the whole page to talk about Mr.
Fields and Miss Dooley, but, as a part of the remarkable revolution-
ary note in the Comic Supplement additions, Norman-Bell Geddes' sets
are masterpieces. Inserted in the conventional surroundings of the
old Follies' scenery, they make it look like a street-drop in an olio.
If The Comic Supplement, with Fields, Dooley, McEvoy, Held and
Geddes, was all like the bits that have been saved for the Follies it
would have been better to close the old Follies and bring The Comic
Supplement in.

None of this should be construed as a retraction of our stand
on Will Rogers. He is still with the show and still moves in an orbit
of his own.

> --Robert C. Benchley in Life
> (April 2, 1925), page 22.

*   *   *

Sadly, with memories of the good old days in our heart, we
witnessed the summer edition of the Ziegfeld Follies. In this new
edition there was no fire, or earthquake, or divorce scandal which
set it apart from any other edition, and there was a great deal of
the old stuff left over from last year. It was a great deal like the
"Extras!" which are always being shouted through the streets: one
pays a nickel and finds only two cents' worth. We suspect that Mr.
Ziegfeld has grown both bored and parsimonious. We recognized a
great many old sets and trappings, not to mention old ideas decorated
afresh--such originalities as a song called "I'd Like to be a Gardener
in a Garden of Girls" with a general parade of the Glorified American
Girls, clad in feathers and tinsel, who stood appropriately on rocks
and steps until the whole stage resembled the aviary of the Bronx
Zoo. We kept sitting there, a little angry at being given so much of
the old stuff, and thinking all the while about the great old days
when in one evening at the Follies one might have seen Fannie Brice,
Will Rogers, Raymond Hitchcock, W.C. Fields, Ray Dooley, Eddie

Cantor, Bert Williams, Dolores, Ina Claire and a dozen other good
entertainers. This year there were only Ray Dooley and Rogers and
Fields left to do all the work, and even these entertainers seen over
and over again in the same evening lose some of their charm. It
was a good enough revue in its way but when one thought of the good
old days it was nothing at all. Still it was the good old days which
gave the Follies their reputation and it is a big enough reputation
no doubt to carry the public through many more new editions of old
stuff.

--Louis Bromfield in The Bookman,
Vol. 62, No. 1 (September 1925),
pages 69-70.

ZIEGFELD FOLLIES OF 1927 (Lyrics and Music by Irving Berlin,
     sketches by Harold Atteridge and Eddie Cantor; New Amsterdam
     Theatre, August 16, 1927)

     Among Mr. Ziegfeld's minor accomplishments in the realm of the
drama has been to make toe-dancing tolerable to this department.
Up until Rio Rita we were hailed from coast to coast as the bitterest
and most vituperative opponent that toe-dancing had in this country.
A campaign of over ten years to put down ballet-dancing in all forms,
and especially toe-dancing, had won for us the nickname, "Anti-
Ballet Bob." We wore it with pride.

     But then came Rio Rita with its Albertina Rasch ballet and we
were horrified to find a definitely localized glow creeping over us as
the young ladies in blue raised themselves in what had hitherto been
to us the dullest manoeuvre in all the field of rhythmic activity. We
were weakening.

     And in the new Follies our capitulation is made complete, again
by the Albertina Rasch cohorts. We don't know what it is that they
do so different from what toe-dancers have always been boring us
with, but whatever it is, they have made a siss out of us. Hereafter we are going to find ourself talking about Beauty and Symmetry
in Motion. And we don't care who hears us.

     A year ago, if you told us that we should derive our greatest
satisfaction in a performance of the Follies from a ballet, we would
have struck you across the face with our gloves. But such seems to
be the case this year.

     It may be part of the degenerative process which has brought
us to liking toe-dancing, but most of our satisfactions at the new
Follies were visual and abstract. For instance, we got quite a kick
out of the mass of yellows in the finale of the first act. But perhaps
we had better not commit ourself further until we look up Freud and
see what liking yellow means.

And speaking of the finale to the first act, it is here that the Follies hits its high point for all concerned, especially Mr. Berlin. After pitching a good steady, unpretentious game for a whole act, Mr. Berlin uncovered a fast one in a counter-melody to "The Stars and Stripes Forever" which is worthy to stand beside his early prize-winning counter-treatment of "America" in Stop, Look and Listen! (Correct us if we are wrong in our history.)

We shall probably have no department on this page next week, as we expect to be very busy trying to learn this new melody. It will probably take quite a time also to find some one who is willing to sing "The Stars and Stripes Forever" while we practice. If there is one thing we love more than another, it is to sing counter-melodies, but we find it difficult to get people to sing straight for us.

From what we have said so far, you might think that there were no comedians in the Follies. Nothing could be farther from the truth. There are more comedians than there is comedy for. Mr. Andrew Tombes again finds himself smoking in the alley during the greater part of a show--unfortunately both for Mr. Tombes and the audience--and it was not until we had consulted our program that we discovered that the old man with a bald wig was Harry McNaughton. And by then he was gone.

There is, however, Eddie Cantor and he has a lot to do. Like ballet-dancing, Eddie Cantor is a comparatively recent enthusiasm of ours, but we yield to no one now in our devotion. Some of his material is good and some of it isn't, but, so long as he is white-face and can register his expressions, the thing is bound to have something. If we hadn't already talked so much about Beauty in Motion, we should say that Mr. Cantor is, rain or shine, an artist. As it is, we will let it go at saying that, good jokes or bad, you don't have to worry about him.

There now remains nothing much to do except to make random jottings concerning this twenty-first edition of Mr. Ziegfeld's Follies. There are some pretty long stretches where not even random jottings can be made, favorable or unfavorable, which is perhaps the worst thing that can be said about the show.

But there are the Brox Sisters, long personal representatives of Mr. Berlin in the presentation of his songs, and still quietly effective. There is a large lady orchestra, called the "Ingenues," who seem able to play anything well--and do. There are Irene Delroy and Ruth Etting and Frances Upton and a large and influential-looking chorus whose mothers have got together and stitched them up some very pretty frocks for the occasion.

A team of dancers named Ross Himes and Peggy Chamberlin performed what promised to be a pretty comical burlesque of "Mon

Homme" but turned into just another rough-and-tumble Apache dance
which reminded us of the Dooleys and made us cry.

So there you have the Follies in several nutshells.
                              --Robert C. Benchley in Life (Sep-
                                 tember 1, 1927), page 21.

INDEX BY CRITIC

INDEX